Virtue Ethics, Old and New

VIRTUE ETHICS, OLD AND NEW

Edited by

STEPHEN M. GARDINER

CORNELL UNIVERSITY PRESS

ITHACA AND LONDON

First published 2005 by Cornell University Press
First printing, Cornell Paperbacks, 2005

Printed in the United States of America

Library of Congress Cataloging-in-Publication Data

Virtue ethics, old and new / edited by Stephen M. Gardiner.
    p. cm.
    Proceedings of a conference held in May 2002 at the University of Canterbury.
    Includes bibliographical references (p.   ) and index.
    ISBN 0-8014-4345-8 (cloth : alk. paper) — ISBN 0-8014-8968-7 (pbk. : alk. paper)
    1. Virtue—Congresses. 2. Ethics—Congresses. I. Gardiner, Stephen Mark.
    BJ1521.V566 2005
    179´.9—dc22   2004030943

Cornell University Press strives to use environmentally responsible suppliers and materials to the fullest extent possible in the publishing of its books. Such materials include vegetable-based, low-VOC inks and acid-free papers that are recycled, totally chlorine-free, or partly composed of nonwood fibers. For further information, visit our website at www.cornellpress.cornell.edu.

Cloth printing   10 9 8 7 6 5 4 3 2 1
Paperback printing   10 9 8 7 6 5 4 3 2 1

For
Anne Louise Gardiner and Peter Gardiner,
and for David

Contents

viii   Contents

Acknowledgments

This volume emerged from the conference "Virtue Ethics, Old and New" at the University of Canterbury, Christchurch, New Zealand, in May 2002. The conference featured twenty-seven speakers from New Zealand, Australia, the United States, Canada, and the United Kingdom. I would like to thank all those who participated, and especially the keynote speakers, Julia Annas, Rosalind Hursthouse, and Christine Swanton, for creating such a lively and productive atmosphere. I also gratefully acknowledge the support of the Department of Philosophy at the University of Canterbury, the Head of Department, Graham Macdonald, and particularly Carol Hiller, who "put in the hard yards" with characteristic warmth, encouragement, and professionalism.

For help with the development of the volume, I'd like to thank Eric Hutton, Sylvia Burrow, the Departments of Philosophy at the University of Utah and the University of Washington, and Roger Haydon, our editor at Cornell University Press. I am especially grateful to Julia Annas and Christine Swanton for their advice, guidance, and support throughout the project.

My debts to Roger Crisp and Terry Irwin are much too deep and broad, and span far too many years, to be recounted here. So let me just say that I am especially pleased and honored to include their contributions to this volume.

I dedicate this volume to my parents, for their love and support across many years and miles, and to my friend and colleague, David Novitz. David intended to be part of the conference and the volume, but passed away before either project could come to fruition. He was an inspiration, and I know that I am just one of very many who continue to miss him.

S.M.G.

Virtue Ethics, Old and New

Virtue Ethics, Here and Now

STEPHEN M. GARDINER

Virtue ethics is both old and new. This makes study of it paradoxical. On the one hand, there are grounds for saying that contemporary work is, if not quite in its theoretical infancy, at least not far out of diapers. And this suggests that we should be gentle and nurturing, allowing it time to flourish before coming to any definitive verdict on its merits.[1] On the other hand, it is hard to deny that modern day virtue ethics is part of a long, sophisticated, and fairly continuous tradition. Not only does the approach have origins almost as ancient as philosophy itself, but its history includes extensive work by such philosophical luminaries as (at least) Socrates, Plato, Aristotle, the Stoics, Aquinas, and (perhaps) Hume and Nietzsche. And this suggests that we should already be in a good position to assess its appeal.

The above paradox is manifest in the contemporary debate about the merits of a virtue ethical approach. Proponents of virtue ethics are typically inclined towards the first, more indulgent attitude, while critics tend to the second. But

---

1. Its newness is well-documented. Elizabeth Anscombe is widely credited with starting a revival of virtue ethics with her seminal paper "Modern Moral Philosophy" originally published in 1958. Anscombe's paper provoked at first a trickle and then a flood or articles on the subject. Many of the major articles, including Anscombe's, are collected in *Virtue Ethics,* ed. Roger Crisp and Michael Slote (Oxford: Oxford University Press, 1997). See also *How Should One Live? Essays on the Virtues,* ed. Roger Crisp (Oxford: Oxford University Press, 1996), and *Virtue Ethics: A Critical Reader,* ed. Daniel Statman (Georgetown: Georgetown University Press, 1997). Statman's introduction provides a useful overview. We are just now starting to see a number of major book-length treatments. Prominent examples include Rosalind Hursthouse, *On Virtue Ethics* (Oxford: Oxford University Press, 1999), Philippa Foot, *Natural Goodness* (Oxford: Oxford University Press, 2001), and Christine Swanton, *Virtue Ethics: A Pluralistic View* (Oxford: Oxford University Press, 2003).

this leads to further puzzles. On one side, the critics are prone to argue that the laborious pursuit of virtue ethics in the tradition has already shown the approach to be fruitless. Hence, they claim that the return to virtue is both a retrograde step and one that fails to appreciate the motivations for and advances of its main rivals. But this attitude is itself paradoxical. For one thing, much of the twentieth-century work in virtue ethics emerged from, and was inspired by, the deficiencies of the utilitarianism and Kantian approaches that remain its main competitors. For another, many of the recent innovations in those traditions have been prompted either by criticisms coming from contemporary virtue ethics or by attempts to learn from its independent appeal. But there are also puzzles on the other side. *Prima facie,* it is paradoxical for contemporary defenders of virtue ethics to distance themselves from their theoretical ancestors. For in confronting external criticisms, they often, and perhaps typically, appeal to particular doctrines of the canonical authors. Indeed, contemporary virtue ethicists often complain that their critics simply fail to appreciate the richness of the virtue ethics approach, relying instead on simplistic caricatures when they make their objections. And usually the charge is that they do this precisely because they have misunderstood the relevant parts of the tradition.

How do we account for the various paradoxical attitudes? Presumably, one partial explanation is that the world views of many past virtue ethicists were, in some respects, quite different from our own in ways which have implications for their philosophical systems.[2] However, real as this concern is, it is important not to draw hasty conclusions from it. For the concern implies neither that contemporary virtue ethics must be unsound (as some critics seem to think), nor that it must begin again from a clean slate (as some sympathizers imply). Instead, the importance of the wider and divergent beliefs of past virtue ethicists—and in particular their scientific and religious beliefs—depends crucially on whether those beliefs play an essential role in their ethical theories and on how widespread their influence extends. But the answers to these questions are not yet clear.[3]

Fortunately, a second partial explanation for the paradoxes is less deep and much easier to address. For some of the puzzles seem to have their roots in an unfortunate historical and institutional bifurcation of the virtue ethics movement itself. As has already been mentioned, much of the relevant early work in ethical theory in the twentieth century was essentially negative: it was focused around a critical reaction to the existing utilitarian and Kantian orthodoxies.

---

2. This suggests another paradox. For the point tends to suggest the "early days" approach; but it is most often made by critics of virtue ethics.

3. Moreover, finding them will probably require projects similar to the ones contained in this volume.

This work not only reestablished virtue ethics as a distinctive position in normative ethics, but also (along with a renewal of interest in the history of philosophy in general, and in ancient philosophy in particular) provoked a reexamination of the classical texts themselves. But for a while, the contemporary and historical projects seemed to proceed at some distance from one another. Important work was being done on both sides; but without much deep synthesis, or in some cases, even evidence of overt engagement.[4]

This bifurcation is now beginning to dissolve, and one aim of this volume is to be part of that dissolution. The volume brings together contributions from authors who share the commitment to virtue ethics, old and new; that is, to the fruitfulness of study of the history of virtue ethics for contemporary work. This commitment is founded not merely on a desire to find historical ways of fighting off standard criticisms and rival approaches, but also, and more importantly, on the conviction that past versions of virtue ethics can illuminate the nature and possibilities of the approach for contemporary audiences, where this might mean self-criticism as well as self-development. This approach helps to resolve the basic paradox: whereas it is indeed early days for the project of virtue ethics, old and new, this fact casts no doubt on the value of the tradition.

The present volume is divided into four parts, with the essays grouped largely on the basis of the increasing severity of the challenges they pose to orthodox (by which I mean "roughly Aristotelian") positions within contemporary virtue ethics.[5] The authors in the first part aim to show how historical approaches can enrich discussion of three central theoretical issues in contemporary virtue ethics: the status of mainstream virtue ethics as a naturalistic doctrine, the role of moral rules in virtuous decision-making, and the problem of coping with apparent moral conflict.

In the first essay, Julia Annas considers one of the concerns that most motivated earlier historical turns away from virtue—the desire for philosophical naturalism. Annas dismisses this argument with three characteristically interesting and provocative claims. First, she maintains that though virtue ethics is not necessarily a naturalistic approach, it is suitably naturalistic in its most prominent

---

4. I am not saying that there was no interaction or no mutual influence. There clearly was. My point is only that the two aspects of work in virtue ethics were substantially divorced from one another. It is only recently that people have begun to accept that historical and contemporary work in virtue ethics are not mutually exclusive but can be integrated into a coherent approach. This is itself puzzling, since the integration has been obvious for decades in much important work on utilitarian and Kantian approaches. One might also adopt a stronger position and say that, at the present stage of the development of contemporary virtue ethics, historical work is instrumentally essential, in the sense that it is by far the most effective means of enriching the approach.

5. Within these divisions, the papers are usually grouped by the historical order of the author they consider.

and attractive versions. Second, she argues that such forms of virtue ethics are truer to the naturalistic aim of respecting modern science than their modern rivals. Indeed, she criticizes prominent twentieth- century approaches for being both unduly impressed with the sciences, and also (and ironically) anti-scientific. Third, she claims that the ancient theorists with the most promising approach to naturalism are the Stoics.

Some of Annas' argument builds on recent work by Philippa Foot and Rosalind Hursthouse. But Annas does not accept the particular characterization of naturalism provided by Foot and Hursthouse, since their accounts are Aristotelian in an important and central respect: they envisage the role of nature as being to provide *constraints* on ethical theory. Annas believes that this approach is deficient in two ways. First, it is open to factual objection. Annas argues that even though it is possible that it might turn out that, for example, men are by nature more aggressive than women, or that women naturally bear the brunt of child-rearing, neither of these "facts" would justify a constraint of human nature on ethical theory, as Aristotelianism implies. Second, Aristotelianism threatens the universality of morality. Annas claims that moral theories "must apply equally to everyone, with no arbitrariness as to what beings are left outside [them]." But Aristotelian theories, she claims, deny this. Because they allow for the possibility of rationality's being constrained by human nature in some cases, they assume that the good life may be simply beyond some people: a person may fail in spite of her best efforts, because of factors outside her control.

Given these (alleged) deficiencies of Aristotelianism, Annas proposes that we accept a Stoic account of the role of nature, as providing the material for rational action. Her suggestion has two main elements. First, she claims that the Stoic account differs from the Aristotelian view in envisioning a completely pervasive role for rationality: rather than human nature acting as a constraint, it is amenable to direction by rationality in its entirety. Second, she maintains that the two contrasting approaches are connected to the debate between Aristotle and the Stoics on whether virtue is necessary (in the Aristotelian case) or sufficient (in the Stoic) for happiness; and that, contrary to much discussion on this topic, the Stoic position on happiness is not only more plausible than the Aristotelian, but also a reason in itself to develop the Stoic form of naturalism.

The second essay is my own. There I consider the place of moral rules within virtue ethics, and argue both that the Stoic Seneca provides an insightful account of how virtue ethics can accommodate the existence of moral rules, and that this account helps to elucidate and resolve some important contemporary issues. My argument begins with a puzzle. One prominent feature of contemporary virtue ethics is its insistence on the normative priority of the virtuous person; another is its skepticism about the place of rules or principles in moral decision making. But the Stoics seem paradoxical on this score. On the one hand, they are great proponents of the authority and privileged position of the sage; on the other, they see moral life as structured by an elaborate system of principles and rules.

I suggest a resolution to this apparent paradox, and in doing so offer an interpretation of Seneca that contrasts markedly with the standard views (such as those offered by Gisela Striker, Philip Mitsis, and Brad Inwood). Seneca endorses two kinds of moral rules, precepts (praecepta) and doctrines (decreta), and argues that both are essential parts of an ethical theory. The precepts, I claim, guide action by referring to descriptive or low-level evaluative properties accessible to most people, while doctrines rely on higher-level evaluative properties such as those captured by the virtue terms. This suggests a way of reconciling the role of rules with the normative priority of the virtuous person: the precepts are useful to the nonvirtuous, but not the virtuous; the virtuous employ doctrines alone, but this is because the relevant doctrines essentially rely on higher-level evaluative concepts such as the virtue terms.

T.H. Irwin's article concerns one of the core theoretical issues facing virtue ethicists: can the virtues conflict? Commonsense views suggest that they can; but most traditional defenders of virtue ethics have argued that they cannot, endorsing instead a doctrine of the unity of the virtues. Irwin considers an attempt by Aquinas to defend and add more detail to the traditional view by appealing to the coordinating role of four cardinal virtues. Irwin explains both how Aquinas provides a general theoretical framework from within which to understand the absence of conflict, and also how he applies it to a case of historical and contemporary importance: the apparent conflict between "pagan self-assertion" and "Christian self-denial."

The essays in the second part argue for the existence and centrality of two values not usually associated with traditional forms of virtue ethics. In the fourth essay, Robert Solomon argues that erotic love (of the sort that characterizes a good marriage) is a moral virtue. In doing so, he takes himself not only to be rejecting modern puritanical attitudes about sexuality and sensuality, but also both Aristotle's claim that passions or emotions are not virtues, and Kant's claim that they cannot be moral, since they rest on inclinations. Solomon also denies that it is friendship alone that makes the best marriages morally good. As he puts it: "*Eros* and *philia* are a wonderful combination, but it is not *philia* alone that makes [the best marriage] virtuous."

In the fifth essay, Daniel Russell argues that Aristotelian virtue ethics can offer a persuasive account of what at first seems to be a distinctly modern ethical notion: self-respect. This account, he claims, has good textual credentials, in that the basis for it can be found in Aristotle's own descriptions of courage, pride, moral development, and love. Moreover, he adds, this is of profound theoretical importance: it implies that self-respect is morally good for its own sake, and one of the most important parts of virtue.

The essays of part three aim to reform virtue ethics in still more profound ways. Kathleen Higgins and Jennifer Welchman employ insights from figures usually considered to be on the periphery of the virtue ethics tradition (the Daoist Zhuangzi and John Dewey) to suggest that some core components of the standard approach should be rejected. In the sixth essay, Higgins claims that contemporary virtue ethics has taken over from Aristotle the notion that virtue essentially requires an active exercise of the agent's powers, but this appropriation is unwise. Higgins argues that an important part of virtue consists in refraining from some activity, in ways which are essentially passive. Correct behavior in these circumstances consists in exhibiting certain "negative virtues" which are more prominent in some of the Asian traditions. Higgins offers a detailed analysis of the work of Zhuangzi to make clear the characteristics and importance of these neglected virtues.

In the seventh essay, Jennifer Welchman argues for an even more fundamental change of emphasis. Welchman claims that traditional forms of virtue ethics have neglected central facts about human growth and development. In particular, they have substantially prioritized the virtues of maturity over dispositions that serve us best at other times, and so have ignored the fact that much of our lives are characterized by dependency rather than autonomous agency. This neglect of the virtues of the dependent is not simply a lamentable omission, Welchman believes, but has profound theoretical implications. For, she claims, such virtues turn out to be better candidates for recognition as primary or central virtues than the traditional virtues of majority. These "minor virtues" are dispositions such as curiosity, sympathy, playfulness, trust, gratitude, and loyalty; and they emerge most directly from John Dewey's pragmatic account of human flourishing.

The last part of the collection is constituted by three essays which, in various ways and to different extents, articulate or assess challenges to traditional virtue ethics from its close neighbors. In the eighth essay, Roger Crisp offers an account of Hume's theory of virtue. Crisp claims that the central place of virtue in Hume's ethics gives Hume an extremely sophisticated position that virtue ethics cannot afford to ignore. In particular, he argues that though Hume's position may ultimately be described as motive utilitarian, it is both an extremely sophisticated form of motive utilitarianism, and one which may remove the very possibility of non-utilitarian virtue ethics.

Among other things, the remaining essays both take issue with consequentialist-minded versions of virtue ethics such as Crisp's. In the ninth essay, Christine Swanton offers a novel account of the content and the structure of a Nietz-schean virtue ethics. Swanton distinguishes two excellent forms of will to power in Nietzsche—life affirmation and health—and tries to account for apparent tensions between them. She also distinguishes the approach from rival, conse-quentialist perfectionist approaches. She argues that Nietzsche's approach is a vi-able and attractive alternative to the versions of virtue ethics usually discussed by contemporary writers, and should not be discounted merely because of fears about Nietzsche's apparent immoralism.

In the tenth and final essay, George Harris takes on a particular manifestation of perfectionist consequentialism recently defended by Thomas Hurka. Hurka offers a recursive account of the perfectionist good of knowledge which relies on understanding the value of knowledge from the impersonal or impartial point of view. But Harris claims that this is a mistake. Instead, the intrinsic value of knowledge is best understood from the personal point of view; and love of knowledge is best understood from the perspective of an agent-centered the-ory of practical reason. This account is, Harris says, of profound importance to a hitherto neglected requirement on moral theories—that they address the se-rious threat posed by pessimism about the value of the world and our own lives. Hurka's account poses such a threat because of the preponderance of our igno-rance in relation to our knowledge. But the agent-centered alternative, as well as being plausible in its own right, raises no such worries.

The essays in this collection aim to enrich contemporary understanding of virtue ethics through reflection on its past manifestations, and some key theo-retical issues raised by them. To the extent that they succeed, such projects sug-gest that consideration of the rich history of virtue ethics should play a central role in the future development of the approach. There is a time and a place for virtue ethics, old and new, and that is here and now.

PART I

HISTORICAL INNOVATIONS ON FOUNDATIONAL ISSUES

CHAPTER I

Virtue Ethics: What Kind of Naturalism?

JULIA ANNAS

Virtue ethics is not by definition naturalistic. It would surely be surprising if it were; most ethical theories are compatible with different positions about their relation to the world. I take it that any ethics based on virtue requires an account of the good life which the virtues enable us to achieve.[1] On this issue of the good life most modern forms of virtue ethics are naturalistic, and often take a form called neo-Aristotelian, harking back to the best-known naturalistic theory from antiquity, Aristotle's. When we are investigating what the good life is, these theories hold, and how living virtuously might achieve it, we are aided by investigating our human nature. This in turn we do by seeing how we humans are a part, though a distinctive part, of the world that the sciences tell us about.

This means that they are rejecting two possible alternative approaches. One is to base ethical theory on a religious or metaphysical theory which gives us an alternative grounding for the virtues. There have been ancient, mediaeval, and modern forms of Christian virtue ethics which do this, and similarly for other religions. Even among the ancient pagans, Plato in some places tells us that being virtuous is becoming like god, and fleeing from mere worldly matters.[2] Some virtue theories, then, urge us to find out about our human nature only to transcend it. Achieving the good life is, on such theories, not a matter of fulfill-

---

1. Theories which reject this and give virtue a more minor role are, I hold, working with a reduced conception of virtue; I have no scope to argue this here, but I think it a plausible claim.

2. Plato's most trenchant expression of this idea is at *Theaetetus* 173d–177b, especially 176a–b, a passage which became very famous in later antiquity. *Flight* from the world is not implied in the mere idea of becoming like God, but it takes this form in the Platonist tradition, in which it was most influential.

ing our human nature but of striving to achieve a different kind of existence, a divine one. This is obviously a perfectly possible form for virtue ethics to take, although it is worth noting that in the period of antiquity when virtue ethics had its most serious and sophisticated development, it was naturalistic candidates which were in play.[3] And nowadays the most prominent forms of virtue ethics do not take this approach; indeed, most seem unaware of it.

The other alternative approach is more radical, namely to take a meta-ethical approach which is non-naturalistic. That is, we could hold that our ethical terms such as "virtue," "good," and so on have their meaning in some other way than by referring to us and the world around us. Their meaning might lie in their being used to pressure people (oneself and others) to act, for example. Or it might lie in their being used to vent or express feelings. Non-naturalist theories were influential in the late twentieth century, and the issue is obviously too large to discuss properly here. I mention them here only to make the point that there is good reason why a proponent of virtue ethics would not be tempted to a non-naturalistic account of virtue and goodness.

We can see this clearly from Philippa Foot's comment, in her recent book.[4] A philosopher, whom she does not name, was asked what account he gave of the goodness of a tree's roots, given that he held that "good" should be understood not naturalistically but in terms of choosing things. Good roots, he said, were roots that we should choose to have if we were trees. Foot refrains from commenting on this, and indeed if it does not seem absurd in itself, it is hard to see what else could serve to render it absurd. Why, though, is it so absurd? I suggest that the absurdity lies in the way human concerns are projected onto trees, and nature generally, as though we were not ourselves part of nature. Non-naturalistic accounts of ethical terms assume that their function, prominently their normativity, is something that arises with humans, or is produced by humans, in a way which owes nothing to the nature which we share with other living things. The way we should live and act, on these accounts, has nothing to do with what we can find out from the sciences about nature, including those aspects of ourselves that form part of that nature. Our ethical terms, on this view, arise in ways cut off from any facts which locate us as parts of nature, so that

---

3. The period from the development of the major Hellenistic schools (Epicureanism, Stoicism and hybrid forms of Stoic/Aristotelian ethics) to the rise of revived forms of Platonism. In discussions of ethics such as Cicero's *On Moral Ends* we find that the debate is structured by "Carneades' division," a framework for discussing ethical theories formulated by the great Academic skeptic Carneades. As a skeptic, he did not introduce ideas or methods of his own, but relied on the positions and methods he found himself arguing against; so it is notable that he pays no attention to "other-worldly" accounts of virtue and happiness such as Plato's in the *Theaetetus*. It seems reasonable to infer that these were not live options in ethical debate. With the rise of revived Platonism these theories had a new lease of life.

4. Philippa Foot, *Natural Goodness* (Oxford: Oxford University Press, 2001), 25–26.

when we try to apply these terms to parts of nature other than humans we have, weirdly, nothing to go on, and have to resort to feeble anthropomorphism. It strikes me as ironical that such accounts often arise (or are presented as arising) from an excessive respect for science. Not only do they cut off our self-understanding from the understanding we have of other things, they prevent us from seeing continuities between us and other living things, and in both these ways reveal themselves as profoundly anti-scientific.[5]

The simple point that the goodness of roots has nothing to do with what we do or don't choose enables us to see why virtue ethics, which makes the goodness of human lives central, is attracted not just to naturalism in general, but to naturalistic theories of an Aristotelian kind, for these locate us humans in the world in a way which makes us, as Rosalind Hursthouse has put it, "part of the natural, biological order of living things."[6] A scientific naturalism which talks in terms of physics is not helpful for ethical discourse, but the level of biology and ethology is one which helps us to make sense of ethics in a way that takes account of all of our nature—our biological nature which makes us part of the world of living things as well as our rational nature which makes us inquire and reflect about it.

What is so helpful for ethics from this kind of biological naturalism is that we find that the normativity of our ethical discourse is not something which emerges mysteriously with humans and can only be projected back, in an anthropomorphic way, onto trees and their roots. Rather, we find normativity in the realm of living things, plants and animals, already. It is part of the great merit of the work of Philippa Foot and Rosalind Hursthouse to have stressed this point. Like many important philosophical points, it is obvious once pointed out, but was rendered invisible for many decades by the ascendancy of non-naturalistic theories of ethical discourse. (Once we appreciate it, we can understand why those theories have been so barren of insight.)

Hursthouse, taking off from Foot's work, spells out, in her recent book, that ethical evaluation—if we are coming from a virtue ethics direction—is analogous to the ways in which we evaluate good, healthy specimens of living things such as animals and even plants. A good cactus is one whose parts and operations are well suited to serve its individual survival and the continuance of its species, in the way characteristic of cacti. We can evaluate good cacti on the one hand, and bad, defective ones on the other, by reference to the norms for cacti,

5. It has always been recognized that, formally, non-naturalistic metaethical accounts of ethical terms have more in common with religious or supernaturalist positions than they do with naturalistic accounts. But the implications, particularly for our attitude to the sciences (and the biological sciences in particular) have generally not been thought through.

6. Rosalind Hursthouse, *On Virtue Ethics* (Oxford: Oxford University Press, 1999), 206.

which are quite complex. With animals, especially social animals, things get more complicated, because there are four ends to consider: individual survival, the continuance of the species, characteristic pleasure or enjoyment and characteristic freedom from pain, and the good functioning of the social group. As ethological studies tell us, a "free-rider" wolf that joins in eating the prey without hunting with the pack is a defective wolf, and a barren female cheetah is a defective cheetah. This is so however much *we* might admire the wolf for getting away with it, or feel sorry for the pregnant cheetah's hard life.[7] The ways in which we are tempted to anthropomorphize nature have nothing to do with the actual ways in which members of species are evaluated: that is entirely in terms of what is appropriate to the species.

This last thought has both encouraged and discouraged philosophers who have suggested that our ethical evaluations of ourselves are recognizably like those we make of other species. In some ways the thought that "our ethical evaluations of ourselves ought to exhibit at least a recognizably similar structure to what we find in the botanists' and ethologists' evaluations of other living things"[8] is quite unsurprising; after all, we are social animals, and unless we are prepared to alienate ourselves completely from our own biology this is what we would expect. The discouragement comes from the attempts by sociobiologists, and some philosophers too reliant on what they think are the truths of biology, to argue that our ethical evaluations should allow for, or even stress, the fact that we belong to a species where by and large males are more aggressive than females, females carry the greater biological burden of child-bearing and -rearing, and so on. The facts about our species that naturalists and ethologists on field trips would report do not, to put it mildly, look like a good basis for ethical theory. It is this depressing history which puts some philosophers off the whole idea.

What is encouraging, however, about the thought that our ethical evaluations of ourselves should reflect the distinctiveness of our species, is the point that there is something which genuinely marks off our species, something which is not so obvious from a field trip and which sociobiologists have strikingly failed to take into account: our rationality. As Hursthouse puts it: "The other animals act. So do we occasionally, but mostly we act from reason, as they do not, and it is primarily in virtue of our actions from reason that we are ethically good or bad human beings."[9] In her book, she develops a form of naturalism for rational beings which belongs firmly in the Aristotelian tradition, seeing our ethical

---

7. Depressing facts about this can be found in ibid., 221 n. 3.
8. Ibid., 206.
9. Ibid., 217.

evaluations of ourselves as robustly based in the nature of us as a species, but taking properly into account the fact that we are a rational species.

Since we are social animals, we will evaluate ourselves on the way in which, and the degree to which, our make-up is fitted to serve these four ends, that is, (a) our individual survival, (b) the continuance of our species, (c) our characteristic freedom from pain and characteristic enjoyment, and (d) the good functioning of our social group—in the ways characteristic of our species. This is, of course, because any naturalistic account of animals—and of us, since we are animals—looks for traits which further the four ends when asking what makes us flourish, live lives which are good, choiceworthy lives.

But, because we are *rational* animals, we flourish in a way different from other social animals, in a way which involves our use of reason, that is, the ways we achieve our four ends in a rational way. And this, as Hursthouse plainly sets out, makes a very large difference. For it is because we are rational that we can *criticize* and *change* what we do, and can *choose* to live and act in a variety of ways. Our conceptions of what it is to live a good life are not just given by the way that biology has left us able to achieve our four ends. One striking example of this is that it does seem to be the message of biology that men are by and large more aggressive than women, and that women bear the brunt of reproduction; but this does not land us with having to think that this must be the way the good life for men and for women has to go. This is because we can, and do, *transform* our conceptions of the good life for men and for women in the light of rational considerations, of what we have good reason to do, and ways of thinking about our lives that we have good reason to go for.

It is because we are rational animals that we can't identify what is characteristic of a good human life in the way that we can for other species. Further, even if we could, we would not thereby be committed to thinking that this *must* be the good life for *us*, just because we are humans. It is one of the most original achievements of the book that Hursthouse not only faces this point, but takes it up into her theory. "Our characteristic way of going on . . . is a rational way. A 'rational way' is any way that we can rightly see as good, as something we have reason to do."[10] This is normative in just the same way as are claims about other species' characteristic ways of behaving. But two points are different with humans. One is that most of us humans don't in fact carry on that way—and thus are defective humans beings. The other is that this gives us a characteristic way of going on only at an extremely high level of generality. It doesn't determine specific ways of life for us, in the way that characteristic ways of behaving do for other species.

10. Ibid., 222–223.

Thus, although virtue must enable us to achieve our four ends, this allows for considerable variation in the lifestyles within which we develop the virtues. For example, the virtues might be practiced by a celibate monk; whether he does so or not depends not on his lifestyle but on whether or not he lives his chosen way of life honestly, with charity and so on. For, as Hursthouse says, "a life lived in accordance with the virtues can take a great variety of forms, including those in which the exercise of at least one virtue figures much more largely and even at the expense of the exercise of others."[11] The virtues practiced in a celibate lifestyle exclude, in an obvious enough way, virtues that can be practiced only in family and social circumstances. How then can they contribute to the ends of the continuance of the species and the good functioning of the social group? Now I agree with Hursthouse that the argument does not just end here. Plenty has been said, in many societies and not just in Christian ones, as to how celibates do contribute to these ends in an indirect way. Celibates often, for example, function as teachers to the young, and serve to maintain rituals important to the cohesive functioning of society. These societies have a conception of the continuance of the species such that you can contribute to it by helping to bring up children, not just by having them, and a conception of the good functioning of the social group which includes participation in various rituals. These can certainly be defended as reasonable conceptions of these ends, and ones that have much empirical support over a vast variety of societies and cultures.

Nonetheless, Hursthouse maintains that "the structure—the appeal to just those four ends—really does constrain, substantially, what I can reasonably maintain is a virtue in human beings. I cannot just proceed from some premises about what it is reasonable or rational for human beings to do to some conclusion that it is rational to act in such-and-such a way, and hence that a good human being is one who acts that way. I have to consider whether the corresponding character trait (if such a thing could be imagined) would foster or be inimical to those four ends."[12] Her example is that impersonal benevolence, beloved by consequentialists, fails as a virtue because it cannot reasonably be seen as furthering the ends of the continuance of the species and the good functioning of the social group. For it looks as though our natural tendency to bond to our own families, relatives, and loved ones does tend to further those ends, and that impersonal benevolence, if taken to be a virtue, would not. Suppose that we did develop impersonal benevolence, and regarded it as a virtue—that is, as a character trait of not just acting in certain ways but of thinking, feeling, and reacting in a complex set of interconnected ways. Then we would be suffi-

11. Ibid., 216.
12. Ibid., 224.

ciently detached from our own families, for example, that I would not be *particularly* bothered if I never had the chance to spend time with my own child, and, if my child were hurt, would not feel that it was anything particularly to do with *me*. How would this further our ends as *social* animals, who nurture our offspring?[13]

Now I agree wholeheartedly with both of these particular conclusions—that it is perfectly possible to practice the virtues in a celibate lifestyle, and that impersonal benevolence of a consequentialist kind could not be a virtue. But that Hursthouse defends both of them raises a problem here, or at least an issue which requires further thought. Reflecting about her position has pushed me to think further about the kind of naturalism that we are concerned with, for I think that we face an alternative here about the kind of naturalism required by a virtue ethics theory.

I shall pose the issue by asking, what is the relation between the four ends which we have because we are social animals, and our human rationality, which enables us to choose and create so many different ways of life? I shall distinguish between the weaker and the stronger relation between them. (We shall see why I characterize them as weaker and stronger, and claim that they go with weaker and stronger forms of virtue ethics.)

The weaker relation is the one which is generally associated with, and expected from, Aristotelian forms of virtue ethics. These rely on a form of naturalism which puts us in our biological place and emphasizes, as Foot and Hursthouse do, continuities between our ways of evaluating ourselves and the evaluative patterns to be found in the lives of animals and plants. I call this the weaker relation because it holds that our four ends that we have as social animals form a robust constraint on the exercise of our rationality, and thus give it a weaker ability to transform them than the stronger view holds.

For the Aristotelian, human nature provides a kind of barrier which rational thinking has to respect, since otherwise it will be frustrated. The example of impersonal benevolence brings this out in a vivid way. Human nature constrains our rationality—our ability to choose different ways of life, to transform what we do and what we are—in two ways. Firstly, some attempts will just be unrealistic. Mothers do care about their own children in a particularly intimate way, and so impersonal benevolence would be peculiarly difficult to inculcate as a pattern of behavior, never mind a virtue. Human nature is not plastic in this re-

---

13. Indeed, there is a familiar problem at this point. What would motivate adults to bring children up to have the correct (on this view) moral outlook—that is, impersonal benevolence? As often, consequentialists are assuming that prolonged care of the young and their upbringing in the right way "come free" with the theory, even though the theory itself gives it no recognition and indeed has no room for it.

spect, as twentieth-century totalitarian regimes have discovered. And secondly, even if we *could* transform and reshape ourselves in this way—even if we could make ourselves more plastic in this respect—this couldn't be a *good* way of life for beings with our human nature. This has been obvious since Plato in the *Laws* rethought the radical suggestions about family life sketched in the *Republic*. We can think up science fiction scenarios in which there are societies of beings for whom (or for which) this could be a good life, but these beings would not be very like us.[14]

Human nature, then—human nature as we find it given in a naturalistic account which respects the right kind of sciences—sets bounds on the kinds of ways in which we can rationally rethink the way we live in these two ways. Firstly, some ways just won't work. People won't act that way, and if they're made to act that way they will resist it. It will have to be forced on them, rather than being, as we say, natural to them. Secondly, even if we *could* make these ways work—somehow change people so that they ceased to resist—this would be a bad idea. Humans wouldn't flourish if they lived in those ways, even if they could be forced or manipulated into trying them out.

This is the weaker relation between our rationality and our human nature as social animals which gives us our four ends. Is it strong enough for an ethics of *virtue,* one which will give our lives *ideals* to pursue in the face of all the self-ishness and short-sightedness that characterize humans as they actually are?

There are, I think, two worries here, of different kinds although they are related. One is that on some points it looks as though we do have *prima facie* reason to worry whether the weaker relation will produce conclusions that are ethically strong enough. For example, Hursthouse is rightly insistent that the way that reproduction weighs more heavily on women than on men gives us no reason to think that because of this the good life for women should be narrowed and constrained in advance, compared to the options for men. But, notoriously, many otherwise intelligent people have thought that human nature did produce exactly this barrier to women as opposed to men. Aristotle famously helped to bring the whole idea of ethically appealing to human nature into disrepute with his easy assumption that, because women unarguably do have a different kind of life from men, therefore the kind of good life they can aspire to, and the kinds of virtue that they can practice, are inevitably going to be different from those open to men. (And no prizes for guessing which is the

14. The Platonist can take up the argument by claiming that a good life will in fact require our transforming some aspects of our human nature into something different (as the *Republic* in fact does argue). This is to reject the naturalistic approach of the Aristotelian, demanding that ethics have a different kind of basis, and taking us away from the present debate.

superior version.) But more reasonable positions than Aristotle's can be defended, and have been. The fact that we care for our families is an important fact about our nature, showing that we can't, and anyway shouldn't, cultivate impersonal benevolence as a virtue; attempts to use our rationality to do this are misguided. This is because it wouldn't be compatible with our being the kinds of social animals that we are, with our characteristic four ends. Why aren't the biological differences between the sexes equally significant when we consider our nature as social animals, with our characteristic four ends? Why can't they be reasonably held to stand in the way of attempts to reason out good ways of living which counteract or overcome the biological disadvantages of women? As I indicated, I'm not in doubt about the right conclusion; I'm here raising a worry as to whether the weaker, Aristotelian view of the relationship between our rationality and our human nature as social animals of a certain kind is really strong enough for us to feel that it fully entitles us to it.

The second worry is more indirect. It concerns the result when we turn to the implications of the weaker view for the agent who raises the question of how living according to the virtues will benefit him as an individual. For the issue of how the virtues enable us to live good lives and flourish as human beings is connected to the issue of how the virtues benefit *me*, if I am virtuous. We can see this particularly clearly with Aristotelian forms of virtue ethics, which hold to the weaker relation, and also hold the thesis that living virtuously is necessary, though not sufficient, for flourishing, living happily. I shall not here be concerned with arguments to show that living virtuously is necessary for flourishing. The worry here concerns the thought that for the Aristotelian view, virtue is not sufficient.

Now this can easily be made to seem a strange worry. The thought that virtue is sufficient for happiness or flourishing is apt to produce Aristotle's response: you can't be serious. But *if* you accept that a flourishing life isn't just one in which you have lots of stuff, or one in which you get success by any means— if, that is, you accept that wicked or selfish people do not in fact flourish, so that only those who live virtuously have a chance of flourishing—then a problem does emerge as to why virtue is not sufficient for flourishing. For it is up to me whether I live virtuously, or at least try to, but Aristotelian theories accept that even if I do the best I can I may still be deprived of happiness by factors that are beyond my control. For Aristotle, happiness is a hybrid combination of living virtuously and of achieving a measure of success in worldly terms. The latter is not under my control, and cannot be guaranteed.

I am not here thinking of the kind of case that Aristotle himself worries most about—what might be called the Priam situation, where an individual lives virtuously and successfully, and then meets total worldly shipwreck, and Aristotle is left holding that he is neither happy nor unhappy.[15] What concerns us here is rather the point that someone may put all her efforts into living virtuously and still be deprived of flourishing because of something which from her point of view is bad luck in the *natural* lottery (as we call it). She may live virtuously and yet fail to flourish because of being, to use Aristotle's examples, friendless, childless, or very ugly. Even if we think these examples are no longer realistic (though I doubt this, given the tremendous emphasis on appearance and popularity in most societies) we get the virtuous person who does not flourish because she is always chronically sick, or dies prematurely. The thought here is that our human nature as social animals makes it impossible for us to flourish if we cannot form normal social contacts, or lead a normally active life, or (in some societies) lack family support in old age, or die prematurely, with projects unfulfilled, even if these disasters are no fault of our own. People in this situation are suffering from a tragedy that they do not deserve, but they are not flourishing.

This worry—that virtue does not guarantee flourishing—takes two forms, both problematic for the status of virtue ethics as an ethical theory. Firstly, is it good enough for an ethical theory to tell us that virtue is the only way to flourish, but that we may fail to flourish because of factors about human nature which are not our fault and which our rationality is powerless to alter? Virtue ethics is a very demanding theory, which requires us to reshape our lives; is it reasonable for it also to demand that we lower our expectations of what it can do for us? Hursthouse makes much of the analogy with health; a healthy diet, exercise, and so on is not just a good idea but the only reliable bet if we want to live a long healthy life, and yet there is no guarantee, since the people who live healthy lives may drop dead young and those that live unhealthy lives may go on to be a hundred.[16] I think that we expect more of a moral theory than this—in the health case, after all, I might turn out to be lucky in my genes, but I can hardly have such a hope with virtue and flourishing. It is reasonable for me to ask why it should be so important for me to make myself into one kind of person rather than another, when my flourishing turns out to depend on factors which have nothing to do with me.

This is connected to the second point, which is that we expect that an ethi-

15. The Priam situation worries Aristotle in the concluding parts of chapters 9 and 10 of book 1 of the *Nicomachean Ethics;* the concluding part of chapter 8 worries about the kind of problem I focus on here (being ugly, childless, and so on). Stephen Gardiner has made the point that external goods and evils can play two kinds of role: they are antecedent materials for action, and also the subsequent results of action. The Priam situation deals with the second role, whereas I am here focusing on the first.

16. Hursthouse, *On Virtue Ethics,* 170–174.

cal theory must be universal, by which I mean, fairly minimally, that it must apply equally to everyone, with no arbitrariness as to what beings are left outside it. (This point is of course problematic when we think of the role of non-human animals, but I shall lay that aside for now.) Virtue ethics, on the weaker interpretation, makes a demand of everyone, that they be virtuous, claims that living virtuously is the only way to flourish, and yet allows that you may fail anyway however hard you try, because of factors outside your control. Not all these factors trace back directly to our human nature as social animals, but some of them plausibly do. So if failure to be universal is problematic for virtue ethics, which I take it that it is, then it seems to be a liability for Aristotelian forms of virtue ethics that they think that the exercise of our rationality in forming the good life is constrained by some aspects of human nature which are not amenable to being transformed by it.

There is a response to this.[17] Aristotelian forms of virtue ethics, it can be claimed, are universal in that it is true for everyone that living virtuously is necessary for flourishing; everyone has the same rationale for adopting the theory. The unlucky, it is true, may fail to flourish because of factors other than virtue, but even the unlucky are better off, if they live virtuously, than the non-virtuous or vicious; for, since virtue is necessary for happiness, these people do not flourish however lucky or unlucky they are. Thus the necessity thesis can make a reasonable demand of everyone. But while this response has merit, it also, I think, has two weaknesses. Firstly, we do need to be assured that even the unlucky can flourish to the extent that they are virtuous; and people unlucky in the natural lottery raise more serious problems here than the Priam situation does. Aristotle himself notoriously thinks that for many people flourishing is just not achievable because of conditions that they can do nothing about, and we need a firm assurance that modern forms of virtue ethics need not be similarly resigned. Secondly, the idea of the unlucky virtuous people still being better off than the lucky non-virtuous needs more support from within the theory. Virtue is not sufficient for you to flourish; for that it needs external goods. Yet it is still powerful enough to make you better off than the non-virtuous with external goods, even when you lack those external goods. Even if we accept this conclusion, we need to know more precisely just what it is about virtue that permits it: just why is it more important for flourishing than external goods for the unlucky, but never enough, without external goods, for the lucky to flourish?[18]

So much for the situation where we have what I call the weaker form of the

17. Both Rosalind Hursthouse and Stephen Gardiner have made me think harder about this.

18. This problem exercised later Aristotelians considerably; for a persuasive but ultimately unsuccessful attempt to answer this problem, see Antiochus' theory in book 5 of Cicero's *On Moral Ends*.

relation between our rationality and our human nature as social animals. It is clear by now why I think of Aristotelian forms of virtue ethics as themselves being weaker forms of virtue ethics.

I turn now to the stronger relation between our rationality and our human nature as social animals. On this view, our human nature is simply the material that our rationality has to work with. I put it in terms of material because of the usefulness here of a metaphor which is very common in ancient thinking on this topic. My practical rationality is seen as a skill or expertise which gets to work on the circumstances of my life, including of course the rest of my human nature, and makes something of it, in the way that a craftsperson makes an object from raw materials. Human nature does not have to be seen as wholly plastic and transformable into anything at all; after all, a good craftsperson will respect the potentials of the materials. This corresponds to the point that we are living beings of a *distinctive* kind, and that projects for living well have to work with this point. But what is distinctive about us is that our ways of living can be transformed *as a whole* by our rationality; we can choose and create new ways of living. To quote from Hursthouse, "Apart from obvious physical constraints and possible psychological constraints, there is no knowing what we *can* do from what we *do* do, because we can assess what we do do and at least try to change it."[19] I can try to turn my life from a mass of materials which are formless in the sense that I haven't given them form, into a product of rational thought, unified by my trying to live by certain kinds of reason and make myself into a certain kind of person, a life which I am *living,* rather than just taking for granted.

On this stronger view, all of our social animal nature is transformed by its being activated, as we live, in a rational way. To take something basic, although we eat to satisfy hunger, and so do lions, we do so in a way which is not simply tied to the satisfaction of hunger, as the lion's is. It involves a number of social aspects—eating is standardly a social occasion, meals are structured in various ways, numerous conventions are involved. It also involves a number of individual choices—we like some foods and not others, and don't eat what we don't like unless to be polite, we make great efforts to prepare food in complex ways, we care about specific results. So even our basic needs and the ways we fulfill them are thoroughly transformed by occurring in the life of a rational animal. I have taken something basic like eating, because it would be easy to think that this aspect of us really is something we share with the other animals in an inevitable way, and so is something that is properly to be seen as a constraint on the way in which rationality can rethink our lives. But if we think about the role that eating plays in our lives, we can see that we don't share it with the other

19. Hursthouse, *On Virtue Ethics,* 221.

animals in a relevant way. Its meaning in our lives is quite different from what it is in theirs; it has been transformed by the fact that we are rational animals. Of course there are some situations where humans are so reduced by starvation that they do think of eating as the other animals do, but these are situations so desperate that considerations of living *well* have to recede.

The same kind of consideration is true of the place in our lives of sexual differentiations and their implications. We do not blame male cheetahs for impregnating the female and then paying no further attention to the birth and upbringing of the cubs. This is just the evaluative pattern for cheetahs, and for us to get indignant is anthropomorphism. Indeed the wide variety of patterns here among other animals should warn us off anthropomorphism, since in the case of so many of them any attempt to see them in human terms rapidly becomes distressing, disgusting, or otherwise clearly inappropriate.[20]

In a human life, sex and reproduction have a completely different significance from what they do in the lives of the other animals. They give rise, for a start, to patterns of family life (which themselves vary, of course, among different societies). So for humans differences of sexual role are already part of a system of living together with other humans. And, unlike other social animals, we see these as socialized, as part of a shared social world that is the product of shared efforts and subject to changes in the ways those efforts are made. Biological differences are already seen as being part of, involved in, social roles and patterns. It is part of the way we see these biological differences that we see them as resulting from and involved in relationships which can be negotiated in different ways. Changes can thus be brought about in different circumstances. Even humans who hold biological differences, and the social roles within which they are located, to be changeless, hold this for reasons: they are seen as fate we have to submit to, imposed on us by God, or the like; they are not, as they are for other social animals, just a given which cannot even be thought about.

This is, of course, as brief and schematic as it could be, but it serves, I hope, to show that on this perspective the biological differences between the reproductive roles of men and women are not to be seen as a barrier to the rational planning of good lives—"it would be nice if women could be the professional equals of men, but they simply can't, because of their special biological role of motherhood" and the like. This whole idea does not get off the ground, because the special biological role of motherhood is already seen as part of human *social* life. Creating ways of life in which it is not a disadvantage to women is not a matter of bringing the merely biological under control, but of changing our views about the proper organization of family life.

---

20. It is often so incongruous as to be comic, as in the *Far Side* cartoons.

What of Hursthouse's point that on an Aristotelian view we can see clearly why impersonal benevolence could not be a virtue? The Aristotelian view seemed to do a good job of showing why this was so. Humans can't live in such a way as to be emotionally indifferent to their children, say; and even if we could be forced or induced to do so, it could not be a *good* way for us humans to live. Here the idea that human nature is providing barriers to reason-driven ways of organizing our lives seemed the right idea. If we think that our human nature is more like material for us to develop into a finished product by the use of our rationality, it might seem that we have little or no defense against the idea that impersonal benevolence could be a virtue for us. We are attached to our own children and families; why isn't *this* an already socialized aspect of our life which is subject to negotiation and to our coming to think of better ways of organizing it?

That is exactly what it is, on the stronger view; but the stronger view also claims that it does allow us a good defense against the idea that impersonal benevolence could be a virtue. More than that, it claims that it actually gives us a stronger defense than the Aristotelian view did.

On the stronger view, we reject impersonal benevolence as a virtue, on the same grounds as the Aristotelian does. Humans do care about their own families, in such a way that they have to be forced to act otherwise; and even if they could be forced or otherwise changed so as to act otherwise, this would not result in a good way of life for humans as we are. On the stronger view, however, this is not presented as a brute fact about humans standing in the way of a rational proposal. Rather, impersonal benevolence as a virtue for humans is rejected as being a bad idea, one that has more rational considerations against it than for it. I can do no more than sketch some of them here. Any project whose success requires forcing people to act in ways that are deeply repugnant to them is dubious on several grounds. It is unlikely to succeed, for a start. It exacts tremendous cost. And it raises sharply the question what this goal is, for which people's lives have to be commandeered. What justifies it? If it is urged that it will make people's lives either better or happier, what grounds such an idea of the goal which people have to be forced to pursue, or fooled into pursuing? And what justifies the idea that this is a *project* in the first place? Who are these people who are proposing to alter other people's lives from the outside, as though they didn't share that kind of life? And where have they got their idea of a good human life? If it's so good, why doesn't it appeal to other people anyway? These are, obviously, all first versions of objections which have been developed with great sophistication over the last few years; here I merely mention them to indicate that the stronger version of virtue ethics does not lack arguments against the idea that universal benevolence might be a virtue for us humans.

Moreover, arguing against the idea on its own terms can reasonably be seen as a more powerful defense than claiming that the proposal is defeated by human nature, as though that were just a barrier about which nothing more could be said. That way of looking at the matter arguably gives too much to the other side, as though the proposal might be a rational one, with human nature as a merely mindless opposition, the spirit being willing but the flesh unfortunately weak. On the stronger view, we are not reduced to thinking of our resistance to a virtue of impersonal benevolence as merely the old Adam part of us rebelling against our rational planning. It is *as rational beings* that we reject it; we are not just social animals but rational ones, who can recognize a bad idea when we see one, and realize that as social, rational animals we would not flourish under such a system: the result would not be good *human* lives, taking all of human nature into account.

Indeed, the weaker, defensive posture arguably grants too much to the consequentialist way of thinking which produced the proposal of impersonal benevolence as a virtue in the first place. For the consequentialist, morality makes a rational demand, and if we fail to meet it this merely shows us to be weak and selfish. The fact that we care about our "near and dear" gives us a "bad conscience" because it appeals to our selfishness; we feel it is "forbidden fruit" because it stands in the way of our achieving more good, which is the rational demand on us.[21] In showing this position to be completely misguided, we are on stronger ground arguing that as rational animals we have every reason to reject it, than if we argued that we would be recalcitrant about it even supposing it to be a rational demand.

This is what I have called the stronger position: is it strong enough to sustain an ethics of virtue, which, as I've insisted, gives us ideals to pursue in the face of

21. This is quite explicitly the view of Torbjörn Tännsjö, "Blameless Wrongdoing," *Ethics* 106 (1995): 126–127: "The recognition of the consequentialist rationale behind love (in general) does give a taste of forbidden fruit to our love, that is true. When, out of love, I pay special attention to a certain woman, rather than to a stranger, I may comfort myself with the thought that it is a good thing that I am the kind of person who is capable of loving someone, but I must also recognize that, if, in this particular situation, I were instead to pay more attention to the stranger, without, for that reason, turning into a person who is—otherwise—not capable of loving someone else, this would be a good thing to do. I could do it but I don't, shame on me, and, therefore, I do make a moral mistake (which makes my love taste somewhat bitter). But that's the way I am. And therefore, I can retain my special concerns, without having to give up my belief in the truth of consequentialism.

"This mixture of love and bad conscience (because of my belief in the truth of consequentialism) is something I do exhibit, and, from the fact that I do exhibit it, it follows that this is something that can be exhibited. My love survives the knowledge of its rationale; it does not erode. Therefore, I stick— without any risk— with my belief in consequentialism.

"As a matter of fact, the observation that there is an element of 'forbidden fruit' in love and friendship, according to consequentialism, is as it should be. This is something most people testify that they feel when, in a world of starvation, they watch TV and show special concern for their near and dear."

the difficulties we have living up to them? The problem here is more likely to be that it is *too* strong. We do not need here to worry about possibly reactionary uses of human nature to constrain ethical thought in indefensible ways. But we might feel uncomfortable about the implication in this case for the agent for whom the question arises how the virtues will benefit her. For, as already stressed, these questions are linked. Just as the weaker relation turned out to go with the weaker, Aristotelian view that the virtues are necessary for a flourishing life, but not sufficient, so the stronger relation turns out to go with the stronger, Platonic-Stoic view that living virtuously is sufficient for flourishing.

On this view, if you draw a short straw in the natural lottery (chronic illness, disfigurement, premature death, and so on) these are not aspects of human nature which, as Aristotle puts it, curtail and maim your ability to flourish however virtuously you live. Rather, they are just more of the material you have to work with, along with your situation in life, your job, your circumstances in general. It is just as much up to you to live a virtuous life in these particular circumstances as it is for someone in circumstances that you would prefer. Someone with a normal appearance, health, reasonable income, and friends can live virtuously; so can the solitary, poor, ill, and disfigured person. The latter is trying to achieve flourishing through a virtuous life just as much as the former person is. On the stronger view, the latter person is not doomed to fail at flourishing if she lives virtuously, just because her circumstances are not those of the former one. This does not imply, of course, that there is nothing preferable about the former person's circumstances. Of course we would all choose to have those circumstances rather than to be poor, ill, and so on. But the fact that we would all prefer the former life, in the sense of the circumstances of that life, does not show that there is something doomed to failure about the second life, in the sense of the *living* of that life.

So, given the stronger relation of our rationality to the rest of our human nature as social animals, all of our natural circumstances, just like the rest of our circumstances, are material for our rationality to work on as we try to live the good life. There are thus no aspects of our human nature required for us to flourish but outside the control of our rationality. What matters is not whether I am healthy, but what I make, in my life, of my health or lack of it. What matters is not how long I live, but the quality of the life I have lived, however long or short. What matters is not whether I have narrow or wide scope for my actions, but how I cope with the range I have.

There is a familiar objection to this kind of view: why, on this view, is it rational for us even to prefer favorable circumstances? Why should I care about being healthy, having friends, and so on, if these do not contribute to my flourishing? I can't deal with this issue here, but I should note that this is not handwaving; this is a point on which much has been thought, and there are power-ful and developed ways available of meeting this point.[22]

Probably the biggest advantage of the stronger view is its stronger claim to universality. Living virtuously is required for flourishing—and nobody will fail at this for reasons which are beyond their control or arbitrary. It is open to any-one to live virtuously given the circumstances of life which they have, and so the poor and ill can flourish as well as the rich and healthy. Epictetus the slave and Marcus Aurelius the emperor can both equally well try to flourish by liv-ing virtuously; indeed we know that the emperor found the slave's book help-ful. It is one of the most attractive features of the Stoic version of virtue ethics that it is universal in this way, and thus appears more like ethical theories like Kant's with emphasis on the thought that living virtuously makes us members of a moral community in which everyone is an equal member no matter what the circumstances of their actual lives.[23]

Because of this, the demands that this stronger version of virtue ethics makes are matched by the point that if we go in for it, we do not have to lower our expectations about success; nobody will fail for arbitrary reasons, and so the ef-fort we put into living virtuously, if we do, will be rewarded on the basis of what we do, not on the basis of facts about us that are outside our competence to do anything about.[24]

But we come to what is for many the biggest objection to the stronger ver-sion of virtue ethics. Does what I have called the stronger version of the rela-

22. This is the major point at issue in much of ancient ethics. The Stoics' answer to this problem is their theory of "preferred indifferents"; we have reason to value, and to choose, things like health and long life, as long as we recognize that they have a quite different kind of value from the sort that virtue has, so that virtue is sufficient for happiness while leaving us with a realistic attitude to the circumstances of our lives. One major advantage of this is that we can reject as confused the Aristotelian hybrid notion of happiness, as constituted both by the living of a life and (some unspecified) level of natural advantages. I have reason to care about the circumstances of my life, and to prefer them to be one way rather than another; but this is a radically different attitude from the one I take to the living of my life; this is some-thing which is up to me whatever the circumstances of my life. Any attempt to think of happiness in terms of a threshold, as the Aristotelians do, will require a hybrid notion of happiness which conflates these two different attitudes, and tries to combine the living of a life with its circumstances. Despite the ingenuity of later Aristotelians I do not think that they succeed in meeting this point, but the issue can-not be fully argued here.

23. But is *virtue* equally available to everyone whatever their circumstances? If not, the theory will not be universal. The Stoic answer is that it is, because to develop virtue you need to develop your rea-son, which is something we all have and can develop. There is another analogy here with Kant, who thinks that it is equally open to all humans to reason morally, not restricted to those with certain natural advantages.

24. The point can of course be raised here that the notions of *success* and *reward* are not being used in ways that are familiar to those who associate them with monetary reward, success in terms of status and so on. For present purposes we should just note that this is a point which has been answered at length by developed versions of the stronger theory.

tion between our rationality and the rest of our human nature as social animals give us a plausible form of *naturalism*? We might think not, if we think that the Aristotelian form is a plausible one. For it stresses continuities between the evaluative patterns in our lives and those that are to be found in the lives of plants and animals. The fact that we are rational animals makes a big difference, but does not nullify the continuities. Because we are rational, we can transform our lives, but it remains true that our four ends as social animals constrain what we can do by way of living well.

A stronger form of naturalism than the Aristotelian kind does have to stress what makes us different from plants and animals. Thus it does not find it particularly helpful from the point of view of ethics to stress the continuities between the evaluative patterns in the lives of plants and animals and those in ours—other than the fact that we are part of nature: we still stress the point that when we examine our own rationality we are examining something of which we can and must give an account acceptable to the sciences. Many forms of ethics which have emphasized our natures as essentially rational animals have taken this to go with a position, associated with Kant, which marks a sharp break between the kind of fact which science can discover about us and the kind of fact which is formed by our rationality. But this is only one way in which the position could be developed, and in the modern world it is far more reasonable for us to think as the ancient Stoics did—that our rationality indeed makes us different from other living things, but is just as much a natural fact about us and the world we live in as are facts about other species, and about us insofar as we are like them and our lives like theirs.

Thus there is nothing unscientific about an approach which stresses that what matters for the living of our lives, from an ethical point of view, is our rationality. We are not cutting ourselves off from the world that science studies, as the non-naturalists do. Indeed, the approach can appeal not only to biology and ethology but to another large and developed area of science, namely psychology. This is the approach of Lawrence Becker, for example, in his book *A New Stoicism*.[25] He develops an ethical theory which he claims has the structure of ancient Stoicism. We begin by considering our natures as creatures with various wants and means to achieve these rationally. We examine the development of our rationality, and the way in which we can come to value not just its instrumental use to get the ends we want, but its employment itself *as* rational agency; thus we come to have a conception of ourselves as rational agents, and to value this in a non-instrumental way. This is all built up from accepted studies and results in the psychological literature. It does not require us to be particularly def-

25. Lawrence Becker, *A New Stoicism* (Princeton: Princeton University Press, 1998).

erential to any particular school of psychology, merely to go along with widely accepted and tested results. I won't here go further into the issue of whether Becker succeeds in showing from this story, which is clearly a modern version of what the ancient Stoics called *oikeiosis* or familiarization, that we can get to a distinctive ethical theory which is of the sort I have sketched here.[26] I think that books like his are the beginning of a discussion, rather than the end. There has been comparatively little development of the stronger form of virtue theory and its associated form of naturalism, compared with the weaker, Aristotelian form and the kind of naturalism appropriate to it. I do think that there is an interesting philosophical issue as to whether it is the weaker or the stronger form of naturalism discussed here which is in the end the most satisfactory version for an ethics of virtue. If this discussion develops, then we may find ourselves seriously discussing whether virtue ethics should hold that virtue is sufficient, or merely necessary for flourishing. If so, then modern ethical discussion will at long last have caught up with its lively state in the first century B.C.,[27] which I for one would consider progress.[28]

26. In particular, we need to examine whether Becker really succeeds in showing that from this psychological basis we can get to the *sufficiency* of virtue for happiness, as he claims we can.

27. This is only half facetious. The discussions in, for example, Cicero's *De finibus (On Moral Ends)* are sophisticated and forceful, and it does not require much interpretation to see that they are about matters which are still relevant.

28. I am very grateful for comments at the very stimulating Christchurch conference, for longstanding friendly discussion with Rosalind Hursthouse and for written comments from Stephen Gardiner and an anonymous referee.

CHAPTER 2

Seneca's Virtuous Moral Rules

STEPHEN M. GARDINER

One prominent feature of contemporary virtue ethics is its insistence on the normative priority of the virtuous person. Another is its skepticism about the place of rules or principles in moral decision-making. But the Stoics seem paradoxical on this score. On the one hand, they are great proponents of the authority and privileged position of the sage; on the other, they see moral life as structured by an elaborate system of principles and rules.

This apparent tension in the Stoic view was noticed even in antiquity.[1] The heretic Aristo, defending the authority and autonomy of the sage, criticises mainstream Stoics for assigning a prominent role to moral rules. Such rules are of scant import, he says, since they are helpful neither to the sage (who has no need of help) nor to the learner (who will not be helped by such things). Hence, Aristo seems to be arguing in the same spirit as contemporary virtue ethicists. (And notice that he is the heretic.)

---

1. A similar paradox is identified by Phillip Mitsis, who questions Paul Vander Waerdt's "radical particularist" account of early Stoicism. Mitsis says: "Surely, it is *prima facie* a little paradoxical to claim that the tradition of natural law begins as a theory rooted in the assumption that moral reasoning is not lawlike, and that when we are faced with forming our moral attitudes or acting morally, natural law can offer no contentful recommendations beyond the immediate moment." Mitsis, "The Stoics and Aquinas on Virtue and Natural Law," *The Studia Philonica Annual* 15 (2003): 35–53; at 36.

Vander Waerdt's solution to this problem is to claim that various philosophical and historical pressures force a move away from particularism from the early to the later Stoa. See Vander Waerdt, "The Original Theory of Natural Law," *The Studia Philonica Annual* 15 (2003): 17–34; "Zeno's Republic and the Origins of Natural Law," in *The Socratic Movement,* ed. Vander Waerdt (Ithaca: Cornell University Press, 1994); and "Politics and Philosophy in Stoicism," *Oxford Studies in Ancient Philosophy* 9 (1991): 185–212. My more moderate account, offered later, implies an alternative explanation of Mitsis' paradox.

Seneca defends the orthodox Stoic position against Aristo, arguing that the Stoic emphasis on the central role of the sage is compatible with their endorsement of two different kinds of moral principle,[2] precepts (the praecepta) and doctrines (the decreta).[3] In this paper, I defend a new interpretation of Seneca's moral principles, suggest a resolution to the apparent paradox, and explain how this Stoic position avoids some of the problems normally attributed to virtue ethics because of its insistence on the normative priority of the virtuous person. In particular, I claim, first, that the focus of some virtue ethics on the rejection of moral principles is misguided (as indeed is the whole debate between proponents of principles and their opponents); and second, that through an appropriate account of rules, the virtue ethicist has a way to meet concerns about the ability of her theory to be action-guiding.

The paper is divided into four parts. The first briefly explains the insistence of many contemporary virtue ethicists on both the normative priority of the virtuous person and the rejection of moral principles, and contrasts this with the basics of the Stoic position in Seneca. The second looks at two rival views of the role of principles in Stoicism (one associated with Gisela Striker and Phillip Mitsis, and the other with Brad Inwood) and argues that neither is attractive, though not for the reasons that they usually offer against each another.[4] This discussion is of interest in part because the rival views mirror some complex positions in contemporary ethical theory. The third part introduces my own interpretation through a survey of the evidence from Seneca. The final part briefly explores the implications of my interpretation for contemporary virtue ethics.

---

2. Actually, Seneca makes the stronger claims (a) that such principles are necessary for any moral theory, and (b) that there is something self-defeating about any attempt to eliminate them. But I will not consider those arguments here. See Seneca, Lucius Anneus, *Ad Lucilium Epistulae Morales,* vol. 3, trans. R. M. Gummere (New York: Heinemann, 1925), 95.60. All translations will be from this volume unless otherwise noted.

3. This distinction between kinds of rules reveals that Aristo's skepticism is more complex than the initial gloss above suggests. Seneca has him saying:

"[T]he greatest benefit is derived from doctrines and from the definition of the supreme good. When a man has gained a complete understanding of this definition and has thoroughly learned it, he can frame for himself a precept directing what is to be done in a given case." (94.2)

This passage appears to establish (1) that Aristo endorses doctrines, and (2) that he believes that it is at least possible (and perhaps even necessary) for the sage to employ precepts. From this, it would seem that Aristo's main targets are the views (3) that precepts are worthwhile for the nonsage, and (4) that they make up an independent branch of philosophy. My account of Seneca helps to make sense of this dispute among the Stoics.

4. This part also builds a philosophical case for a position of the kind I defend on textual grounds in the next part.

1. Virtues and Rules

One way to think of virtue ethics is simply as the thesis that "the basic judgments in ethics are judgments about character."[5] By this, virtue ethicists typically mean to suggest that judgments about virtue are independent of,[6] and
justificatorily prior to, at least some other kinds of moral judgments, and, in particular, judgments about the rightness and wrongness of acts.[7] Thus, virtue, it is
sometimes said, has a certain kind[8] of normative priority.[9]

5. In this section I rely heavily on Daniel Statman's introduction to his edited volume, *Virtue Ethics:
A Critical Reader* (Georgetown: Georgetown University Press, 1997), 1–41; For quote, see 7.

6. Typically, this is thought to mean "not reducible to."

7. For example, Statman says, "What is essential [to virtue ethics] is the idea that aretaic judgments,
i.e., judgments about character, are prior to deontic judgments, i.e., judgments about right and wrong,"
ibid., 8; Gregory Trianosky claims that the way to understand virtue ethics is in terms of two claims: "(1)
At least some judgments about the value of character traits are independent of judgments about the rightness or wrongness of actions; (2) The notion of virtue justifies the notion of right conduct" (Trianosky,
"What is Virtue Ethics All About?" *American Philosophical Quarterly* 27: 335-44, reprinted in Statman, 42–
55); and Roger Crisp says that "A virtue ethicist can be characterized as someone who allows the virtues
to ground at least some reasons, perhaps alongside other moral reasons or non-moral reasons grounded
in the good of the agent" (Crisp, "Modern Moral Philosophy and the Virtues," in *How Should One Live?*
ed. Roger Crisp [Oxford : Oxford University Press, 1996], 7). John McDowell proposes that the question "How should one live?" is approached via the notion of a virtuous person, so that a conception of
right behavior is grasped, as it were, from the inside out ("Virtue and Reason," *The Monist* 62:3 [1979]:
331–350, at 331; cited by Statman, ibid., f. 32). There are various views about the extent and character of
both independence and explanatory priority. See Statman.

8. Ultimately, my account tends to dissolve, or at least reduce the importance of, the priority claim.
Still, it may be worth pointing out that it makes a difference whether one considers the priority thesis
to be primarily ontological (concerning the character of moral facts) or epistemological (concerning the
structure of moral knowledge). Though virtue ethics is not identical to particularism—so that one should
avoid assimilating the two—it is relevant here that Jay Garfield distinguishes between ontological versions of particularism— which he associates with Jonathan Dancy—and epistemological versions—
which he associates with John McDowell. Dancy, of course, is not a virtue ethicist; but McDowell is, and
inspires much of the work in this area. See Garfield, "Particularity and Principle: The Structure of Moral
Knowledge," in *Moral Particularism,* ed. Brad Hooker and Margaret Little (Oxford: Oxford University
Press), 178-204, at 181. Gerard Watson suggests that in Cicero at least "No attempt is made to preserve a
clear distinction between what we might call the ontological and epistemological order," since "his whole
purpose is to demonstrate the essential identity of the reason which directs the universe and the reason
of the good man." See Watson, "The Natural Law and Stoicism," in A. A. Long, ed. *The Problems of Stoicism* (London, 1971), 227–8.

9. Notice that virtue ethicists do not necessarily endorse full normative priority: the claim that judgments about virtue are independent of and justificatorily prior to *all* other kinds of moral judgments.
This is important when it comes to the Stoics, since they believe in a natural law which both grounds
and justifies claims about virtue, and so appear to reject full normative priority.

Does this mean that the Stoics are not virtue ethicists in the sense of interest to contemporary theorists? Not necessarily. First, other prominent virtue ethicists may also reject full normative priority. Consider, for example, the role played by *eudaimonia* in Aristotle's ethical theory, or that played by the bases
of moral responsiveness in Christine Swanton's theory. Second, the Stoics believe that nature is normative, and that the life of virtue is both coextensive with following nature and constitutive of it. So, at least
as far as human beings are concerned, there might be no meaningful distinction between virtue and the

This emphasis on the primacy of virtue tends to go hand in hand with a skepticism about the status and point of moral rules. This skepticism is in marked contrast to the central place of rules in the major rivals to virtue ethics, traditional utilitarian and Kantian theories of morality. As Daniel Statman puts it, according to such views:

> Ethical theories see it as their primary task to formulate principles . . . that should guide human behaviour. According to such theories, when we face a practical quandary, we are supposed to go through this list of principles, determine which principle applies to the particular case, and 'apply' it. When we face a conflict of considerations we are supposed to turn to some higher-order principle to resolve the conflict. In this manner, the ideal person is one whose principles govern everything he or she does, and the best theory is the one that provides the most comprehensive and consistent system of principles.[10]

But proponents of virtue ethics typically argue that this project has failed. Statman offers two reasons for their view. The first is that there seems no way to generate a completely exceptionless, universal moral principle that can simply be applied in this way; the second is that there are no really useful moral rule books that can be used in this simple deductive way. The principles are too abstract to guide conduct, and in most situations more than one principle might be applied, calling for the need for still more higher-level principles, which are even more abstract.[11]

Virtue ethicists claim that these problems can be explained by the fact that rule-based moralities overlook the importance of character and judgment. In particular, they fail to recognise that people with good moral characters are already sensitive to the morally salient features of situations, and do the right thing on the basis of that sensitivity, without appeal to principles. Hence, principles seem "neither necessary nor sufficient for right behaviour," and so "redundant."[12]

---

natural law, and so no relevant priority of the latter over the former. (According to my account, the rules that would be relevant here—the decreta—include the virtues.) Moreover, it is the fact that it is divine which would give nature priority on the Stoic view, not its being structured by rules. Finally, as a practical matter, the aspect of the Stoic position here that is of most interest to contemporary work is the place of virtue relative to rules, since it is the part that does not depend on the deeply controversial aspects of Stoic cosmology (e.g., that nature is normative, manifests a divine purpose, and that this purpose is communicated to the sage). This makes it reasonable to focus on the relative normative priority of virtue, even if ultimately the Stoics believe that there exists something beyond virtue with priority over it. (See my introduction to this volume.)

10. Ibid., 6.
11. Ibid., 6.
12. Ibid.

In light of the standard criticism, how might the Stoics defend their appeal to rules? In the contemporary discussion of Seneca's account, we find two main camps. According to the first, led by Gisela Striker and Phillip Mitsis, the Stoics escape the paradox by being extreme proponents of the primacy of moral principles, and characterizing the virtuous person as simply the embodiment of those principles. According to the second, represented by Brad Inwood, they escape it by asserting the primacy of the sage: the principles have only a minor role as rules of thumb for the nonvirtuous learner, and the sage is free to break them.

Now, I believe that there is something right about each of these views; yet as they stand, both are too extreme. Instead, Seneca's actual position occupies a much more appealing middle ground: while it is true that the sage has normative priority (as Inwood says), it is also true that moral principles are (at least partly) constitutive of practical rationality (as Striker and Mitsis maintain). The resolution of the apparent paradox depends on a new understanding of moral principles, and of the opposition of virtue ethicists to them.

2. Rules as Constitutive of Virtue: The Striker-Mitsis View

Let us begin with the Striker-Mitsis view.[13] Mitsis claims that rules are absolutely central to the Stoic account of ethics. He says, "for the Stoics . . . moral judgment and development are structured at every level by rules"; and, "the Stoics . . . are convinced that moral development depends *solely* on a deepening cognitive grasp of both universal and more determinate moral principles . . ."[14]

13. See Gisela Striker, "Origins of the Concept of Natural Law," *Proceedings of the Boston Area Colloquium in Ancient Philosophy* 2 (1987): 79–94; and "Following Nature: A Study in Stoic Ethics," *Oxford Studies in Ancient Philosophy* 9 (1991): 1–73. Both are reprinted in her *Essays in Hellenistic Epistemology and Ethics* (Cambridge: Cambridge University Press, 1996). For Mitsis, see Phillip Mitsis, "Seneca on Reason, Rules and Moral Development," in *Passions and Perceptions*, ed. J. Brunschwig and M. Nussbaum (Cambridge: Cambridge University Press, 1993), 285–312; "Natural Law and Natural Right in Post-Aristotelian Philosophy: The Stoics and their Critics," *Aufstieg und Niedergang der romischen Welt* II 37.7 (1994): 4812–50; "Moral Rules and the Aims of Stoic Ethics," *Journal of Philosophy* 83 (1986): 556–557; and "The Stoics and Aquinas."

The label "the Striker-Mitsis view" comes from Inwood. Mitsis (personal communication) tells me that he dislikes this characterization, since he views himself merely as defending a traditional view that goes back at least to Sidgwick and Zeller. I shall focus on Striker and Mitsis because they seem to have worked out the view in more detail in print. I should note, however, that I do not assume that their positions are identical—indeed, there is some evidence that they differ in what they say about, for example, moral conflict—rather, the idea is simply that they share the same general background assumptions about the centrality of rules. I assume that Inwood has the same position in mind.

14. Mitsis, "Seneca," 291 and 290, respectively, with emphasis added. Mitsis also says: "[T]he Stoics'

According to this reading, the Stoics are not merely opposed to the view that moral principles are unnecessary for ethics. Rather, they take precisely the contrary view: that moral judgment is *exclusively* a matter of understanding and applying moral principles. Furthermore, they believe this partly because their view directly confronts the main objection of contemporary virtue ethics: that it is appropriate sensitivity to situations that is vital, not the application of rules. According to Mitsis, the Stoic view is that:

> . . . moral rules can structure our understanding of a particular moral situation in ways that *guarantee* our sensitivity to its specific demands. For the Stoic, *developing the requisite sensitivity to moral particulars is strictly a matter of cognitively grasping the applications of such rules.*[15]

So the Stoics claim that sensitivity to particular situations is *itself* to be understood purely in terms of the grasp and application of rules.

Mitsis' interpretation provides an interesting theoretical position for the Stoics. Three features are particularly worth spelling out. First, for Mitsis' Seneca, even the sage's judgment is structured at every level by rules. Indeed, that is *just what it is to be the perfectly virtuous agent.* Hence, we get the result that there is no conflict between the authority of the rules and that of the moral agent: the virtuous person's judgments simply *embody* the authority of the rules. And even though this may be a particularly deep kind of embodiment (since the virtuous person's judgments are constituted by the rules), it remains true that it is ultimately the rules themselves that play the primary role in justification. Hence, on Mitsis' reading, the Stoics reject the normative priority of the virtuous person in favor of the normative priority of rules; indeed, the initial appearance of normative priority for the virtuous person is created simply by the deep way in which such people embody the rules.

Second, Mitsis has a particular reason for moving from the coextensiveness of the rules and the virtuous person's psychology to the normative priority of rules. For he regards it as crucial that Seneca's rules, as he understands them, refer to "objective, repeatable features of moral situations" and "fixed, external patterns" that "exist independently of us."[16]

---

programme . . . takes morality to depend crucially on knowing how to grasp and apply moral rules." Ibid., 290.

15. Ibid., 290; my emphasis.

16. Mitsis maintains that the Stoic account "remains in jeopardy until it can be shown to meet . . . general sceptical attacks on rules." Ibid., 292. He characterises these attacks as follows:

> By denying that rules are objective patterns that extend, without limit, "independently of where we

Third, Mitsis offers a particular way of distinguishing between the two different kinds of moral principle articulated by Seneca. On the one hand, precepts are principles of moral salience. Their role is to lead us to see that particular situations need moral attention. They rely on morally-salient, rather than factual, features and "alter the structure of our beliefs" to develop "a new framework for our moral awareness."[17] By contrast, doctrines embody active, dynamic principles of reason and judgment. Their role is to govern the precepts by providing "limiting or categorical conditions" which are necessary for further articulating and guiding them.[18]

I will eventually argue that each of these three views is mistaken. But first, let us consider some rather different objections to Mitsis' view in order to gain a better appreciation for the position.

3. Substance and Exception: Inwood on Striker-Mitsis

Brad Inwood objects to Striker and Mitsis because they conceive of Stoic rules as universal, substantive, and exceptionless.[19] This interpretation, he says, founders quickly. For neither precepts nor doctrines are both substantive and exceptionless: doctrines are exceptionless, but not substantive; precepts are substantive, but not exceptionless.

---

ourselves take them," they attempt to undermine the claim that there are any objective, repeatable features of moral situations that can guide us in making moral judgments or forming moral intentions. By the same token, such sceptics reject the view that our actions depend on an ability to understand and make determinate projections based on fixed, external patterns. (Ibid., 292)

Furthermore, he admits in a footnote:

This rides roughshod over several difficult issues since it fails to factor in internalist defences of rules based on linguistic practices and so-called communal "forms of life"; nor does it take into account the extent to which non-externalist theories can claim to be realist or objective, etc. I take it, however, that for the internalist, the Stoic view that moral norms exist independently of us must come to grief as must their belief that grasping a rule guarantees future behaviour (as opposed to the internalist claim that rules go where we take them, i.e., it is because we behave in certain ways we can be said to have grasped a rule).

I contest these claims below.

17. Ibid., 298 and 304, and notes 37 and 41; and "Natural Law," 4847 and 4850. Mitsis bases his account of rules of moral salience on Barbara Herman's. See Barbara Herman, "The Practice of Moral Judgment," *Journal of Philosophy* 82 (1985): 413–36, at 420.

18. Mitsis, "Natural Law," 4849–4850; see also "Seneca," 302–304.

19. Inwood, "Rules and Reasoning in Stoic Ethics," in *Topics in Stoic Philosophy*, ed. Katerina Ierodiakonou (Oxford: Oxford University Press, 1999), 95–127. See also, "Goal and Target in Stoicism," *Journal of Philosophy* 83 (1986): 547–56; "Commentary on Striker," *Proceedings of the Boston Area Colloquium in Ancient Philosophy* 2 (1987): 95–101; and "Natural Law in Seneca," *The Studia Philonica Annual* 15 (2003): 77–95. This kind of view was pioneered by Vander Waerdt in the articles cited earlier. However, Inwood has developed the position in more detail in those aspects of concern here, so I will focus on his work.

There is something to Inwood's criticisms, but in order to see it we must first take care that Striker and Mitsis do not turn to straw. For there is a sense in which they admit that Stoic rules are neither exceptionless nor substantive. Consider Striker's comments on exceptions. She says:

> [The] Stoics begin with the notion of goodness as rational order and regularity, and then define virtue and just conduct in terms of obedience to the laws of nature.[20]

But then she adds:

> This does not mean that the Stoics thought they could produce a set of moral rules that would admit of no exceptions. Indeed, as Professor Inwood has pointed out in his comments[21], the Stoics were quite aware that rules of conduct will be subject to exceptions under unusual circumstances. Hence their belief that only the sage who knows when and where an exception is justified will achieve perfect virtue. . . . But those exceptions would not be seen as infringements of rules. Rather . . . they would be justified by *appeal to higher-order rules.* That is to say, *exceptions occur, according to Stoic theory, when there is a conflict of rules, and in such cases one needs some order of priority among rules to decide* which rule should override which other.[22]

Hence, Striker does not claim that individual rules are exceptionless; indeed, she is explicit that such exceptions are made in cases of conflict.

Nevertheless, there is a claim about the lack of exceptions to rules that is important to Striker's view. First, since the exceptions that Striker accepts arise only because a lower-level rule conflicts with a higher-level rule, and since these exceptions do not constitute an infringement of the rules considered together as a set, what Striker seems to believe is exceptionless is *the complete set of rules.* Hence, the claim is that any situation falling under a rule ought to be resolved in accordance with either that rule, or another rule that applies to that situation. Second, if Striker accepts Mitsis' claim that the sage's judgment is structured at every level by rules (so that, like moral development, it "depends *solely* on . . . [the] cognitive grasp of both universal and more determinate moral principles"), then it seems likely that every situation calling for moral choice must fall under some rule or other. Hence, the set of rules must cover all possible actions and

---

20. Striker, "Origins," 219.

21. These comments of Inwood's (and Striker's reply here) pre-date the main paper of Inwood's presently under discussion.

22. Striker, "Origins," 219–220, note 8; emphasis added.

situations that call for moral choice.[23] And this leads to a stronger sense in which the rules can be said to be exceptionless: all situations which call for moral choice will be governed by the overall set of rules and ought to be resolved in accordance with that set.

Now these two claims about the exceptionlessness of moral rules—i.e. (1) that any situation falling under a rule ought to be resolved in accordance with either that rule or another rule that applies to that situation; and (2) that every situation calling for moral choice must fall under some such rule or other—seem to me both questionable in their own right, and questionable as an account of the Stoic view.[24] However, one cannot establish the questionability of either claim merely by showing either that individual moral rules admit of exceptions or that the Stoics thought that their individual moral rules admitted of exceptions. Instead, if one wanted to object to the view in this way, what one would have to show is that some exceptions to individual moral rules come about for reasons other than that they conflict with other moral rules. And this is a much more difficult task.

This point deserves discussion and emphasis. Presumably, in order to show that some exceptions to individual moral rules come about for reasons other than that they conflict with other moral rules, one would try to defend the view that at least some exceptions arise because individual rules conflict with what the particulars of the situation determine should be done, where it would be a

---

23. To add to the complications, in a later paper ("Following Nature") Striker concedes that the Stoics do not succeed in carrying off this project. For she claims that they are unable to resolve the conflict between the two fundamental components of *oikoiosis*: self-preservation, and concern for others.

> What seems to be lacking is a ranking of values within the field of things preferred or dispreferred such that acting in conformity with the priorities so determined results in morally good conduct. But while the two tendencies that are said to underlie preferences and rejections are rather uncontroversially natural, it seems far from clear whether nature can also provide the appropriate rules of priority. However, rather than criticizing the Stoics for their failure to find a solution, I would suggest that we should admire them for having attempted the task at all. (Ibid., 261)

24. Mitsis (personal communication) suggests that there is little room for my questioning given the following passage from Diogenes Laertius: "The end may be defined as life in accordance with nature . . . a life in which we refrain from every action *forbidden by the law common to all things, that is to say, the right reason which pervades all things,* and is identical with this Zeus, lord and ruler of all that is." (Diogenes Laertius, *Lives of Eminent Philosophers,* translated by R. D. Hicks [Cambridge, Mass.: Harvard University Press], 7.87; my emphasis.) I have two quick responses. First, while I agree that the passage shows that Stoic natural law as such pervades all things so that, for example, it is always right to "follow nature," I do not think that it shows that natural law operates exclusively through an all-encompassing system of subsidiary rules, which is the issue here. Second, one consideration on the other side is provided by Seneca's countenance of the possibility of commands that override standard laws of nature (*De otio* 5.5, referred to by Inwood, "Natural Law," 83, 89). Even though such commands count as "laws" for Seneca—and so might satisfy (1) and (2) strictly speaking—they are at least in tension with both the spirit of a claim of exceptionlessness, and the alleged explanation of this: that the sage's psychology is structured at every level by the rules.

mistake to understand these particulars as embodying some new rule. Now, on the one hand, it would be surprising if one could conclusively establish this, and so decisively defeat the rule-based view. But, on the other hand, it is not clear that the opponent of the Stiker-Mitsis view should accept this burden of proof. For at this point the contention that all cases are covered by rules is an entirely theory-driven idea. At least, it certainly does not seem to be a straightforward, uncontroversial component of our pre-philosophical way of looking at things. There is no reason simply to presuppose that even rules that are in themselves exceptionless would cover the full *range* of practical reason.[25]

So much for the Striker-Mitsis claim that the moral rules are exceptionless. Consider now Inwood's claim that their rules fail to be substantive. It is not clear to me what Inwood means by 'substantive.' But one possibility would be that 'substantive' means informative. (At one point, Inwood does seem to have this in mind: he says that Aristo accepts only "vacuous" prescriptions such as "follow virtue.") If this is the idea, how we understand Inwood's objection depends on which of Seneca's two kinds of moral principle are under discussion. Suppose we begin with decreta, which (according to Mitsis' view) seem to be principles like "follow nature," or "act virtuously." Mitsis explicitly rejects the claim that such prescriptions are vacuous in the sense of being uninformative. He says:

> We might reasonably claim, for instance, that "One should always be virtuous" informs us exactly what to do in a particular moral situation: it informs us that we should be virtuous. The problem seems be not so much one of information, but of our needing further help in the form of more determinate principles to recognize particular actions that are in fact virtuous. But this need for further determination hardly demonstrates that general principles are uninformative, unless we assume that a principle provides information only if we apply it directly to an individual situation without the help of more determinate principles. It is not clear, however, what makes this latter requirement a reasonable test for principles.[26]

Hence, if what is meant by 'substantive' is informative, Mitsis claims that even quite high-level principles are substantive.

However, if for a principle to be "substantive" is for it to be capable of being applied directly to an individual situation without the help of more determinate principles, Mitsis explicitly rejects the claim that individual moral principles need to be substantive in this sense. Consider first the doctrines. Mitsis claims that on Seneca's account (1) "one may have a grasp of general moral principles (decreta) and yet still be unable to discover what a particular moral situ-

---

25. I thank Julia Annas for discussion on this point.
26. "Seneca," 301.

ation demands," and (2) that more determinate principles, the precepts, are needed to provide supplement in these cases. Hence, echoing Striker's remarks about exceptionlessness, he seems to be asserting that what is important about Stoic moral rules is that they can be applied to particular situations as a set. And this renders largely irrelevant the indeterminacy of particular doctrines when considered in isolation.

Suppose then that Inwood's objection about substantiveness is applied to Seneca's praecepta, or precepts. But Mitsis claims that precepts are substantive in the requisite sense: they "[teach] agents to recognize what individual cases require and therefore [enable] them to act."[27] It is just that, according to Mitsis, precepts are not in themselves *decisive*. Instead, they are what Barbara Herman calls "rules of moral salience." As such, precepts can be overruled by the presence of other precepts, and so in some sense admit of exceptions. But we have already seen that this, by itself, is not a decisive objection.

We can conclude then that Inwood's objections to the Striker-Mitsis view do not quite hit the mark. Still, they are suggestive. First, they reveal the possible sophistication of a view based on a deep commitment to moral rules. In particular, on the one hand, they suggest that even the proponent of rules needs to think of moral judgment *holistically*, as invoking a network of principles. For it is this holism that provides the sense in which principles might be exceptionless and substantive. But, on the other hand, they suggest that holism by itself will not quite solve the problem: for holism does not establish that the rules actually are exceptionless and substantive, nor that (if they were) they would cover the full range of practical reason.

Second, the invoking of holism suggests an important point. For there is now one way in which the perfect moral agent is more central than the individual rules: the rules have to be considered in combination (with each other, and perhaps also with judgments about particular cases), and *the virtuous agent provides the context for that combination,* as well as the circumstance of choice. So, the appropriate holism tends to bring the virtuous person back into the center of the theory.

Third, this centrality of the virtuous person suggests that two assumptions of the Striker-Mitsis account (and indeed of many normal rule-based views) may be erroneous. Consider first Mitsis' requirement that the rules refer to "fixed, external patterns" that "exist independently of us." As a general claim, this seems a mistake. On the one hand, there is no reason to presume that rules which derive their meaning from the context supplied by the virtuous person will refer exclusively to features of the world that can be tracked externally by just any

27. Mitsis, "Seneca," 291.

kind of agent. Indeed, this seems in conflict with the core Stoic idea that virtue is a kind of skill, requiring expertise. On the other hand, if the rules do not refer to such features, then it seems that they will rely on concepts embedded in the sage's psychology—such as the virtue terms. But then it seems unlikely that claims about external specifiability will undermine the central role of virtue.

More specifically, Mitsis seems to believe that the Stoic commitment to the claim that "moral norms exist independently of us" in the form of natural law rules out a primary role for virtue. But it is not clear why this should be so. For example, according to my later account, the norms constitutive of natural law are structured by the virtue terms that appear in doctrines; and the discussion above suggests that these cannot be understood outside of the context provided by the virtuous person.[28]

Consider next Striker's idea of conflicts between rules. On the alternate picture, if the virtuous person is primary, we might instead expect that the general context of rules circumscribes the domain of application of particular (and especially lower-level) rules in such a way that it is inappropriate to speak of conflict. This might seem odd, given Mitsis' model of externally specifiable rules, but such circumscribed rules seem natural if one is thinking of the virtuous person as employing thick moral concepts, which are defined in part through their relations with one another.[29]

These largely theoretical concerns suggest reasons to move away from a rather austere conception of individual exceptionless and externally-specifiable rules towards a more holistic, less conflict-ridden system of virtues, which are themselves to be understood in the context of the virtuous person. Hence, they move

---

28. Watson puts the point this way:

Human reason may be in agreement with divine reason either because it accepts the suggestions of divine reason or because the two are simply manifestations, from different points of view, of the same principle. In the latter case the agreement could be expected to be perceptual. This perfect agreement would have been realized in the case of the Sage. (Watson, 223; see also the remarks on 222.)

The key difference here may have something to do with the difference between ontological and epistemic claims of priority. See earlier note.

29. This is one theoretical reason to think that Mitsis' claim that precepts are rules of moral salience may not be quite right. There are also some textual reasons. First, Seneca recounts Aristo as saying that precepts should be "definite," "certain," and "binding in all cases" (94.14–16). Second, he conceives of precepts as commands to be obeyed (94.37; 94.50). This suggests that precepts are decisive considerations, not merely salient ones. Similarly, while Seneca rejects Posidonious's claim that nothing is more foolish than a law with a preamble ("*Warn me, tell me what you wish me to do; I am not learning but obeying,*" 94.38), he does not do so because precepts are not decisive. Indeed, he seems to accept the basic characterization of laws as precepts with threats attached (94.37). But laws thus conceived are not rules of salience.

I. G. Kidd suggests that Seneca is guilty of a "muddled conflation" in his conception of precepts. See Kidd, "Moral Actions and Rules in Stoic Ethics," in *The Stoics*, ed. John M. Rist (Berkeley: University of California Press, 1978), 247–258, at 252.

us towards more familiar territory in contemporary virtue ethics. Soon I will argue that Seneca himself occupies that territory, and in an interesting and relevant way. But first I should address Inwood's similar attempt to mark out a middle ground.

4. Rules of Thumb: Inwood

Inwood argues that the Stoics, and Seneca in particular, occupy a middle position, between Aristo and the Striker-Mitsis account, which asserts the primacy of the virtuous person while still allowing for a substantial, but subsidiary, role for moral rules. The possibility of such a middle position emerges, he says, once we appreciate an alternative account of law and its relation to rules, such as is found in contemporary legal theory.

Inwood's account begins with a problem. It is obvious, Inwood says, that when applied to a particular situation, an individual rule can conflict with its own background justification. The legal theorist Frederick Schauer points out that we have three options when such a conflict occurs. First, we can regard the rule as a defeasible rule of thumb. If so, we will reassess the situation and decide in view of the values and assessments underlying the background justification. Second, we can find reasons to relocate the case outside the scope of the rule to which it *prima facie* applies. Third, we can engage in hardcore rule following. This constitutes entrenching the rule: we follow it even when it conflicts with the substantive justification for its own existence.[30]

Inwood claims that the usual views of rules "force us to choose between (1) regarding them as mere rules of thumb without independent normative force and (2) a view that endows them with some ultimate and general normative power independent of particular situations."[31] He does not make explicit why the forced choice between these two views is problematic, but I take it that he has in mind problems that are familiar from contemporary discussions of rule-utilitarianism. On the first possibility, that we treat a rule as a mere rule of thumb, we threaten to undermine its authority: if the rule is defeasible, won't we end up having to assess the background justification in each case anyway? On the second possibility, that we entrench the rule, following it seems to have become an irrational fetish (or, mere "rule worship").

Inwood claims that Schauer's own view suggests a more acceptable mixed position. According to this position, there are two levels of moral reasoning. At

---

30. Schauer's major work on the topic is *Playing By the Rules* (Oxford: Oxford University Press, 1991).
31. Inwood, n.13.

the first, lower level, ordinary moral agents make decisions in accordance with entrenched moral rules; at the second, higher level, idealized moral reasoners are allowed to set aside these rules, treating them as mere rules of thumb.[32] Moreover, he argues that something like this account captures the essence of the Stoic view. The Stoic will allow the wise man to reason directly in terms of substantive justifications in particular situations, giving him the authority to act in violation of the rules. However, all other moral agents will be provided with "entrenched but modifiable general rules prescribing appropriate actions as a framework for their thinking."[33]

Inwood's account naturally raises the question of what the nonvirtuous person is missing that prevents her from reasoning directly about situations. Presumably, we should be able to work this out by considering what role the rules actually play. Seneca claims that precepts are needed because (1) the majority of deliberation turns on the immediate circumstances; and (2) the nonvirtuous, even if motivated to be virtuous, lack the experience to work out what each situation requires. However, since he also claims that the peculiarities of an action cannot be dictated universally, he must respond to Aristo's charge that any rules must be useless to the nonvirtuous person. Aristo's objection depends on the claim that people's circumstances and roles are so varied that any rules must be unfeasibily detailed and specific. How might Seneca respond to this claim?

According to Inwood's Seneca, precepts, though they don't prove anything by themselves and don't demonstrate the goodness of a particular course of action, nevertheless aid us in deciding what to do, and so enable us to do the right thing before our characters become well formed. But how do they achieve this task? In his paper, Inwood suggests four relevant functions which precepts perform: (1) they remind us of moral facts which we once knew but have forgotten; (2) they can make the relevant facts of a particular case perspicuous in a way that the vagueness of a more general principle cannot; (3) they can wake up moral intuitions; and (4) they allow the untrained mind to synthesize previously unconnected guidelines in a way which bears on the specific needs of the immediate situation.

Unfortunately, it is not clear that these roles make sense of precepts as Inwood describes them.[34] Consider (1): the claim that precepts remind us of moral facts which we once knew but have forgotten. First, (Plato's theory of recollection

---

32. This may remind some readers of Hare's distinction between the levels of moral reasoning characterized by the Prole and the Archangel. See R. M. Hare, *Moral Thinking* (Oxford: Oxford University Press, 1983).

33. Inwood, "Rules," 109.

34. Similar considerations assail other attempts to account for rules. See, for example, the efforts of contemporary particularists, such as Jonathan Dancy and Martha Nussbaum.

notwithstanding) this is simply an odd way of understanding the nonvirtuous person's inexperience. Why should we think that the nonvirtuous person's problem is that he has forgotten something, and, in particular, something moral? Second, even if we ignore the oddness of the claim about recollection, and assume merely that the precepts get us onto the genuine moral facts, it is not clear how they do so. One possibility would be that they directly pick out such facts. However, this seems problematic. For if precepts pick out genuine moral facts, it would seem that they pick out facts that are always morally relevant. But if this is the case, it seems odd to regard them as mere rules of thumb, and hence defeasible. Indeed, it seems more reasonable to suppose that Striker and Mitsis are right, and that such rules can only be discarded in the presence of a further overriding rule.

Fortunately, (2) and (3)—precepts can make the relevant facts of a particular case perspicuous in a way that the vagueness of a more general principle cannot; precepts can wake up moral intuitions—seem to suggest that the precepts pick out nonmoral natural facts, rather than moral facts, but that these are natural facts that are often relevant, and so some kind of guide, to the moral facts. Furthermore, Inwood's examples of precepts suggest that he himself does not believe that the precepts pick out moral facts directly. For those examples are: "don't commit suicide," and "return deposits"; and the features these pick out seem to be nonmoral natural facts, rather than moral facts.

Now, nonmoral natural facts of the kind Inwood's examples identify do not seem always to be morally relevant. So, they seem compatible with the claim that precepts are rules of thumb. However, now there is reason to wonder why they would ever become entrenched. For the first three features seem, in themselves, to provide no reason to entrench precepts. Once (1) we have been reminded of the moral facts, (2) the relevant facts of this case have been made perspicuous to us, and (3) our moral intuitions have been fully woken up, why should we *then* regard ourselves as bound by the rules if their role was just to facilitate these three things? Having been directed to the moral facts of the case by the precepts, why can't we reason directly about these facts and the role they play in this case? Nothing about the role of precepts as messengers seems to tell us.[35]

The fourth feature of precepts Inwood identifies is more promising. It is that precepts synthesize previously unconnected guidelines in a way the nonvirtuous person otherwise could not. However, there remain several problems. First,

---

35. Though it may be irrational to shoot the messenger, surely it is equally irrational either to prize him above the message, or to insist on entrenching his message by understanding it only in light of what he himself says, and not in a wider context.

though this feature suggests that the nonvirtuous person should at least be reluctant to act against the precepts, it does not really tell us why this should be so, since it does not tell us what the source of the nonvirtuous person's inability to synthesize actually is. Second, it seems implausible to regard Inwood's examples of precepts as rules that synthesize a number of other considerations. This is because Inwood's precepts are not very detailed and so seem to be lower rather than higher-level principles. And it seems implausible to regard them as integrating a number of different subsidiary moral concerns. Third, there is something odd about the suggestion that entrenched precepts respond to the fact that the nonvirtuous person lacks an appropriate understanding of how different considerations fit together into something more global. Since what it is to entrench a rule is to follow it even when confronted with a more detailed background justification, there is some tension in saying that the precepts ought to be followed because they synthesize more information for a nonvirtuous person than she would otherwise be able to integrate. Fourth, the synthesizing rationale may imply that the nonvirtuous person is really not in a position to understand the background justification in the first place, but if this is her problem, the circumstances for genuine entrenchment ought never even to arise. Hence, there ought to be no need to regard precepts as entrenched. Instead, even the person who lacks virtue should regard the precepts as rules of thumb, albeit with the knowledge that she will never be in a position (in her current nonvirtuous state) to act against one.

Before concluding, it is worth mentioning one more general difficulty for Inwood which picks up the other side of Aristo's complaint against Stoic rules. This is that even if the learner does need moral rules of a specific sort, it is unclear why the sage would also use them. In particular, even if we were to concede that the sage has some use for rules of thumb (which is itself dubious, since he is supposed to have internalized the relevant information needed for decision), why should we assume that these will be the *same* rules that the learner must take as entrenched? Indeed, this seems particularly unlikely, given that it seems best to regard the learner's rules as directly picking out merely natural facts, which happen to be related to moral facts as a matter of empirical generalization. Why would the sage be concerned with such empirical generalizations? Won't he simply rely directly on the moral facts?

So, I conclude that Inwood's account of Seneca's rules is also unsatisfactory. Still, his discussion is instructive. In particular, it brings into focus: (1) the contrast between nonmoral and morally-loaded kinds of rules, (2) the worry about potential conflict between rules and their background justification,[36] and (3)

---

36. On my view, this worry turns out to be misplaced because (a) the rules are circumscribed by their

the distinction between the sage's rules and those of the nonvirtuous. These are all matters that should be resolved by a satisfactory account of the role of principles in moral life; and I shall argue that the interpretation I am about to offer does resolve them.

5. Seneca's Precepts

So far I have examined two main interpretations of Seneca. These interpretations are representative of more general positions on moral rules, but both are found philosophically wanting. Now it is time to begin my own textual account of Seneca's rules and to argue that Seneca's position meets the philosophical burdens already identified. I shall begin with Seneca's precepts.

What kind of principle is a precept? Seneca says that precepts are to be found in nonmoral domains (such as sailing and religious observance) as well as in morality. Moral precepts, he maintains, concern questions such as: how a man should conduct himself towards his wife; how a father should bring up children; or how a master should rule his slaves (94.1). He offers the following examples: refrain from bloodshed; stretch forth a hand to the shipwrecked sailor; point the way to a wanderer; share a crust with the starving (95.51); a man should fight for his country, sweat forth his last drop of energy on behalf of his friends, and know that keeping a mistress is the worst kind of insult to his wife (95.37); friendship is honorable; and a man should not have a double standard about chastity (94.25).

How are we to understand precepts in light of these examples? The first thing to note is that there appear to be a range of cases. To begin with, in his religious examples Seneca seems to invoke very straightforward and easily applied nonmoral rules. These rules (involving such activities as lighting lamps and bringing towels) do not appear to rely on specialist knowledge or enhanced perceptual capacities for their application. And perhaps Seneca's advice about refraining from bloodshed and not committing adultery are similar.[37]

But matters are more difficult in some of the other cases. First, when talking of sailing, Seneca refers to making use of a fair wind and making the best of a shifting and variable breeze. But these notions of "a fair wind" and "making the

holistic setting, and (b) their content is largely circumscribed by the thick evaluative terms, or by social context. The precepts would never be entrenched, except by the setting. Furthermore, if one really had access to the thick terms, one wouldn't need the precepts anyway, and so would not be entrenching them.

37. There is an obvious inconsistency between refraining from bloodshed and fighting for one's country, so these precepts cannot be mechanical in the sense that one can safely use a given precept so long as it applies to a situation.

best of" will not be straightforwardly understood from outside the practice and distinctive aims of sailing. So, some specialist knowledge is required. Second, advice such as that we should stretch forth a hand to the shipwrecked sailor, share a crust with the starving, and point the way to a wanderer seems to require careful application. Should we extend a hand if our boat is full and in danger of sinking? How much aid should we give to the starving? Should we tell the wandering Nazi storm trooper where to find his Jewish quarry? Third, the claim that friendship is honorable introduces a term that is a straightforwardly evaluative.

So, in each of these cases, the precept by itself will not give clear guidance. Further interpretation is required. Still, what is required for such interpretation is not too demanding—or at least does not involve the skills of the master craftsman or sage. By that I mean: although expert knowledge may be required for correct usage of the precept on all occasions—i.e., under all possible circumstances—a reasonable grasp is sufficient for standard cases, and this is relatively accessible, at least after some training.

How do we understand precepts in light of this? My suggestion is that the precepts rely on features which are either quasi-descriptive and nonevaluative (such as natural properties, or easily identified cultural properties), or else involve low-level moral or evaluative concepts or properties[38] that are relatively easy to pick out and apply.[39] This suggests that their main role is to give guidance to the novice. Such principles are substantive, but not in themselves exceptionless. They are useful insofar as that, under appropriate conditions, they pick out behavior that is reasonably coincident with what the virtuous would do, or at least conducive to the attainment of virtue. But they are not co-extensive with virtuous behavior, and could not hope to be.

Some evidence in favor of this suggestion is provided by Seneca's remarks about the need for precepts. First, on the one hand, he says that precepts are necessary because the absence of vice is not sufficient to tell us what to do in life.[40] Rather:

38. I do not think that much turns on my use of "properties" here. Those with an ontological axe to grind may translate the term to mean simply "considerations."

39. Nicholas White argues that precepts rely on "non-evaluative expressions, such as could be determined to apply by either sensation or memory." See White, "Nature and Regularity in Stoic Ethics," *Oxford Studies in Ancient Philosophy* 5 (1985): 289–305, at 303. Similarly and relatedly, Paul Vander Waerdt's account of the difference between *kathekonta* and *katorthomata* relies on a distinction between "the intensional rather than the extensional characteristics of virtuous actions" ("Zeno's *Republic*," 275; cf. "Origins," 18), and emphasizes the dispositions of the sage and his infallibility. My account is in the same general spirit as these, but (1) allows for the low-level evaluative terms occurring in the examples I cite and (2) makes no assumptions about the role of the sage's dispositions and the extent to which the morally relevant features of situations are to be found externally.

40. This claim is odd, since official Stoic doctrine claims that there is no middle ground between virtue and vice. But I will not pursue that issue here.

"We are hindered from accomplishing praiseworthy deeds . . . by lack of practice in discovering the demands of a particular situation";[41] and hence "the mind . . . needs many precepts in order to see what it should do in life."[42] This suggests that the role of the precepts is to tell the nonvicious person what to do in particular situations. And it seems that precepts as I have described them provide such advice by relying on those properties which are accessible to such a person.

Second, on the other hand, Seneca provides an explanation of why it is difficult to know how to act well. He believes that the right thing to do is difficult to discern because the actions required by virtue change from case to case: "If we would hold men firmly bound and tear them away from the ills which clutch them fast, they must learn what is evil and what is good. They must know that *everything except virtue changes its name and becomes now good and now bad*." This suggests, at a minimum, that principles that do not crucially rely on the virtue terms, such as the precepts, will necessarily not always get the right answer.[43] Hence, Seneca is very clear that precepts alone are not sufficient to make a person virtuous.[44] In order to overcome this difficulty, one needs, in addition to precepts, both a receptive mind,[45] and to act for the right reason.[46]

6. Seneca's Doctrines

Of particular importance in overcoming the limitations of precepts is the second kind of principle, the doctrine. Again, Seneca gives some examples. Nonmoral cases include the soldiers' oath of allegiance, love for the flag, and horror of desertion. Moral examples include declaring allegiance to honor, judging honor and its results to be the only good and other things only temporarily good, and regarding god and men as part of one organism.[47] In addition to these examples, Seneca also makes claims about the nature and role of doctrines. Doctrines are firm beliefs deeply implanted, that apply to life as a whole, determine acts and thoughts, and supply the purpose and manner.[48]

As one would expect, doctrines make up for the key deficiencies of precepts. For one thing, they combat the feelings of recklessness and sloth that render the

41. 94.32.
42. 94.19.
43. 95.35. It may also imply something stronger: that principles always require interpretation, and so *never* get the right answer when considered in isolation. I thank Julia Annas for this possible reading.
44. 94.21.
45. 95.4; 95.38.
46. 95.4; 95.5; 95.38–9; 95.40.
47. 95.43–44; 95.51–52.
48. 95.56; 95.43–44.

precepts inefficacious. Such feelings are caused by mistaken attitudes of admiration and fear.[49] But the doctrines combat these attitudes[50] by providing a stable standard to which to refer when making decisions.[51] This makes the mind receptive to precepts. For another, the stability of doctrines seems to arise because they are entrenched in an ideal of life as a whole.[52] Seneca says that doctrines get their point from ideals, which set the goal for human conduct. Once such a goal is set up, doctrines are necessary to guide the way.[53] Doctrines concern good and evil, and especially virtue.[54] They bring with them the right reasons for moral action, and also stability, since virtue is the only thing that does not change from good to bad.

We learn more about doctrines when Seneca contrasts them with precepts. In one place, he uses the following analogy:

> . . . [B]ranches are useless without *roots,* and roots are strengthened by their growths. Everyone can understand how useful the hands are. But the heart the source of the hands growth and power and motion is hidden. Similarly, precepts are manifest while doctrines are concealed, and as only the initiated know the more hallowed portion of the rites, so in philosophy the hidden truths are revealed only to those who are members and have been admitted to the sacred rites. But precepts and other such matters are familiar even to the uninitiated.[55]

Hence, precepts are manifest to all, while doctrines are hidden and available only to those with special knowledge. Elsewhere, Seneca says that doctrines are more general than precepts;[56] that they play a role of integrating and supporting the various precepts; and that they do this by taking a wider viewpoint.

---

49. 95.37. See also 95.32–34.

50. 94.52–3; 94.54; 94.55; 94.59.

51. "Peace of mind is enjoyed only by those who have attained a fixed and unchanging standard of judgment; the rest of mankind continually ebb and flow in their decisions . . . because nothing is clear to them, because they make use of a most unsure criterion—rumor. If you would always desire the same things, you must desire the truth. But one cannot attain the truth without doctrines, for doctrines embrace the whole of life." 95.57–8.

52. 95.57–8.

53. "We must set before our eyes the goal of the supreme good, towards which we may strive, and to which all our acts and words may have reference—just as sailors must guide their course according to a certain star. Life without ideals is erratic: as soon as an ideal is to be set up, doctrines begin to be necessary." 95.45. See also 95.35; 95.61; 95.62; 95.63.

54. "Some people would advise us to rate prudence very high, to cherish bravery, and to cleave more closely, if possible, to justice than to other qualities. But this will do no good if we do not know what virtue is . . ." 95.55.

55. 95.64.

56. See 94.8. Mitsis is strongly critical of the idea that this is the principal difference between precepts and doctrines. See "Seneca," 299–300.

Given these characteristics, how are we to understand doctrines? First, it seems clear that there is some sense in which doctrines subsume precepts. They are more general than precepts and more fundamental. Like the roots of the tree, they ground the infrastructure on which the precepts depend. And they do this by providing the reasons for precepts, which alone simply deliver verdicts. Still, doctrines cannot replace precepts and by themselves they are ineffective. This seems to be because they are hidden to all but the initiated; and the reason for this is that they refer to virtue and to the structure of the good.

So far, so good. But we soon run into a problem. From Seneca's description of the roles of precepts and doctrines, two things seem clear: that precepts are principles primarily meant to guide the conduct of the uninitiated, the nonsage; and that the doctrines pick out high level structural principles in a general theory of ethics. I have claimed that the precepts perform their role through referring to nonevaluative and low level evaluative features of the world. But it is less clear how the doctrines operate. In particular, *it is not clear where the Stoic's favored moral terms, the terms for the individual virtues themselves, should appear;* and so what the status of principles such as "Act justly" or "justice is always compatible with generosity" is. For such principles appear to be neither precepts, since their content is not accessible to the nonsage, nor doctrines, since they seem not to have the characteristics—of being narrowly theoretical, and at the higher level of abstraction—suggested by Seneca's actual examples of doctrines.

It is worth noting that this tension appears in Seneca's own descriptions of doctrines: on the one hand, doctrines are described as theoretical, and the examples given are rarefied and abstract; on the other hand, Seneca expects doctrines to play the grounding practical role—giving the reasons for the precepts, being merely more general than them and being connected with virtue. But it is not clear how these roles are to be reconciled: how can abstract theoretical principles (such as those concerning "whether he who has one virtue possesses the other virtues also") give the reasons for precepts, and be construed as just more general versions of them? This question is especially pressing given Seneca's examples, which seem to be largely of the structural kind, rather than principles with evaluative content.[57]

---

57. See, perhaps, the full version of a passage quoted earlier: "Some people would advise us to rate prudence very high, to cherish bravery, and to cleave more closely, if possible, to justice than to other qualities. But this will do no good if we do not know what virtue is, whether it is simple or compound, whether it is one or more than one, whether its parts are separate or interwoven with one another; whether he who has one virtue possesses the other virtues also; and just what are the distinctions between them." 95.55.

I want to consider two possibilities. The first is that principles based on the individual virtues can be classified as doctrines. There seems to me strong indirect evidence for this: they are exceptionless; they provide the standard of judgment; they are opaque to the nonsage; they provide the reasons for the precepts; they provide the stable grounding for the precepts. However, this evidence is indirect, and we might wonder why. One answer would amount to a rival interpretation: that Seneca does not see the virtue-terms as useful or appropriately captured in principles at all. Textual evidence for this interpretation might include his silence about the virtues in examples of doctrines, together with the fact that his actual examples can be grasped without virtue and do not seem to have heavy evaluative content.

Now, it seems to me that the second view is more textually parsimonious. But overall I prefer the first. There are two reasons. First, though Seneca does not offer clear examples of doctrines based on thick virtue terms, there is some indirect textual evidence for this reading. For one thing, when introducing the notion of a doctrine, Seneca uses the example of declaring allegiance to honor. This is both a thick moral term, and (arguably in the context) one that always guides us to right action. Hence, it is structurally identical to a virtue term. For another, given this example, and also Seneca's nonmoral examples of doctrines (such as the one involving the trainee soldier), it seems that we can say by analogy that the nonsage should declare allegiance to virtue, to the genuine individual virtues, and to principles such as "Act justly," "Be generous," and so on.[58]

Second, and more importantly, whereas on the second view, the remarks Seneca makes about the connection between doctrines and precepts are mysterious; according to the first, they are not. For on that view it is clearer how doctrines support precepts, why they are hidden, and indeed, why they constitute a distinct kind of principle to precepts (rather than simply a higher-level of the same kind of principle). For the thick virtue terms are not accessible to just anyone, regardless of training or experience, and it is clear that they are needed to support the correct application of the thinner precepts.

---

58. Formulae such as "Act justly" are ambiguous. They may mean (a) "act according to the virtue in question under all circumstances" or the more limited (b) "act in accordance with that virtue whenever it is applicable." See John Cooper, "The Unity of Virtue," *Social Philosophy and Policy* 15 (1998): 233–74. Reprinted in his *Reason and Emotion: Essays on Ancient Moral Psychology* (Princeton: Princeton University Press, 1998). Cooper attributes (a) to Chrysippus and (b) to Aristotle. It is not clear to me to which version Seneca would subscribe. Point (b) would pose no immediate difficulties; but under (a) there would be a sense in which the rule would not be exceptionless if the particular virtue were not always applicable. So, accepting (a) for decreta would pose a prima facie problem. I thank Eric Hutton for bringing this point to my attention.

7. Seneca on Virtue

It remains for me to spell out the role of the doctrines and to consider how both kinds of principle—precepts and doctrines—operate with respect to the role of the virtuous person. Seneca's remarks on this subject have two aspects. The first is that he believes that precepts and the giving of examples of virtuous action both play essential roles in moral education.[59] Indeed, he says that they are functionally equivalent:

> [The] function [of examples] is the same as that of precept. For he who utters precepts says: "If you would have self-control, act thus and so!" He who illustrates, says: "the man who acts thus and so, and refrains from certain other things, possesses self-control." If you ask what the difference here is, I say that the one gives the precepts of virtue, the other its embodiment.[60]

Now, this might suggest that the virtuous person has no special primacy.[61] But this is too quick. In this context, Seneca is understanding examples of virtue in a restricted way, as illustrations of particular virtues which involve giving what he calls the "signs and marks" of each virtue and vice. And this mention of signs and marks suggests that the illustrations pick out the descriptive or low-level evaluative features of situations in which particular virtues are exhibited. So, it is no surprise that they function in the same way as precepts.

This contrast seems confirmed by the second aspect. For Seneca contrasts the utility of both kinds of guidance with what he calls "much more useful" robust accounts of the qualities and lives of good men:

> These illustrations, or, to use a commercial term, samples, have, I confess a certain utility; just put them up for exhibition well-recommended, and you will find men to copy them. [. . .] But *how much more useful it is to know the marks of a surpassingly fine soul*—marks which one may appropriate from another for oneself [e.g., from a portrayal of a brave man, such as Cato].[62]

Still, there are also difficulties of interpretation here. For what Seneca says about exposure to the sage pulls in different directions. First, he claims that *nothing is more successful* in moral education than association with good men.[63] But, sec-

---

59. 95.54.
60. 95.66.
61. And perhaps, even more strongly, Mitsis' embodiment view.
62. 95.66–67; my emphasis. See also 95.72.
63. 94.40.

ond, he immediately explains this by drawing a parallel between such experiences and precepts: "[T]he frequent seeing, the frequent hearing of [good men] little by little sinks into the heart and *acquires the force of precepts.*"[64] And this might suggest that the previous equivalence of precepts and experience of virtuous behavior holds—that virtuous behavior simply serves to pick out the sort of descriptive and low-level evaluative properties that precepts make available.

There is, however, good reason to resist this relapse. For Seneca then immediately adds something that does not fit this account at all. He says that the reason why association with the sage is beneficial is mysterious:

> We are indeed uplifted merely by meeting wise men; and one can be helped by a great man even when he is silent. *I could not easily tell you how it helps us,* though I am certain of the fact that I have received help in that way. Phaedo says: "Certain tiny animals do not leave any pain when they sting us; so subtle is their power, so deceptive by a swelling for purposes of harm. The bite is disclosed by a swelling, and even in the swelling there is no visible wound." That will also be your experience when dealing with wise men; *you will not discover how or when the benefit comes to you, but you will discover that you have received it.*[65]

This seems to fit better with the idea that the benefit of association is that one is exposed to action on the thicker, more heavily evaluative concepts of the doctrines, and so brought closer to grasping them.[66] (One experiences examples and then "cottons-on," as John McDowell puts it.) For it is these, not the precepts, that are hidden. Precepts, Seneca says, are available to all.[67]

I am inclined to think that this second, doctrine-based, interpretation is more plausible, and philosophically more attractive. The idea then would be that experience of the sage gives something with the practical force of precepts (in terms of giving practical guidance), but not of the same character (it does not rely on the merely descriptive or low-level evaluative, but on the more "mysterious" thick evaluative terms).[68]

---

64. 94.40.

65. 94.40–41; my emphasis.

66. Julia Annas has suggested to me that Seneca may have something much less grand in mind in this passage. Perhaps he is merely telling us to guard against an overly literal understanding of the virtuous person's actions, such as in Epictetus' story of the friend who "copied" Socrates by insulting the jury at his trial (and so lost his case). This reading would be quite compatible with my interpretation.

67. But note that Seneca also seems to think there is something mysterious about the effects of precepts (94.44; 94.43), which are similar to the effects of oracles (94.42).

68. One aspect of this, which tends to be obscured by the talk of grasping thick properties instantiated in given instances, would presumably be a sensitivity to how important moral questions arise and are framed in a life well lived. The sage will simply avoid getting into some morally charged situations, but will actively bring on others. Similarly, he will refuse to regard some popular issues as important, but

This understanding gains credibility from Seneca's remarks about the appropriate audience for precepts. At one point, Seneca considers the objection that once one has knowledge of what to do and the appropriate psychology to do it, one has no need of precepts in addition, since it is simply derived from them.[69] To this, Seneca responds:

> That which you mention is the mark of *an already perfect man,* of one who has attained the height of human happiness.[70]

Hence, he seems to accept the premise that someone who already has both the doctrines and the relevant psychology does not need precepts in addition. Moreover, he then continues by arguing that precepts are necessary for the nonvirtuous, both for those with weak characters, and for the more fortunate who are approaching virtue. He says:

> But the approach to these qualities is slow, and in the meantime, in practical matters, the path should be pointed out for the benefit of one who is still short of perfection, but is making progress. [. . .] Wisdom by her own agency may perhaps show herself this path without the help of admonition; for she has brought the soul to a stage where it can be impelled only in the right direction. Weaker characters, however, need someone to precede them, to say "avoid this" or "do that."[71]

And elsewhere he says:

> Hence come the choice minds which seize quickly upon virtue, or else produce it from within themselves. But your dull, sluggish fellow, who is hampered by his evil habits, must have this soul-rust incessantly rubbed off. [. . .] As the former sort, who are inclined towards the good, can be raised to the heights more quickly: so the weaker spirits will be assisted and freed from their evil opinions if we entrust to them the accepted principles of philosophy.[72]

All this suggests that the precepts play an important developmental role on the path to virtue, but are superceded by the doctrines and virtue in the virtuous person.[73]

---

be a strenuous advocate of other, neglected causes. I assume that these are some of the reasons for Aristotle's insistence on the importance of role models, and part of what he means by claiming that a vital component of moral education is imitation of the virtuous person doing virtuous actions.

69. 94.48.

70. 94.50; emphasis added. Shortly afterwards he speaks of the soul "becoming able to guide itself." 94.51.

71. 94.50.

72. 95.36–37.

73. There is a parallel with the gods here:

8. The Primacy of the Sage

My interpretation of Seneca provides the beginnings of an account of how the role of precepts and doctrines might be reconciled with the primacy of the virtuous agent.[74] To begin with, the precepts pick out natural and low level evaluative facts that novices can access perceptually, and which are empirically likely to be associated with the right action, because they are in some way connected to real moral facts. Considered alone, we would not expect such rules to be exceptionless. But they might become so when embedded in a wider theoretical framework.

Next, that framework is provided by the doctrines. Doctrines ground the precepts, providing the reasons for them and the general setting within which they operate. I have claimed that this is best understood if the virtues themselves are reflected in doctrines. This implies that at least some doctrines embody the sage's evaluative concepts (e.g., bravery, virtue). Hence, if precepts are guided by doctrines, they become exceptionless, because their appropriate application is ensured by the background evaluative concepts. The virtues *circumscribe* the application of precepts.[75]

Now, so far this account leaves open the possibility that the sage might use precepts. For, since his perceptual abilities are not defective, he will not be led astray by the imperfections of precepts for judgment—his background theoretical framework is such as to guarantee that the domain of application of the precepts is appropriately circumscribed. Still, the comments cited above suggest that

---

Just as the immortal gods did not learn virtue—having been born with virtue complete, and containing in their nature the essence of goodness—even so certain men are fitted with unusual qualities and reach without a long apprenticeship that which is ordinarily a matter of teaching, welcoming honorable things as soon as they hear them. (95.36)

74. It also addresses Mitsis' "two key points of disagreement" with Inwood and Vander Waerdt: that they "slight the best evidence for the role of rules in Stoic thinking, and that is our reports of the debates between Aristo and orthodox Stoics over the usefulness of general and particular moral recommendations"; and that they "understand the differences between the moral deliberations of sages and the non-wise" as either a "historical shift" (in Vander Waerdt's case) or "a timeless divide between sage and non-sage" (in Inwood's). See Mitsis, "The Stoics and Aquinas," 49–50. My account can allow for the disagreement between Aristo and the mainstream Stoics as perhaps an empirical disagreement about the availability of purely descriptive and low-level evaluative properties that track right action. It does not understand the difference between sage and non-sage as a "timeless divide," but rather as, in the relevant respect, a matter of degree.

75. This might be thought to create a problem for the account in explaining the phenomenology of conflict between competing moral considerations. For it suggests that precepts are silenced in cases where they don't apply, and so leave no moral remainders. This is too big a topic to address here. But two remarks may be helpful. On the one hand, the precepts do not (in this sense) have moral weight independently of the backing of doctrines (which supply the reasons), so it does not seem correct to look to them to explain moral remainders. On the other, I have not presupposed that each precept is subsumed under only one doctrine, nor that doctrines themselves are one-dimensional. So there is conceptual space for an account of moral remainders.

Seneca himself did not believe that the sage needs precepts.[76] (Hence, Seneca is closer to Aristo than one might have thought. He denies that principles are never useful, but accepts that only doctrines are useful to the sage.)[77] Instead, Seneca's idea seems to be that if the sage's judgments reflect rules at all, he would either rely on, or (merely as a matter of fact) act in accordance with, rules that are properly connected to the correct conceptual scheme, and which (hence) require perceptual judgments that are made in accordance with that scheme.[78]

The above interpretation has several advantages. First, it accounts for at least some aspects of the relationship that Seneca posits between precepts and doctrines. For example, doctrines are primary, but less accessible; precepts must ultimately be interpreted in light of doctrines; precepts refer to descriptive natural facts or low-level evaluative ones, and doctrines to more evaluative facts. Second, it explains why the nonvirtuous person would need to rely exclusively on precepts, and not appeal to doctrines. For the nonvirtuous lack the conceptual framework (and the corresponding perceptual capacity) which makes it possible to understand (and to apply) doctrines correctly. By contrast, the virtuous person has the necessary framework and capacity. But once she has these, she has no need of precepts; for she has no need of second-best rules. Finally, the account allows for the primacy of virtue. For the deep evaluative concepts replace the nonevaluative and shallow ones; they justify them; and they are necessary to stop lower-level rules leading people astray. But these concepts are hidden, and properly accessible only to the virtuous person.[79]

There is one important point about the primacy of virtue that I want to emphasize at this point. It may initially appear that much of the grounding for virtue ethics here rests on a quasi-empirical claim: "nothing except virtue does not change its name." For the core idea seems to be that correct behavior does not co-vary with those empirical properties of actions which are easily accessible to the nonvirtuous person, so that grasping the virtue concepts themselves

76. This appears to be disputed by David Sedley. Sedley claims that "there is an exact one-to-one correlation between *kathekonta* and *praecepta.*" Given that "*kathekonta* in the generic sense . . . include the proper conduct both of the non-wise and of the wise," the sage employs *praecepta.* See Sedley, "The Stoic-Platonist Debate on Kathekonta," in *Topics,* ed. Ierodiakonou, 128–152; at 129 and 132.

77. Mitsis, by contrast, says: "Orthodox Stoics claim that knowing the fundamental doctrines or principles of morality (*decreta*) is not enough to insure correct moral action; one also needs more determinate moral rules to pick out the morally salient situations to which they apply (cf. Seneca, *Ep. Mor.* 94.32). *This applies to those who are wise and those who are not equally.*" Mitsis, "The Stoics and Aquinas," 51; emphasis added. Against this, see, for example, 94.50–51, as discussed in the main text above.

78. These would be the first-best rules, couched in theory and value-laden language; and perhaps (if the Stoics accept such rules) these are also doctrines. If they are precepts, they would have to be of a different kind to those employed to educate the novice.

79. Note that Seneca himself does not think that the quasi-empirical nature of the need for precepts means that the need for them is contingent in any strong way. For he goes so far as to offer a strong conceptual argument—the self-refutation argument mentioned in an earlier footnote—against those who would do away with rules of either kind. See 95.60.

is necessary for right action. But this impression turns out to be misleading in an important way. Though there is clearly an empirical edge to the Stoic claim, there is a more important *nonempirical basis* for it. For even if some coextensive relations were found between virtue and generally accessible properties of right actions, this would be an empirical fact too. The concepts of the virtues would still be primary in justification—one would be justified in using the easily accessible empirical features to form rules *only because* of their coextensiveness with virtue, not because they themselves were normatively prior to virtue.[80]

Despite the insistence on the primacy of virtue, rules play an important role for Seneca. Precepts are necessary in moral education; and doctrines are always necessary, and can count as guiding principles. Furthermore, Seneca's account helps to resolve the core difficulty for the rule-based views: that rules can be exceptionless but substantive. For the idea of nested or circumscribed rules gives a clear sense to these claims. On the one hand, precepts considered in isolation are substantive, but are not exceptionless. But they are not meant to be considered in isolation. Instead they are framed by and nested in the doctrines and the wider purview of virtue. This is the background that is taken for granted in their application—like the guiding hand of the master to the pupil scribe.[81] One needs the example of good people's behavior to see how they are circumscribed (in experience of them, through role models in history, and so on).[82] On the other hand, doctrines are exceptionless but nonsubstantive for the nonvirtuous person. But they are nonsubstantive just because the nonvirtuous person is not in a position to apply them, because she is not in a position to employ the thick evaluative terms they contain. For the virtuous person, they are substantive and exceptionless.

9. Implications

Seneca's account has two important implications. The first is that conceiving the debate between virtue ethics and its modern rivals as being primarily about the existence of moral principles is a mistake. Seneca thought that rules were

---

80. Some particularists also suggest that theirs is a fundamentally empirical doctrine. But I agree with Jonathan Dancy, who suggests that particularism is primarily a modal notion: that moral judgment does not *require* moral principles, but would be *possible* without them. See Jonathan Dancy, *Ethics Without Principles* (Oxford: Oxford University Press, forthcoming).

81. 94.51.

82. Seneca also seems to think that (either as an addition or alternative) social structure and environment are important. For example, in several places he extols the virtues of rural life. See, for example:

A quiet life does not of itself give lessons in upright conduct; the countryside does not of itself teach plain living; no, but when witnesses and onlookers are removed, faults which ripen in publicity and display sink into the background. (94.69)

See also 95.18.

necessary, and yet believed in the priority of the virtuous person, and his view is perfectly coherent. This might seem to be a surprising result. But reflection suggests that it should not be. For, at least pretheoretically, a principle is in the first instance simply a verbal form;[83] hence most moral claims can be expressed in terms of principles.[84] The key issue is not, then, whether we can express certain foundational moral claims in terms of principles. We clearly can ("be virtuous," "act justly"). What is really at stake is (1) whether or not the necessary rules appeal to evaluative concepts which are accessible to all, and (2) whether they have to be understood in a holistic way, that is, as nested into a wider framework of decision.

Moreover, in these two matters the virtue ethicist seems to be on firm ground. First, it seems entirely reasonable to hold that correct moral judgment depends on a grasp of concepts which are not immediately available to just anyone, regardless of their psychological condition. This is simply one aspect of the appealing Stoic idea that virtue is a skill. Moreover, and perhaps more importantly, this is a natural default position: if some people think that transparent moral principles are available, or that they need to be, then the burden of proof is on them to show it. Second, holism is to be expected on a virtue ethics framework, and does not seem an unreasonable starting-point. On the first point, the foundational concern of virtue ethics is to establish how to live virtuously, as a virtuous agent would. But this is a holistic notion: the concept of a life subsumes the concept of how to act on a particular situation. On the second, we should not simply assume that good action can be made sense of without appeal to the background notion of living a good life.

The second implication of Seneca's view is that we should not be swayed by a familiar objection made against virtue ethics: that it does not provide practical guidance. For one thing, we should not start out with the presumption that all the information needed for living well will be immediately accessible to all, without effort and regardless of the state of the mind receiving it and its previous history.[85] For another, Seneca has shown us how a virtue ethicist might accept this point and yet still accommodate our need for accessible practical guidance for the novice. For he has shown how the primacy of the virtuous agent can coexist with several kinds of moral rules.

---

83. At least, anyone with a more rigid account needs to defend that on theoretical grounds.

84. Indeed, Seneca himself makes these points: the first with his claim about precepts and examples of virtuous behavior; and the second with his argument (which I did not discuss here) that precepts and doctrines are ineliminable.

85. Also, as Rosalind Hursthouse points out in her classic article, other traditions have notions that are initially as opaque as virtue (such as "respect" and "happiness"). See Hursthouse, "Virtue Ethics and Abortion," *Philosophy and Public Affairs* 20 (1991): 223–246. Reprinted in Statman, *Virtue Ethics*.

10. Conclusion

This paper has accomplished two main tasks. It has provided a new interpretation of Seneca's position on moral rules; and it has shown how this position helps to resolve a central debate within contemporary virtue ethics. Seneca can escape Aristo's paradox; and so can his philosophical descendants. Virtue ethics is compatible with genuine practical guidance, for there can be virtuous moral rules.[86]

---

86. A distant ancestor of one part of this paper was presented back in 1998 at Cornell University as a commentary on a paper of Brad Inwood's. I thank Todd Blanke, Charles Brittain, Brad Inwood, T. H. Irwin, and Jennifer Whiting for comments on that occasion. More recently, I have profited from discussions with the participants of the Christchurch conference, and especially Julia Annas, Eric Hutton, Bob Solomon, and Christine Swanton. Shortly before this paper went to press, I received some extremely generous, extensive, and stimulating comments from Phillip Mitsis. A full response to his arguments would require another long paper, and here I have had time to make only a few minor adjustments. Nevertheless, I am grateful for his encouragement and for his continued interest in raising the level of debate about these issues.

CHAPTER 3

Do Virtues Conflict? Aquinas' Answer

T. H. IRWIN

I.

The Secunda Secundae (or Second Part of the Second Part) of Aquinas' *Summa Theologiae* occupies over 900 pages of Latin text and contains 189 Questions. But in the Prologue he tells us with a perfectly straight face that it results from his effort to discuss the area of morality (materia moralis) more compactly than other people have discussed it. On this point it carries out the aim of the *Summa* as a whole (cf. 1a, Prol.). To avoid repetitive and unsystematic treatment, he proposes to consider in turn a given virtue, the gift corresponding to it, the vices opposed to it, and the relevant affirmative or negative precepts. Hence the whole area of morality will be derived from the consideration of the virtues. Moreover the virtues themselves will be derived from the three theological virtues as the basis of the infused virtues, and from the four cardinal virtues, as the basis of the acquired virtues.

This attempt to organize the acquired virtues around the four cardinal virtues is Aquinas' innovation in mediaeval discussions.[1] But is it a good idea, and does it throw any light on the virtues of character and on the moral principles connected with them?

To answer this question, and to see the relevance of the cardinal virtues, we must go back to a still more basic level in his theory. For we might wonder why

---

1. M. D. Jordan, "Ideals of scientia moralis," in *Aquinas' Moral Theory*, ed. S. C. MacDonald and E. S. Stump (Ithaca: Cornell University Press, 1999), 79–97, at 91–5, discusses the organization of *ST* 2–2, and emphasizes Aquinas' innovation in making the cardinal virtues the principle of organization.

we have any right to expect a systematic account of the virtues. It might be convenient for mnemonic or expository purposes, but why should it reflect any facts about morality itself? Human life, both individual and social, is untidy. Why should moral virtues that respond to the untidy complexity of life be part of any system?

Aquinas is aware of some reasons for skepticism about attempts to represent moral virtues as a system. In his analysis of the different virtues, he often rejects the suggestion that one virtue could be opposed to another.

> It follows, accordingly, that favoritism (personarum acceptio) is opposed to distributive justice in that it is pursued beyond <proper> proportion. Now nothing but sin is opposed to virtue: and therefore favoritism is a sin. (2–2 q63 a1)
>
> Further, no virtue is opposed to another virtue. But magnanimity is opposed to humility, since "the magnanimous person counts himself worthy of great things, and despises others," as is said in *Ethics* IV. Therefore magnanimity is not a virtue. (q129 a3 obj4)
>
> Nothing except a vice is opposed to a virtue. But insensibility is opposed to the virtue of temperance . . . Therefore insensibility is a vice. (q142 a1 sc)
>
> For no virtue is opposed to another virtue. Yet both of these [sc. clemency and mildness (mansuetudo)] appear to be opposed to severity, which is a virtue. Therefore neither clemency nor mildness is a virtue. (q 157 a2 obj1)
>
> Further, no virtue is opposed to another virtue. But humility appears to be opposed to the virtue of magnanimity, which aims at great things, whereas humility avoids them. Therefore it appears that humility is not a virtue. (q161 a1 obj3)

When we face apparent evidence that two virtues are opposed, we have three choices: (1) We may reject the general principle that two virtues cannot be opposed, and hence we may conclude that these two virtues really are opposed. (2) We may accept the general principle, and conclude that at least one of these opposed conditions is not a genuine virtue. (3) We may accept the general principle, and conclude that these two states are not really opposed.

Aquinas never tries the first answer. The condition opposed to a virtue is its corresponding vice, and so if we were to allow virtues to be opposed to virtues, we would be confounding virtues and vices. He adheres to the principle that good cannot be opposed to good (q47 a9 obj3; q101 a4), and always tries the second or the third answer. Most often he tries the third. Hence he argues that clemency and mildness are not opposed to severity (q 157 a2), that carefulness is not opposed to the promptness needed for prudence (q47 a9), that honoring one's parents is not opposed to religion (q101 a4), and that humility is not opposed to magnanimity (q161 a1). Since the allegedly opposed states are not really opposed, we cannot cite their opposition as a reason for refusing to count them both as virtues.

Aquinas' refusal to consider opposition between virtues is so central in his description and comparison of the virtues and vices that we may reasonably expect him to give good reasons for it. In looking for his reasons, we may ask two main questions: (1) Why is this a reasonable general expectation for an account of the virtues? (2) How far do we find this expectation confirmed by the details of our account?

An answer to the first question does not settle the second question. We might have good reasons to look for a unified account of the virtues that avoids any opposition between virtues, but we might fail to find what we are looking for, once we examine the states that we normally count as virtues, or the states that it seems reasonable for human beings to cultivate as virtues.

Aquinas does not believe that his answer to the second question requires him simply to stipulate that the virtues are the states of character that meet the general expectation for no opposition between virtues. He believes that he can show that the states we reasonably count as virtues also meet the general expectation. That is part of the reason for the length and detail of the Secunda Secundae.

An opponent of Aquinas' position might argue that the reputed virtues seem to display the sorts of conflicts that Aquinas denies. One might argue that Aquinas has made a moral error. Different virtues promote, preserve, or respect different values, and since these values conflict, the virtues themselves conflict. The virtue of justice seeks fairness and equality between individuals. The virtue of benevolence aims at the total good. These are incompatible aims, and the corresponding virtues conflict. Alternatively, his error might be psychological rather than moral. Even if the aims of different virtues do not conflict, the characteristics, traits, and emotions that we need for one virtue conflict with those we need for another. The cold impartiality and detachment of a judge will conflict with the sympathy and warmth we might value in a nurse or a parent or a friend. Though the aims of the judge are consistent with those of the nurse or parent or friend, perhaps we cannot cultivate the traits needed for one virtue without weakening the traits needed for another virtue. The virtues require the development of immediate and unreflective spontaneous reactions that cannot always be controlled on particular occasions, and so cannot be switched on and off according to the needs of one or another virtue.

2.

Aquinas believes the virtues form a system because they all require prudence. Virtuous people need the right conception of the end they pursue in their actions.

For each virtue operates because of the good of virtue. Hence if one aims at the good of virtue, as is appropriate for the virtuous person, one does not turn one's aim away from that end. Hence the Philosopher says that the wasteful person, who spends without concern for the good, easily turns away to any evil.[2]

The correct conception of this end is prudence.[3] Prudence itself is a systematic practical science because it is concerned with 'the whole of human life' (in EN #1163), and the end it grasps is 'the common end of all of human life' (in EN #1233).

He [sc. Aristotle] says "being one," because, if there were different prudences concerned with the matters of different moral virtues, just as there are different kinds[4] of artifacts, it would be quite possible for one moral virtue to exist without another, each of them having a prudence corresponding to it. But this cannot be the case, because the principles of prudence are the same for the whole matter of morals, so that everything is derived from the standard of reason. And that is why because of the unity of prudence all the moral virtues are connected with one another. (in EN #1288)

Virtuous people, therefore, need the right conception of the common end for practical reasoning (EN 1144a31–6; in EN #1273–4).

This general claim may seem too slim a basis for useful claims about the virtues. We might agree that we need passions and wills guided by reason and virtue if we are to pursue our good correctly. But this seems to give us no clear view about what the virtues are—whether, for instance, they include the control of appetites or the formation of rational plans for the maximum satisfaction of appetites. We might agree that the human good requires us to act in accordance with reason, but still not agree that acting in accordance with reason requires temperance and bravery, as he understands them. It seems still more obvious that we might agree about acting in accordance with reason, but deny that such action includes action for the good of others that does not provide some antecedently desired good for ourselves.

Aquinas, however, believes that deliberation about one's ultimate end yields not only an account of virtue, but also a sufficiently detailed account of the virtues. Deliberation shows (for instance) that the moral precepts of the Decalogue are among the actions required by the virtues, and that we have reason to

---

2. *Scriptum de Sententiis* [cited as *Sent.*], 3 d36 q1 a1 c.
3. See Aristotle, *Nicomachean Ethics* [cited as *EN*] 1142b31–3; Aquinas, *in Ethica Nicomachea* #1233 [cited as *in EN*, by paragraphs of Marietti edn.].
4. The Leonine edition reads "genera." The Marietti edition prints "genere," which appears to be a misprint.

care about the interests of other people for their own sakes. The considerations
he has appealed to so far seem to him to support a detailed account of the virtues.

This detailed account is mostly presented in the *Secunda Secundae*. This part
discusses a bewildering variety of virtues and vices. Moreover, it clearly belongs
to moral theology more than to moral philosophy, since it presupposes the su-
pernatural additions (infused virtues, and so on) to the acquired moral virtues.
Still, its main structure and aims are fairly clear; it tries to answer some of the
questions about the virtues that we might ask when we reflect on the ultimate
end, prudence, and deliberation.

3.

The main argument of the *Secunda Secundae* rests on Aquinas' claim that the
matter of morality is "derived from" (reduci ad) the subject-matter of the four
distinct cardinal virtues (*3 Sent.* d33 q2 a1 sol.4).[5] How is this derivation to be
explained?

Following his usual practice, Aquinas develops his central argument through
a discussion of his apparently conflicting sources. Different authorities explain
the nature of the cardinal virtues, and their relation to other specific virtues, in
different ways. In commenting on these different explanations, Aquinas works
out his distinctive position on the nature of the cardinal virtues and on the
grounds for recognizing them as "cardinal" or "principal."

The list of four virtues—bravery, temperance, justice, and wisdom—is familiar from Plato's early dialogues. A later dialogue, the *Republic,* explains them by
reference to the rational and non-rational parts of the soul.[6] But Aristotle's classification of the virtues seems to give no special primacy to Plato's four virtues.
Bravery and temperance are listed among the different specific virtues of character, discussed in *Nicomachean Ethics* 3–4; justice is the last virtue of character to
be discussed, and is postponed to book 5; and wisdom is treated separately, in both
its theoretical and practical forms (*sophia* and *phronêsis*) among the intellectual
virtues in book 6. The Stoics, by contrast, treat the four cardinal virtues as generic
virtues and classify the other virtues of character as specific virtues "subordinate"
(*huptetagmenai*) to one or the other of the "primary" virtues.[7]

5. Cf. *De Virtutibus Cardinalibus* [cited as *Virt. Card.*], a1 ad5.

6. I have discussed the cardinal virtues in "The parts of the soul and the cardinal virtues" in *Platon:
Politeia,* ed. O. Hoeffe (Berlin: Akademie Verlag, 1997), ch. 6.

7. See Stobaeus, *Eclogae,* ii 60.9–11 [Wachsmuth]); *Stoicorum Veterum Fragmenta,* iii 262–75. These are
partly translated by A. A. Long and D. N. Sedley (eds.), *The Hellenistic Philosophers* (Cambridge: Cambridge
University Press, 1987), #61H.

As usual, Aquinas takes himself to expound an Aristotelian position. But the Christian sources that he includes among his authorities are influenced by the Stoic classification, and hence recognize four cardinal virtues; indeed, the term "cardinal" itself comes from Ambrose's exposition of the Stoic position. He derives a doctrine of four cardinal virtues especially from Ambrose and Gregory the Great (1–2 q61 a1 sc; *Virt. Card.* a1 obj2; a2c).

Aquinas tries to show how some of his different authorities can be reconciled. But he also revises earlier views of the cardinal virtues so as to present a significant alternative of his own. In his view, the cardinal virtues are neither simply (as Aristotle seems to imply) specific virtues co-ordinate with the other virtues of character nor (as the Stoics believe) simply generic virtues. He believes that we can treat the cardinal virtues in different but complementary ways that help to explain the systematic character of the virtues.

Aquinas does not directly confront the apparent disagreement between the Aristotelian and the Stoic treatment of the cardinal virtues. Instead, he considers two other ways one may understand these virtues and tries to show how each conception of them is reasonable.

4.

According to one conception, the cardinal virtues express the "perfect character of virtue, which requires correctness of desire" (1–2 q61 a1). To act virtuously, according to Aquinas, we must act on the cardinal virtues, no matter what special virtue we exercise in a particular action. These virtues are like hinges (*cardines*) because they are those "in which the moral life turns and is founded in a certain way." They are fundamental to the moral life, because that is the life proper to a human being, in contrast to a non-rational animal or an angel; this is the life of practical reason, the "active life, which consists in the exercise of moral virtues" (*Virt. Card.* a1).[8]

We discover the virtues by examining the "formal principle," which is the good of reason.

> [The cardinal virtues] are called principal, being general, as it were, in comparison with all the virtues: so that, for instance, any virtue that causes good in reason's act of consideration may be called prudence; every virtue that causes the good of what is correct and due in operation may be called justice; every virtue that curbs and

---

8. He cites *Proverbs* 26:14 ("As a door turns on its hinge, so does an idler in his bed") as his Scriptural authority for the term "cardinal," and he cites Ambrose as his patristic authority for the use of "cardinal" for the canon of four virtues. See *Virt. Card.* a1, corp; *ST* 1–2 q61 a1 sc; *3Sent.* d33 q2 a1 sol.2.

represses the passions may be called temperance; and every virtue that strengthens the mind against any passions whatever may be called bravery . . . (1–2 q61 a3)

The formal principle consists both in consideration by reason itself and in direction by reason imposed on other things. These other things are actions and passions; the passions are those that can turn us away in bad directions or prevent us from going in good directions. We need prudence, for proper consideration by reason. We need justice, to achieve rightly-ordered action. We need temperance (understood broadly, as Aquinas points out) as the virtue that regulates potentially distracting passions. We need bravery (also understood broadly) as the virtue that regulates potentially inhibiting passions. The same conclusion results if we consider the subject of the different aspects of the correct formal principle. One subject has to be the rational part, of which prudence is the virtue. Another has to be the part that is rational by participation; this part is divided into the will, the irascible part, and the appetitive (*concupiscibilis*) part (q61 a2).

Aquinas infers the pervasive features of a virtuous life from Aristotle's account of acting virtuously.

> But for actions in accord with the virtues to be done temperately or justly it does not suffice that they themselves have the right qualities. Rather, <actions are done justly or temperately> if the agent acts being in a certain state. First, if <he acts> knowing. Secondly, if electing, and electing because of this.[9] Thirdly, if he is in a firm and unchanging state and acts. (*EN* 1105a28–33)[10]

Aquinas sometimes takes this passage to introduce the cardinal virtues (*Virt. Card.* a1). Aristotle's demand for knowledge introduces "directive" knowledge, and hence prudence. His demand for correct election for the right end introduces justice. His demand for firm and unshakeable election introduces temperance and bravery (cf. 2–2 q123 a11).

These claims do not perfectly fit the specific passage in Aristotle that Aquinas cites. Aquinas himself does not introduce them into his commentary on the *Ethics*. The claim about knowledge is most clearly inappropriate. As Aquinas recognizes elsewhere, Aristotle does not refer to prudence, but simply to the sort of knowledge that is necessary for voluntariness.[11] Aristotle's reference to

---

9. I follow the Leonine edition's reading propter hoc, supported by Aquinas' commentary (#283). Marietti reads propter haec, which agrees with *dia tauta* in the manuscript Kb. Editors of the Greek texts that I have consulted prefer the reading of the other mss, *di'auta*. Aquinas' commentary understands propter hoc as equivalent to "for their own sake."

10. I have adapted the translation slightly to fit Aquinas' Latin version (*in EN* #177).

11. Cf. 2–2 q58 a1.

the right sort of election does not clearly allude to justice. His conception of the range of bravery and temperance does not give them a special role in ensuring a firm and unshakeable election in all areas that concern the virtues.

But though Aquinas' description of Aristotle's position does not fit the passage he attaches it to, it fits Aristotle's general conception of virtue. His reference to prudence fits Aristotle's remark that the mean must be determined by the reason by which the prudent person would determine it (1107a1).[12] The demand for the correct end is plausibly extracted from Aristotle's claim that the correct election is needed. Aquinas' introduction of justice to explain the correct end fits Aristotle's view that general justice is complete virtue, because just people practice virtue everywhere it is relevant, especially in relation to other people (1129b31–3). Aquinas infers that Aristotle attributes a distinctive aim, and hence a distinctive sort of election, to justice; it aims as the common good (intendit ad bonum commune, #912).[13] Firmness and control fit Aristotle's demand for a firm and unchanging state. Firmness and constancy depend on the condition of our non-rational desires and passions; if they are misdirected, they will make us waver even if we make the correct (in some ways) election on occasions where strong passions are not involved. Bravery is connected with firmness, even outside the primary area of brave action. Though bravery is primarily about the danger of death in battle, it makes the brave person firm and constant in other situations as well (1115a32–b6). Similarly, lack of temperance explains why incontinent people waver in their attachment to the virtuous course of action (1151a20–8).

For these reasons, Aquinas' view that the cardinal virtues mark pervasive features of all virtuous action is defensible by appeal to Aristotle. But it is especially characteristic of Stoicism. The Stoics claim that in every virtuous action we act in accordance with each of the cardinal virtues, even though we exercise some specific virtue in a way in which we do not exercise all the others. The cardinal virtues, understood broadly, are pervasive, because all circumstances require us

---

12. Curiously, Aquinas' Latin version (#202) renders *phronimos* by sapiens here, not by the usual prudens. But Aquinas' comment (#323) recognizes that Aristotle is referring to the prudent person.

13. Aquinas' description of the aim of justice is supported by Aristotle's description of "just things" as "those that produce and maintain happiness and its parts for a political community" (1129b17–19). Aquinas introduces the reference to a common good by reference to Aristotle's division between different constitutions, alluded to in 1129b14–16; see #902: "sicut est in rectis politiis, in quibus intenditur bonum commune"; Aristotle does not use any phrase here corresponding to "in rectis politiis," but Aquinas implicitly appeals, legitimately, to the *Politics*.

The Latin version obscures the reference to a political community. It renders *tê(i) politikê(i) koinônia(i)* (for the political community) by politica communicatione (by political common life), inaccurately rendering the Greek dative by the Latin ablative, as though the Greek were an instrumental dative. But Aquinas implicitly corrects this error. His paraphrase per comparationem ad communitatem politicam (#903) captures the Greek better than it captures the Latin he is commenting on.

to exercise all of them; we do not exercise prudence or temperance, say, as opposed to some other virtue, on certain types of occasions rather than others. This feature seems to distinguish cardinal virtues from a virtue such as generosity or wit; if we are not in the right situation, we cannot exercise wit, but if we are in any situation that calls for any of the virtues, we have to exercise the formal principles of the different cardinal virtues (cf. 2–2 q123 a11; q141 a7).

5.

Aquinas also recognizes a second conception of the cardinal virtues, which is easier to recognize in Aristotle.

> They may be taken in another way, in so far as they are named from what is most important (praecipuum) in the subject matter of each. And in this way they are specific virtues, distinguished on a level with the others. Yet they are called principal in comparison with the other virtues, on account of their subject matter's being principal. For instance, the virtue that prescribes is called prudence; the virtue about due actions between equals is called justice; the virtue that restrains appetitive desires for the pleasures of touch is called temperance; and the virtue that strengthens against dangers of death is called bravery. (1–2 q61 a3)

According to this view, as opposed to the first view, we exercise temperance (e.g.) on particular occasions on which we do not (in the same way) exercise other virtues as well.

This second view of the cardinal virtues is recognizably Aristotelian to the extent that it implies that they are distinct virtues with distinct subject matters, not (as the first view claimed) pervasive features of all the virtuous person's actions. But the second view also seems un-Aristotelian; for Aquinas treats his favored four virtues as cardinal or principal, but he seems to have no clear Aristotelian basis.

He introduces Aristotle's treatment of the moral virtues (EN ii 7) by criticizing the Stoic view that the cardinal virtues are generic (in EN #337). He prefers the view he ascribes to Aristotle, that the four virtues are principal because they are to be distinguished in accordance with different principal areas of operation. Though Aristotle postpones justice until book 5 and prudence until book 6, he deals with bravery and temperance and with "certain other secondary virtues" in books 3–4. These are secondary because they can be derived from (reduci ad) the principal virtues. Among the virtues that deal with passions (those discussed in 3–4), bravery and temperance are about "principal passions, concerning human life itself," and others are about "some secondary passions, concerning external human goods" (#528).

Aquinas' claim that the virtues described in *EN* 4 are all secondary to, and derivative from, the cardinal virtues does not rest on any explicit remarks of Aristotle's. Though Aristotle discusses bravery and temperance first, and at greater length than he discusses the non-cardinal virtues, he does not say that they are more fundamental or more important than generosity, magnificence, and so on. If Aquinas' position is genuinely Aristotelian, he needs to defend it by appeal to the content of Aristotle's analysis of the virtues.

In his view, the cardinal status of these four virtues supports and justifies the Aristotelian view that they are different specific virtues exercised in distinct ranges of action. This claim seems especially difficult to connect with Aristotle, since Aristotle's treatment of bravery and temperance is conspicuous for its restrictive view of their scope. Whereas we might take Socrates and Plato to accept a broad conception of bravery and temperance, linking them with the control of fear and appetite in all circumstances where such control is morally necessary, we seem to find the opposite attitude in Aristotle. Bravery, as Aristotle describes it, belongs only to some situations in which fear needs to be controlled—those that involve danger of death in battle. Similarly, temperance requires the control of only some appetites—those for food, drink, and sex; continence and incontinence are similarly limited.

Aquinas argues that the pervasive virtues are exercised "principally" or "especially" in different ranges of action (1–2 q61 a3; 2–2 q123 a11; 141 a7; *Virt. Card.* a1). Whenever we act virtuously, we must exercise the appropriate firmness; we especially exercise it, however, in facing the danger of death; hence, it is appropriately exercised in bravery, which is the virtue concerned with facing this danger. A similar argument applies to temperance. The claim that these are special or "principal" exercises of the relevant pervasive virtues supports the claim that these are distinct virtues with their own range of actions.

In claiming that these are "special" or "principal" exercises, Aquinas perhaps has two points in mind: (1) These are cases in which it is especially difficult to exercise the pervasive virtue of (say) bravery, because the danger of death is especially likely to impede us from following the right course of action. (2) Sometimes it is especially important to exercise the pervasive virtue, because (for instance) we must exercise firmness in this area if we are to be capable of standing up for what we value. The importance of a given exercise may be determined by its effect on some especially central goal of virtuous action, or by its effect on the states of character that make a person virtuous.

These two points sometimes pick out the same actions. The difficulty of restraining certain fears that tend to inhibit actions that promote some central aim of virtue (say, achieving the safety of the community) may partly explain why it is especially important for us to restrain these fears. But difficulty and importance do not always go together; in particular, the most difficult actions are not always the most important. A gymnast may show a principal or outstanding degree of physical agility in doing something that is especially difficult, but it may not be important for other people, given their reasonable aims, to cultivate precisely this degree of agility. Similarly, we may not all need the firmness of the people who face death in battle bravely, if most of us do not face that situation; instead, we ought perhaps to cultivate firmness in sticking to our convictions on the appropriate occasions, if that trait affects more of the ends that a virtuous person pursues.

Aquinas does not always clearly distinguish these two types of principal exercise of the virtues. Sometimes he mentions difficulty (2–2 q123 a11), but sometimes he seems to have importance in mind. When he argues that prudence, rather than other virtues of practical intellect, is cardinal, he seems to mean that prudence makes the decisive and most important difference to our action.

> But through prudence comes reason that prescribes well . . . Hence it is clear that what is most important (praecipuum) in directive cognition belongs to prudence, and on this account prudence is counted as a cardinal virtue. (*De Virt Card* a1)

Here it is the importance of good prescriptive reasoning for a well-ordered moral life, not its difficulty, that makes prudence a principal virtue.

The discussion of temperance distinguishes difficulty from importance. Self-control is especially praiseworthy in the case of the pleasures of touch, which concern temperance:

> On the one hand, because such pleasures are more natural to us, and therefore it is more difficult to refrain from them and to restrain appetite for them; on the other hand, because their objects are more necessary for the present life. (2–2 q141 a7)

Aquinas distinguishes the strength of desires for pleasures of touch (a4) from their connection with the necessities of life (a5), and he recognizes these two facts as distinct grounds for taking temperance to be a cardinal virtue.

The case of justice highlights the question about difficulty and importance. It seems to be more difficult to exercise virtue when we have to consider the interests of others than when we have to consider only ourselves. On this ground, other-directed action principally manifests pursuit of the correct end. Does it also manifest it principally in the other sense, by being especially important? That depends on whether concern for the good of others is especially important for the good aimed at by the virtues; we apparently need to be convinced on this point before we can be convinced that justice, as Aquinas understands it, is really a cardinal virtue.

6.

Aquinas does not merely combine the restrictive Aristotelian account of the cardinal virtues with the broader Stoic account. He also argues that once we understand the point of the Aristotelian emphasis on principal exercises of the virtues, we can also understand why the virtues have a broad scope. In this way, the Aristotelian account actually supports part of the Stoic account.

Bravery, for instance, is concerned with fears and confidence, but more specifically with the fear of death, not simply because it is difficult not to be moved by the fear of death, but also because love of one's own life is natural (2–2 q123 a4 ad 2). The naturalness of the love of life explains why it is important, and not merely difficult, to control one's fear of death, and therefore explains why this is a principal exercise of bravery in both senses. Moreover, bravery is properly concerned with the danger of death in war, not with all danger of death equally.

> Certainly the brave person is also intrepid on the sea and in sickness, but not in the same way as seafarers are. For the one lot have given up hope of safety, and object to this sort of death, whereas the experience of the other lot makes them hopeful.[14] Moreover, people act like brave men on occasions when one can use one's strength, or when it is fine to be killed; and neither of these applies to perishing in these circumstances. (1115a35–b6)

Aquinas takes Aristotle to mean that the principal exercise of bravery is confined to cases in which bravery is praiseworthy (*laudabilis*) or it is good[15] to die; and it is good that a person gives his life for the common good (#542).

Following the view he ascribes to Aristotle, Aquinas distinguishes those dangers that result from our pursuing a good from those that happen to us whether

14. I have used this awkward rendering to capture the ambiguity of *hoi men . . . hoi de* in the Greek. The Latin (hi . . . hi) is equally ambiguous. Aquinas (agreeing with most translators and commentators) takes *hoi men* to be brave people, and *hoi de* to be experienced sailors (#541). Alternatively, one might (following Burnet and Rowe) take *hoi men* to refer generally to people who are not experienced sailors. At any rate, Aquinas misinterprets the Latin aspernantur, used to render *duscherainousi* (object to). He takes it to mean that brave people despise (contemnentes) death on the sea, because they are not excessively concerned about it.

15. As usual, the Latin renders *kalon* by bonum.

or not we are pursuing a good, and he argues that dangers of the first sort are especially appropriate concerns of a virtue. The danger of death resulting from illness or storms or robbers or (Aquinas might have added) earthquakes or road accidents "do not seem to threaten someone directly because of the fact that he is pursuing some good" (2–2 q123 a5). They happen to us anyhow, and we do not avoid them by becoming less active in the pursuit of goods. We expose ourselves, however, to the danger of death in war precisely because we "defend the common good through a just war," and we would be less exposed if we failed to defend the common good in this way. This is a good reason for claiming that it is especially important to form a state of character that is not deterred from active pursuit of the relevant good by the danger of death in war; for (Aquinas assumes) the fact that we expose ourselves to this danger is not a sufficient reason to give up the pursuit.

But once we see Aquinas' reasons for picking out the danger of death in war as a special concern of bravery, we can also see why we might want to reject Aristotle's view of the scope of bravery. For danger in battle is not the only danger that deserves special attention. Aquinas recognizes this; he points out that even the dangers he initially dismissed are proper areas for bravery in the right circumstances. We may face the danger of death from disease if we continue to visit a friend who suffers from an infectious disease, and we may face danger from shipwreck or robbers if we "pursue some pious undertaking" (e.g., a pilgrimage; 2–2 q123 a5).

Recognition of these cases affects not only our decision about the sorts of actions we should call brave, but also our judgment about the common features of different dangers, and about the common features that we should be trained to respond to. Aquinas sees that it would be a mistake to train people to face the danger of death in war without leading them to see the same reasons for facing the danger of shipwreck or illness. Death in war, therefore, need not be the exclusive or primary focus of bravery.

What, then, becomes of Aquinas' claim, on behalf of Aristotle, that facing danger in battle is a "principal" exercise of bravery? This is a principal exercise not because it is the sort of action we would most readily call brave, but because it illustrates the type of danger that should be the primary focus of bravery and helps us to see why it is primary. Aristotle is right to suggest that not every case of facing danger is relevant to bravery. But we ought not to infer from Aristotle's account that facing danger is the only principal exercise of bravery. We find principal cases of bravery wherever we find the occasion of praiseworthy firmness in the face of danger for the common good. Since other types of danger may be equally relevant to bravery, according to this criterion, they may equally allow principal exercises of the virtue.

If bravery embraces all the dangers that might wrongly deter us from the appropriate pursuit of good, has Aquinas' conception become unrealistically broad? We might try to support an allegedly Aristotelian position by pointing out that some people might be good at facing one sort of danger without being good at facing others. Are we to deny that someone is brave if he is completely fearless in war, but completely weak and vacillating if it will cost him something to stick to his convictions?

This combination of fearlessness and weak vacillation may appear even with a narrowly defined area of activity. We might argue, for instance, that Hector's fearlessness in the face of danger makes him brave, even if he shows other weaknesses of character. But it is not so simple. Though he is usually unafraid of danger and death, he is afraid to change his strategy or tactics; he is afraid to admit he has failed, and unwilling to expose himself to criticism and humiliation. Aristotle believes that this attitude falls short of bravery (*EN* 1116a21–9). Does Hector have one sort of bravery without another? Or does his fear show that he really lacks bravery?

It is easier to answer this question if we recall that the discussion of the cardinal virtues is not meant to describe features of every virtuous action, but to describe necessary conditions of acting virtuously. A virtuous action is the sort of action that proceeds from a virtuous character, whether or not it actually proceeds from one. But to act virtuously we must perform the virtuous action from a virtuous character. Perhaps we could be trained to face one sort of danger without being trained to face others that are equally important for the pursuit of the good, but it is not so clear that we would be brave if we did not see the point of resisting all the dangers that would wrongly impede us in the pursuit of the good. If we did not see that, we would not see the point of bravery at all, and we would not be brave.

The demand that a brave person should see the point of brave action and bravery clarifies and supports Aquinas' belief in the connection between prudence and the virtues of character. To see what dangers ought to be faced, and hence to see the point of facing this or that danger, we need to connect facing danger with the human good, and thereby to connect virtue with the "common end of all of human life."[16] Prudence grasps this connection, and in grasping it shows why the ends promoted by bravery are promoted by other virtues as well.

But even if we see the point of resisting all these dangers, we might nonetheless be better at resisting some than at resisting others. Even if we have been trained to resist all sorts of dangers, we may be more used to some than to oth-

---

16. See the passages quoted in sec. 2 above.

ers, and unfamiliar ones may be difficult to resist. Aquinas explains such cases through his doctrine of "sudden motions" of passions. Sometimes passions cause us to reach judgments about goodness that are independent of the will, so that the sensory faculty "does not compare or inquire into the particular circumstances of the situation, but has a sudden judgment" (1–2 q45 a4). Sometimes a sudden motion moves us to action "beyond the command of reason, even though it could have (*potuisset*) been impeded by reason if reason had foreseen" (q17 a7). Hence the passions are not invariably obedient to reason (1a q81 a3 ad 2). Even if we have the appropriate virtue, we may need to get used to the sound of gunfire in a battle, or to the sight of blood in a hospital, before we can face the situation appropriately. Aquinas' claims about the extent of bravery do not imply that brave people can resist every sort of danger the first time they encounter it.

Aquinas' argument about facing danger in war makes it easier to recognize bravery in cases that Aristotle does not even contemplate. He treats martyrdom as an exercise (*actus*) of bravery (2–2 q124 a2). From Aristotle's point of view, it might appear inferior to death in battle, since it is rather passive, and does not involve the active prosecution of one's ends that Aristotle regards as characteristic of brave actions (*EN* 1115a35–b6). Aquinas' account of why bravery is a virtue shows that active prosecution is not necessary. The martyr pursues the good by resisting danger; since the good he pursues in this case is the supreme good, his resistance to danger exercises bravery.

This example shows how Aquinas' account of a cardinal virtue helps him towards an appropriately flexible account of the scope of each virtue. His appeals to prudence give us the means to endorse or to correct his views. It is reasonable to draw the lines between the virtues where he draws them, and to single out some actions as principal exercises of the virtues. If his account needs to be corrected, he shows us the appropriate form of any correction.

7.

Though Aquinas does not believe that the four cardinal virtues are the genera of which the other virtues are species, he believes none the less that the other virtues are in some way subordinate to the four. He expresses this subordination by distinguishing three different sorts of parts of the cardinal virtues (2–2 q48 a1; cf. q79; q80; q128; q143): (1) The subjective parts are species of one cardinal virtue—for instance, the types of prudence that are exercised in different areas (2–2 q48 a1). (2) The integral parts "must concur to produce a perfect act of that virtue," and so are aspects of the virtue, inseparable from it in the way that beams and foundations are inseparable from a house. (3) The potential parts are those that are "annexed virtues that are directed towards some secondary acts or materials, as not having the whole power of the principal virtue" (q48 a1). They apply the virtue to areas that are less difficult than the areas of the primary exercises of the virtues. Though they are less difficult than the principal cardinal virtue itself, they are inseparable from the principal virtue.

Once we recognize potential parts, we can explain some further Aristotelian virtues, especially some of those that seem to cause special difficulties for Aquinas. By organizing the virtues around the cardinal virtues, Aquinas argues that the virtues do not conflict. If they are virtues, they respond to the requirements of prudence, and the appearance of conflict disappears once we recognize these requirements.

We can briefly illustrate Aquinas' argument by considering how he deals with a historically significant charge, that "pagan" and "Christian" virtues conflict. One might take this charge to underlie some of Machiavelli's claims about the conflict between the civic virtues needed to preserve a republic and the (allegedly) anti-civic Christian outlook. A related charge underlies some of Hume's attack on the "monkish" virtues. Mill refers to another version of this belief in conflict, in his contrast between pagan and Christian outlooks. In the course of attacking a conception of humanity and human worth that he calls Calvinistic, Mill introduces a different conception.

> There is a different type of human excellence from the Calvinistic: a conception of humanity as having its nature bestowed on it for other purposes than merely to be abnegated. "Pagan self-assertion" is one of the elements of human worth as well as "Christian self-denial." There is a Greek ideal of self-development, which the Platonic and Christian ideal of self-government blends with, but does not supersede. It may be better to be a John Knox than an Alcibiades, but it is better to be a Pericles than either; nor would a Pericles, if we had one in these days, be without anything good which belonged to John Knox. ("On Liberty," ch. 3)

Mill suggests that the two conceptions he describes cannot be embodied in one person; his comparison is part of his argument for individuality and variation. He does not suggest that Pericles would actually have manifested the Christian self-denial that was characteristic of John Knox, but only that he would have had anything that was good in John Knox's character. Hence he seems to suggest that the specifically Christian aspects of Christian self-denial are not good after all, apparently because they conflict with the appropriate sort of self-development.

Aquinas confronts an aspect of the alleged conflict between the pagan and the Christian virtues, in his examination of magnanimity and humility. In his view, the two virtues do not really conflict, and we can see this when we understand their relation to the cardinal virtues. Magnanimity is a potential part of bravery and humility of temperance. Since each of them is subordinate to the overriding aims of the cardinal virtues, they do not conflict. Magnanimity strengthens us in the pursuit of appropriately great actions, while humility restrains us from the distractions that would result from illusions about our own importance; hence, we need both magnanimity and humility to pursue the right ends without distraction (q161 a1). Once we understand why both "self-assertion" (or "self-development") and self-denial are virtues, we see why it is superficial to suppose that Christian self-denial conflicts with the desirable version of self-assertion.

Some people might take the Aristotelian virtue of magnanimity to display the appropriate sort of self-assertion: since they believe that magnanimity includes contempt for one's inferiors, they take contempt for one's inferiors to be part of appropriate self-assertion. Those who object to this contempt assume that magnanimity conflicts with a characteristic attitude of Christian humility. In Aquinas' view, however, these views reflect a misunderstanding of both proper self-assertion and proper self-denial. The magnanimous person's contempt is directed only towards the evil aims of others. Such contempt prevents the magnanimous person from accepting or acquiescing in the evil projects of others, and so he needs it if he is to be independent enough to stick to the right course of action. This contempt for others is not opposed to humility; for we can honor other people in so far as they exercise the gifts of God, and we can recognize our own failure to use the gifts of God given to us. Determination to use the gifts given to us for great results, and rejection of the evil aims of others that would impede the proper use of our gifts and theirs, are two aspects of magnanimity. In recognizing our own failure to use all our gifts, and in appreciating the gifts shown by others, we exercise aspects of humility (q129 a3 ad 4). Neither magnanimity nor humility can do its proper work without the other.

Humility also prevents a false sense of self-importance. This is why it does not always reject actions that would sometimes betray a lack of self-respect. Sometimes "abject" services are required by charity, and in these cases a person without false self-importance will not refuse to do them.

> It is not, therefore, characteristic of humility, but of stupidity, if one accepts whatever is abject, but <it is characteristic of humility> if one does not refuse because of its abjectness what is necessary to do because of virtue; for instance, if charity demands that one carry out some abject task for one's neighbours, because of his humility one does not refuse to do this.[17]

17. *Summa contra Gentiles,* iii 135. Please note that this paper pursues some issues that arise out of two previous papers: "The scope of deliberation: a conflict in Aquinas," *Review of Metaphysics* 44 (1990) 21–42; and "Practical reason divided," chap. 7 in *Ethics and Practical Reason,* ed. G. Cullity and B. Gaut (Oxford: Oxford University Press, 1997).

It is not abject to belong to a mendicant religious order, even though it would be abject to beg from others simply because one did not feel like supporting oneself. The humble person does not refuse the abject course of action in the right circumstances, though he does not accept it indiscriminately.

The connection between magnanimity and humility suggests that some reasons for believing that they conflict rest on superficial contrasts. Contrary to first impressions, the traits that support one virtue do not impede the development of traits that support the other. We can see that the two virtues do not really conflict once we understand the circumstances in which contempt for others or belief in our own unworthiness is appropriate; for the two virtues have the same aim, and do not conflict, but complement each other. Neither would be a genuine virtue if it were not regulated by the other; for we would not know which actions betray an abject attitude lacking proper self-respect if we did not know when virtue might require us to do some service that might (in some circumstances) be abject. Recognition of the connection between the virtues requires reference to prudence, since it requires reference to the end promoted by the specific ends of the different virtues.

The example of magnanimity and humility suggests how the cardinal virtues, as Aquinas understands them, make the other virtues intelligible. The subordinate virtues are specific ways of promoting or facilitating or protecting the various goods pursued by the cardinal virtues. I have sketched some of his arguments for the systematic character of the virtues in order to show that his arguments against conflict deserve serious consideration. They lead us away from rather inconclusive disputes about traits that we may intuitively regard as virtues, to some worthwhile questions about the sorts of connections between virtues that an adequate theory ought to exhibit. If we are impressed by his arguments about the proper shape of a theory of the virtues, we ought to look more attentively at his attempts to show how an account of individual virtues exhibits their systematic connections.[18]

18. I have benefited from helpful comments by Stephen Gardiner.

PART 2

A REAPPRAISAL OF SOME CENTRAL VIRTUES

CHAPTER 4

Erotic Love as a Moral Virtue

ROBERT C. SOLOMON

In this essay, I would like to defend an unusual and perhaps counterintuitive claim: that erotic love is a moral virtue and thus an important consideration for virtue ethics. Indeed, the claim that even non-erotic love (say, *agapé* or *philia*) is a moral virtue has received plenty of opposition, both because passions or emotions as such are not supposed to be virtues (Aristotle's argument), let alone *moral* virtues (Kant's separation of morality as practical reason and the "inclinations"). In the case of erotic love (*eros*), the denial gets quite vehement, initially, one suspects, because of the puritanical view that any thought or behavior is corrupted by the least taint of sexuality, and, then more generally, because *eros* is often characterized as self-interested desire, even when it is not downgraded to mere lust. To be sure, many people would want to insist that erotic love is a *good thing,* but this is considerably less than saying that it is a virtue. Even in that rare case where love is defended as a moral emotion, for instance, by David Velleman in an already classic essay published just a few years ago, it is not altogether clear to what extent his analysis applies to the defense of *erotic* love, as opposed to the love of close friends and relations, although Velleman has assured me that he does indeed intend it to include erotic love.[1]

I believe that there are good reasons for thinking of erotic love as a virtue, for rejecting Aristotle's distinction between the passions and the virtues (as "states of character"), and for rejecting Kant's distinction between morality and the inclinations. I also want to challenge Velleman's neo-Kantian defense of love. More

---

1. Velleman gave me this assurance in unpublished correspondence and in a comment on a shorter version of this paper at the American Philosophical Society meeting in Philadelphia (December 2002).

basically, I want to reject the puritanical[2] attitude toward sexuality and sensuality. It may be that the passion that characterizes teen-age raunchiness, one-night stands, and at least some illicit affairs is certainly no virtue, but I do not want to conflate *eros* and mere sexual desire, much less *eros* and lust. The erotic love I have in mind is the love that one can find in a good marriage, though I do not want to restrict it to that. I have no doubt that the same is true of many long term affairs, same sex relationships, and perhaps even multiple and more complicated arrangements. I would not deny for a moment that the best marriages (and the best loves, in general) are also paragons of friendship, but it is not as if a sexual relationship (that is, a relationship that is in part characterized by sexual desire and passion) becomes virtuous or moral only when the sex has diminished or moved into the background. *Eros* and *philia* are a wonderful combination, but it is not *philia* alone that makes love virtuous.

Perhaps the place to start is with an infamous passage from Kant.

> Love out of inclination cannot be commanded; but kindness done from duty—although no inclination impels us, and even although natural and unconquerable disinclination stands in our way—is Practical, and not Pathological love, residing in the will and not of melting compassion (*schmelzender Theilnehmung*).[3]

I read Kant's disjunction as I think most philosophers do as a distinction between the familiar feeling or emotion of love and something else for which I do not have a ready-made name, perhaps something like "respect" or "reverence."[4] However, this is not what most of us would identify as love. Respect, in particular, seems too impersonal. It is too cool, too detached, whereas love requires intimacy, immediacy. Or to put it a different way, respect is *impartial*, at least as Kant conceives of it, whereas love is thoroughly partial, concerned with a particular person for particular (even if by no means explicit) reasons.[5] Reverence raises more complicated issues, many of which are complicated by the Kantian literature, but going back to the ancient Greeks and Chinese, who took reverence very seriously as a virtue, it clearly applies to matters much larger than

---

2. I use the adjective "puritanical" in its popular, not its historical usage. There is good evidence that the Puritans, both in England and then in America, had not unhealthy attitudes toward sex, at least within the confines of a religiously sanctioned marriage. I have more in mind Mencken's characterization of a Puritan as someone who is always offended by the fact that someone, somewhere, is having a good time.

3. Kant's "*schmelzender Theilnehmung*" is to be found in *Grundlegung, Werke,* Band IV:399; *Grounding of the Metaphysics of Morals,* translated by James W. Ellington (Indianapolis: Hackett, 1981). The phrase is translated as "melting compassion" by H. J. Paton (New York: Harper and Row, 1964), 67, as "tender sympathy" by Lewis White Beck (Indianapolis: Bobbs-Merrill, 1959) and by Elliston (12) from whom the rest of the quotation is borrowed. Neither translation seems to capture what I read as Kant's irony.

4. For a good account of Kantian respect, see Stephen Darwall, "Two Kinds of Respect," *Ethics* 88 (1977): 36–49. On reverence, see Paul Woodruff, *Reverence* (Oxford: Oxford University Press, 2000).

5. I have defended to idea of "love for reasons" in "Reasons for Love," *Journal for the Theory of Social Behavior* (March, 2002).

the merely interpersonal (which is not necessarily to take it as a religious notion).[6] But despite his devotion to Christian morality, Kant evidently didn't think
much of "pathological love" even in its most benign versions, as *agapé* and compassion (which he elsewhere calls "beautiful").[7] Needless to say, he was much less
keen on the erotic and more sexual manifestations of that emotion as *eros*.

For the Greeks, by contrast, love often appeared as a virtue, or something very
much like a virtue. In the *Symposium,* Plato offers us many comments in honor
of love (*eros*) as a virtue, especially in the long speech by Socrates (via Diotima).
Aristotle lists friendship (*philia*) as among the most important virtues. So what
I would like to do in this essay is to make a bold suggestion, one quite in harmony with Plato and Aristotle but not (in the usual interpretations) with Kant.
I want to suggest that love itself is or can be a virtue, and by this I mean not
only benign and "beautiful" compassion and that general sort of sentiment that
one might (following Hume and others) identify as *benevolence* but *erotic* (romantic, truly "pathological") love. But when I say that erotic love is a moral
virtue I also want to say something about what love is. I want to join Velleman
in rejecting the now standard "conative" conceptions of love in terms of desire,
but I want to (strongly) disagree with him regarding the nature of love. I especially want to say something about the particularity of love, and whether love
in its concern for a particular person is compatible or in conflict with the supposed impartiality of morality. As a virtue ethicist, I find this latter concern not
very troubling. The virtues, as opposed to the Moral Law, are clearly personal
(though whether their "objects" are necessarily particular is a matter I also want
to address.) What will make my defense of love as a virtue more than a bit peculiar is that I will be concerned primarily with erotic love, not love of the more
generalized sorts (such as *agapé*) that can more easily be rendered universal.

Is a Virtue a Passion or a State of Character?

> Since things that are found in the soul are of three kinds—passions, faculties, states of char-
> acter—virtue must be one of these . . . [But] neither the virtues nor the vices are passions
> . . . If, then, the virtues are neither passions nor faculties, all that remains is that they should
> be states of character.
>
> Aristotle, *Nicomachean Ethics*

If love is a virtue, as opposed to a mere emotion, what sort of thing must it
be? Aristotle insists that a virtue is a state of character, not a passion. But are the

---

6. Woodruff makes a powerful case for the co-optation and corruption of "reverence" by Judeo-
Christian religious thinkers. As Woodruff understands the notion (going back to the ancient Greeks and
Chinese), it is not a synonym for religious belief or faith.

7. Immanuel Kant, *Observations on the Beautiful and Sublime* (1770).

two in fact so distinct? A virtue is, according to Aristotle and just about everyone else who has written on the topic, a distinctive and enduring positive characteristic of a person. But "characteristic" here is ambiguous. A characteristic of
a person might be continuous and always in evidence, like proud posture, or it
might be a disposition manifested in any number of episodes, as a tendency or
a trait. Presumably it would not be a single episode, such as a momentary oc-
currence of a passion. But is protracted love (or protracted compassion) a continuing feature of a person or a disposition? I think the question, episode or
disposition, ultimately makes little sense in such cases. Or, we might shift our attention to the "object" of the emotion: does it remain one and the same (as in
love) or is it open to several or many different "objects" (that is, directed at different people)? Thus we might distinguish between a "loving person" (as in
Erich Fromm's famous work, *The Art of Loving* (Perennial Books, 2000) and
someone who is (exclusively) in love with a single person. An emotion might
be a disposition not in the sense that it is manifested in discreet episodes but
rather that it is open to various objects (directed at different people).

Is love a disposition, a state of character, in this sense? In the case of exclusive
erotic or "romantic" love surely not (although, as is often commented, a person
in love may well alter his or her attitude toward everyone else as well). But need
a virtue be underdetermined in this sense? Wouldn't we call a person generous
if the beneficiary of his or her generosity were a single person or charity exclusively? Can't virtues in general be circumscribed by "qua" qualifications—as
in "he is courageous when it comes to dealing with the government but not in
dealing with his Dean"? (Perhaps he is not thereby courageous *overall,* but it
does not follow that he is not courageous.) But if this is true of generosity and
courage, why should it not be true of love, just because it is exclusively directed?
One might object that such love rigidly designates a single object but virtues
must be open to various situations and objects; however, at this point I think
that the definition is getting rather precious. Getting back to basics, if a virtue
is a distinctive and enduring positive feature of a person, it would seem that love
fits in perfectly. What feature of a person better defines that person and his or
her attitude toward the world?

It is sometimes argued, by way of underscoring the particularity of all of the
virtues, that a virtue is not a matter of rule or principle. Thus some virtue ethicists, such as Michael Slote, want to sharply separate an ethics of virtue from an
ethics of impartial rules, while others, such as William Frankena, try to understand the virtues as no more than personal instantiations of universal moral principles.[8] If the virtues were no more than personal instantiations of abstract

8. Michael Slote, for example, in his recent collection, *Virtues* (Oxford: Oxford University Press,
2000); William Frankena, in the last edition of his *Ethics* (Englewood Cliffs, NJ: Prentice-Hall, 1990).

principles—a disposition to do one's duty or to act for the greatest good for the greatest number, for example, then questions about good character and obedience to rational principles would presumably dovetail and ultimately come to the same conclusion. A virtue would be a disposition to act on principle, and the apparent conflict between virtue ethics and rule-bound approaches to ethics (at least in general) would be easily resolved.[9] But I think that a virtue is not this (although a clever philosopher could always manufacture some more or less encompassing principle). A virtue is "personal" in a powerful sense, the sense in which a virtue is what is *distinctive* about a particular person, and it is irrelevant whether it is an instantiation of any general principle.

The sense in which a virtue is strictly personal in this sense is one that Nietzsche perhaps carries to excess (in his *Zarathustra*) when he insists that every virtue is "unique" and should not even be identified by the use of a "common" name. I would certainly not go this far (which would make "virtue ethics" all but impossible), but I do want to argue that a virtue is indeed something distinctively personal, even if several people (ideally, perhaps, all people) might share that virtue. I think we should also avoid confusing the virtues with virtue. There are various virtues—generosity, courage, and such, and these have different characteristics and are ascribed differently to different people. Virtue ethicists for the most part (even those who insist on the "unity of the virtues") insist on the plural—"the virtues"—and reject the singular, "virtue," as the source of considerable confusion. Kant wrote enthusiastically of virtue, but he put much less emphasis on the specific virtues, since he thought that morality as such was something singular (thus "*the* categorical imperative," despite its various "formulations"). Virtue ethicists rather presume that ethics is more varied, that the truth is in the empirical details, and that what is a virtue for one person in one society or situation might not be a virtue in another person or another society or situation. This is not to deny that there might well be "non-relative virtues," but their existence is something that would have to be shown empirically, not argued a priori (as in "if *x* is a virtue for anyone, *x* must be a virtue for everyone").[10]

So, too, the passions are distinctively personal. They are not merely instantiations of emotion-types, and if different people have "the same" emotion they nevertheless each have their own emotion.[11] But the passions are personal in a more important sense. They involve personal perspectives, personal investments,

9. This was William Frankena's purported resolution in the last edition of his *Ethics* (Englewood Cliffs, NJ: Prentice-Hall, 1991).

10. Martha Nussbaum, "Non-Relative Virtues," in Peter French et al, eds., *Midwest Studies in Philosophy* 13 (1988): 32–53.

11. This is not to deny that there can be shared emotions, but it is not enough that two or more people have the same emotion directed at the same object.

personal engagements, personal commitments. It is a mistake, I have long argued, to think of the passions—or what we more generally call the emotions—as merely short term, primitive desires or feelings.[12] Emotions are complex and often enduring cognitive and evaluative engagements with the world. Love, in particular, involves a long-term engagement (whether it is "requited" or not), and if it is to count as love at all, the passion must endure. One might be angry for five minutes or experience a "twinge" of jealousy. But such episodes will not count as love, even if extended for weeks or months. One might object that Romeo and Juliet's love lasted but three days when it was cut short by death. But it is only on the assumption that their love *would have* continued (and not have been a mere youthful infatuation) that we dare call it love at all. Thus love is personal in the strong sense that it distinctively defines something about the person. Moreover, the demand that a virtue must be enduring is at least in that regard satisfied by erotic love, and just as one honest answer does not make an honest man, one brief erotic experience—no matter how powerful—does not constitute love. There is little that is more definitive of a person and distinctive for that person over a long period of time than loving someone.

Just as an episode of feeling, alone, does not count as love, no single act, no matter how beneficial or praiseworthy, is considered a virtue, even if it is a sign of virtue. A single courageous act, "out of character," by a man who has always seemed to be a coward, might well make us re-think our opinion of him and wonder what special circumstances prompted such behavior. Thus there is good reason to say that a virtue is some durable and continuing behavior rather than a single brief episode, but it should not be too quickly concluded that it is therefore a disposition or it is not emotion. A virtue cannot be too routine or ritualized. Good habits are (in general, at least) not virtues. A person who routinely writes a check to a charity every month is not necessarily generous. It may be an unthinking or unfeeling habit. So that if one has set up an automatic contribution scheme sometime in the past that might indicate earlier generosity, having forgotten all about it involves an utterly mindless repetition that does not count as virtue. Moreover, we would want to make several exclusions on the basis of neurotic pathology, for example, compulsive disorders, and we would certainly want to restrict candidates for the virtues according to their functional utility.[13] But, as both Aristotle and Confucius insisted, every virtue must be motivated at least in part by the right kinds and amounts of emotion. What makes

12. This idea that emotions are short-term is wide spread in psychology, esp. by defenders of the "affect program" view of emotions, that is, as brief but very fast neuro-muscular-hormonal reactions. Carroll Izard, for instance, begins his comprehensive article on "Emotion" in the *Encyclopedia Britannica* with the definition, "An emotion is a brief subjective, behavioural, and physiological response . . ."

13. What this means, of course, is in considerable dispute. There are virtue ethicists who lean toward

a virtue a virtue is in part the enduring emotion behind it and, at least sometimes, the virtue is no more than the emotion, fully realized.

Steve Gardiner has suggested to me that Aristotle has a concept of the place of emotion in virtue that is even more complicated than this. He suggests, for instance, that shame is a "quasi-virtue." Gardiner suggests that Aristotle's idea is that shame (for example) is not itself a virtue but a mean state concerned with feelings (*Ethics* 2:7).[14] Such, I would agree, is the case for many of Aristotle's virtues. But this example, like the role of fear in courage, is marked by the fact that no one would call shame—or fear—good as such. (I do not mean to imply that some emotions, e.g. love, is good as such or "good in itself.") But it is the *capacity* to feel shame that is necessary for virtue, and it is a capacity best not activated. It is the *overcoming* of fear that is the virtue, not fear itself. Erotic love, by contrast, is neither a capacity nor a passion to be overcome, though to be sure (like all virtues) it is to be cultivated and is sensitive to time and appropriateness.

A virtue must be somewhat general, but this generality need not entail that the virtue be impersonal, much less dispassionate, nor need it preclude exclusivity with regard to its object. The generality is of a different kind. A virtue must be manifested in many different sorts of actions and feelings, not just one or two (what Gilbert Ryle once called a "multi-track disposition"). A virtue need not dictate any particular action, and those actions manifesting the virtue might well differ from person to person and from situation to situation. What love is may be in some essential sense the same for everyone (despite love's personal aspect and despite a common cliché to the contrary), though the object, the manner, the timing, the expression, may radically vary from case to case.[15]

What is certainly not necessary, if we are not to invite absurdity, is that everyone who loves must love one and the same object of love. There are many lovers, but (happily) there are (more or less) the same number of beloveds. Everyone who loves loves someone or other and, indeed, it is possible that everyone might love just the same someone, but everyone who loves must love someone particular.

---

utilitarianism, as I do, and those who lean more toward Kantian deontontology, who take it that some virtues are virtues regardless of their (usual) consequences. There are also eudaimonistic virtue ethicists (e.g. Rosalind Hursthouse and Julia Annas) who, following Aristotle, take human flourishing to be the end of all virtuous activity and those (such as Christine Swanton) who reject any such requirement in favor of a prior conception of right action. I myself want to hold a more relativist position, that for something to be a virtue it has to (generally) function beneficially in that particular social context and, perhaps, for that particular person in that context.

14. Steve Gardiner, personal correspondence.

15. There is, however, what the Scholastics called the "formal object" of an emotion, "the feared" in all instances of fear, "the offensive" in all instances of anger, "the funny" in all instances of mirth, "the beloved" {writ large] in all instances of love. Whether or not such a conception ultimately makes sense, however, is both beside the point raised here and beyond the scope of this essay.

This particularity (but not the exclusivity) is true not only of love but of all virtues. Several people might be generous, but the beneficiaries of their generosity need not be the same person. Yet there must be (for each act of generosity) a particular recipient (or a designated group of recipients). Giving away money (as such, regardless of context) is not being generous. Giving away money to a particular individual or group (plus the other necessary qualifications) is generous. There is the general attitude that might be called "loving," defended by Erich Fromm and others as the greatest virtue,[16] but one cannot be loving without loving someone. Loving everyone or loving indiscriminately is not love. The distinctive emotion of *agapé*, which is often said to have this feature, is not the same as the erotic or romantic love that concerns us here. That love is specifically directed. (I would argue that the whole idea of *agapé* is in this sense a philosopher's fantasy, but I will not argue that here, at least not yet.) The simple point to press here is that every lover has a particular beloved. The virtue of love is defined in each case not just by one's loving but by one's very particular affections for a particular other person. (I am not begging the question here whether it is possible to [romantically] love two or more people at once. Evidently one can. But each of the beloveds must be a particular person, however difficult the logistics or the emotional strategies.)

Love may be distinctively personal, and the object of one's love may necessarily be particular, but is one's love for a particular person merely particular? This is the odd but subtle question that has recently and persuasively been raised by David Velleman in his essay "Love as a Moral Emotion." I agree with his titular thesis, the idea that love is a moral emotion, although Velleman, a Kantian, is not particularly concerned with whether or not love might also be a virtue. But Velleman makes his case (and thus reconciles love and Kant's morality) not by suggesting that morality might be less than impartial (a suggestion with which I and most virtues ethicists would be much in agreement) but by challenging the thesis that love is concerned with particulars.[17] I want to argue, to the contrary, that love is (as most people think) inescapably partial and particular, whether or not morality might better be conceived more along the lines of virtue ethics and partiality. I confess that my own attraction to virtue ethics (and more particularly to Nietzsche) was based on a personal antipathy towards impersonal, rule-bound morality and Kant's "stern and for-

---

16. Erich Fromm, *The Art of Loving* (New York: HarperCollins, 2000).

17. Others who resist Velleman's claim and hold onto the position that both love and morality are concerned with particulars include Julia Annas, "Personal Love and Kantian Ethics," in *Friendship: A Philosophical Reader,* ed. Neera Badhwar (Ithaca: Cornell University Press, 1993), 155–173; Neera Badhwar, in a recent paper given at the University of Texas; and Lawrence Blum in his *Friendship, Altruism, and Morality* (London: Routledge and Kegan-Paul, 1980).

bidding tone."[18] (What this implies about my personality and upbringing I would rather not delve into here.) And love, it has always seemed to me, provides an obvious alternative to that kind of morality. How Kant combined love as *agapé* and morality in his strict sense together in Christian ethics is a tantalizing question and no doubt one of the main motives for many Kantians tackling the problem of reconciling them. But since I am not defending *agapé* (although I do believe in respect and reverence) and I do not accept Kant's rather extravagant concept of morality, I do not feel particularly motivated to do so. But before we get to love and erotic love in particular, we have yet to answer Aristotle's question, whether a virtue is a passion, a faculty, or a state of character.

Aristotle insists that a virtue is a state of character.[19] It is not merely a faculty, that is, a capacity for virtue. A state of character, unlike a faculty, must be activated and exercised. But the case is not so clear regarding the passions. Passions are not mere potentials. They are by their very nature active. (One can have an angry disposition, of course, but if one is said to have an angry disposition, it is on the basis of his or her many bouts of anger, not the other way around.) But there is a strong tendency, even in Aristotle, to think of the passions in an overly spontaneous, even "stimulus-response" way. Emotions, unlike virtues, are said to be nothing more than reactions to the particularities of a situation. A virtue is a state of character because it operates not just in a single situation but in an open ended number of situations. A virtue is a trait that endures, not a passion that appears and disappears. But I think that this is a wrong-headed or in any case extremely narrow view of the passions.[20] Some passions may be transient, but others endure, even a lifetime, and define a person's character just as surely as do such traits as generosity and courage. Passions (or emotions) are not random bursts of enthusiasm or ire, as Aristotle well knew (considering his analyses in *De Anima* and the *Rhetoric*). Emotions are more or less systematic in that together they form a person's "temperament." And when an unusual emotion "bursts" forth (falling in love, or finding oneself wholly absorbed in affection for a new baby), such emotions are not to be construed as a literal "burst" but as a dramatic new constellation which, if it is to be counted as love at all, reconstitutes and redefines the life of the individual.

18. Velleman, 344.

19. Aristotle, *Nicomachean Ethics*, bk. 2, chap. 5.

20. One currently much in fashion, I should add. Neuropsychologists have now identified an emotion with the reaction that lasts a fraction of a second, insisting that all else—including both the emotional experience and the expression of emotion in action, is secondary, mere "aftermath." See Antonio Damasio, *The Feeling of What Happens* (New York: Harcourt, 1999) and Joseph Le Doux, *The Emotional Brain* (New York: Simon and Schuster, 1996).

Generosity and courage might be characterized as virtues just because they are not bound to particulars, whether or not they are context sensitive in any number of ways, but friendship, by contrast, is not like this. ("Friendliness" may be, but that is a very different kind of virtue—like "being a loving person"—than friendship as such, the focus of Aristotle's books 8 and 9.) Friendship is not just a capacity—that is to say, a faculty for making friends or being a friend. It is the actual having of friends, and that means *particular* friends. One might be generous to all sorts of people, including strangers, but friendship is particular. Of course, one might have several friends (but even then, having "lots of friends" tends to cast doubt on the intensity and integrity of any particular friendship).[21] As Aristotle writes of friendship, it seems pretty obvious that it is the friendship with particular friends, not the mere capacity (faculty) of friendship or the fact that one has friends that constitutes the virtue.

Which brings us back to our general worry about whether love essentially involves particulars and whether it can therefore qualify as a virtue even if it is also an enduring state of character. Generosity and courage are always concerned with particulars, even if they are not bound to particulars. Kant would want to go further, I take it, and insist that generosity and courage are examples of moral virtue (in his singular sense) only if they are also instantiations of universal moral law. But the question is whether the virtues in general must be so understood. Aristotle's powerful defense of friendship suggests that another interpretation is possible. A virtue must be an enduring feature of a person, one that defines his or her character and explains his or her behavior (within a certain field or domain).[22] It need not be general. (Thus being friendly is a very different virtue than having friends.) Both friendship and love (as *agapé*) would seem to satisfy these conditions but this doesn't yet make a case for *eros* or erotic love. An Aristotelian (or neo-Aristotelian) might well accept both friendship and *agapé* as virtues but yet draw the line at *eros*.

The Degradation of *Eros* in Ethics

It (love) does not hesitate to intrude with its trash. . . . Every day it brews and hatches the worst and most perplexing quarrels and disputes, destroys the most valuable relationships and breaks the strongest bonds . . . . Why all this noise and fuss?. . . It is merely a question of every Jack finding his Jill. (The gracious reader should translate this

21. I have often commented that with the elevation of the importance of romantic love in our society, the value of friendship has been diminished. Even passing acquaintances and political allies are listed as "friends," while love remains exquisitely precious, in concept if not in practice.
22. Christine Swanton, this volume.

phrase into precise Aristophanic language.) Why should such a trifle play so important a role?'

Arthur Schopenhauer, The World as Will and Representation

Needless to say, erotic love has not usually been considered a virtue. As *lust,* erotic love is one of the seven deadly sins. (Freud, in one of his darker moments: "Love is nothing but lust, plus the ordeal of civility.") Hesiod in the *Theogony* warned against *eros* as a force contrary and antagonistic to reason. Sophocles and Euripides both denounced *eros,* in *Antigone* and *Hippolytus* respectively, and even Virgil had his doubts. Schopenhauer, much more recently, thought all love to be sexual, contributing more than any other desire to our perpetual unhappiness. Today we are much more likely to invoke the cynical wit of Oscar Wilde or Kingsley Amis than the saccharine pronouncements of our latter-day love pundits, but even the latter de-emphasize the erotic aspects of love, preferring instead to stress the virtues of *agapé* or sexless caring.

Looking through the history of ideas in the West, one cannot but be struck by the ambivalence surrounding this central and celebrated concept. Plato all but commanded it, the early Christians roundly condemned it. The history of the word *eros* is also conflicted and revealing. Since early Christianity, the distinction between *eros* and *agapé* has attracted a great deal of theorizing and moralizing, the former usually translated as sexual love, the latter as selfless and certainly sexless love for humanity.[23] The distinction is often drawn crudely. For instance, *eros* is taken to be purely erotic and reduced to sexual desire, which it surely is not. Or *agapé* is characterized as selfless giving, opposed by *eros,* which thus becomes selfish taking (or at least craving). *Agapé* is idealized to the point where it becomes an attitude possible only to God, thus rendering it virtually inapplicable to common human fellow-feelings. *Eros* by contrast is degraded to the profanely secular and denied any hint of spirituality. To think of love as a virtue, therefore, is first of all to expand (once again) the domain of *eros.* ("Romantic" love, I am presuming, is one historical variant of *eros.*) One need not deny the desirability (or the possibility) of altruistic agapé to insist that erotic *eros* shares at least some of its virtues.

Plato's celebration of *eros* turned a once sleazy concept—consider Sappho's poetic complaints about *eros* as misfortune and physical illness—into a virtue. But to do so, Socrates pretty much de-sexed it. Thus the transformation of Platonic *eros* to medieval Platonic love borrows from Plato love's transcendent reach but eliminates what remains of the erotic. Insofar as *eros* continues to be praised,

23. Andres Nygren, *Eros and Agape* (London: Peter Smith, 1983), Søren Kierkegaard, *Works of Love* (Princeton: Princeton University Press, 1998.

it also continues to be sexless. That explains why Freud caused such a stir back at the turn of the last century when he not only greatly expanded the realm of sexuality but also—at least sometimes—seemed to reduce all of love to sex. David Velleman rightly makes a good deal of this reduction and quotes several contemporary philosophers (notably Richard Rorty[24]) as to the impact it made. Velleman also makes the point that (analytic) philosophers have continued to de-sex love when they talk about it, thus bringing it closer to the ancient concept of *agapé* and reducing prurient and puritanical interest and criticism of the concept. But I note that Velleman seems to join the philosophers he criticizes in leaning toward an still too de-sexed conception of love—"what I have in mind is the love between close friends and relations—including spouses and other life-partners, insofar as their love has outgrown the effects of overvaluation and transference."[25] I take it that erotic love, whatever else it may be, blatantly displays the effects of overvaluation and transference, so I infer that *eros,* as opposed to other forms of love, is irrational insofar as it does not see things as they really are.

Velleman has rejected this inference of mine, insisting that "I do not think that erotic love is necessarily blind or irrational, and I did not mean to set it aside when I set aside cases of love that is still under the influence of overvaluation and transference. When I spoke of the love between spouses as having outgrown these distortions, I did not mean to imply that it had also outgrown *eros.*"[26] But I think this matter of "overvaluation and transference" is critical to erotic love, as I shall argue. Love is not just "seeing clearly" but seeing *erotically* (to be trivial about it), and this has to do with not only desire but with the particularities of the beloved as experienced by the lover. It involves what Irving Singer referred to as "bestowal and appraisal," not universal Kantian or Platonic insight.[27]

One of the reasons why Freud's reduction of love to sex undermined love's claim to virtue did not have to do with the timidity of philosophers toward sexuality. It had to do with Freud's understanding of sex—and consequently of love—as a *drive.* Velleman makes a lot out of this, and I think that he is right to do so. First of all, if love (sex) is a drive, it is one's own satisfaction that one seeks, and this—as opposed to the desired satisfaction of the other person—is hardly a virtue. With this in mind, however, we might also remind ourselves of Kant's less than celebratory account of human intercourse.

24. Velleman, 349; Rorty, "Freud, Morality, and Hermeneutics," *New Literary History* 12 (1980): 175–85.
25. Velleman, 351. Velleman ascribes the phrase "overvaluation and transference" to Freud.
26. In his APA comments, 12/30/02.
27. Irving Singer, *The Nature of Love,* 3 vols. (Chicago: University of Chicago Press, 1966–84).

Because sexuality is not an inclination which one human being has for another as such, but is an inclination for the sex of another, it is a principle of the degradation of human nature, in that it gives rise to the preference of one sex to the other, and to the dishonoring of that sex through the satisfaction of desire.[28]

I would argue that such selfishness and degradation need play no part in erotic love. I think that the emphasis on one's own satisfaction repeats one of the most elementary fallacies in arguments about egoism and selfishness, namely that all behavior is selfish insofar as it involves the satisfaction of one's desires. Surely it depends on what those desires are, and when the desire is, for instance, the satisfaction of the other person, or better, the expression of mutual love, it makes no sense to characterize sex as a degrading "use" of the other person as a mere means.

The idea that *eros* is selfish pervades the literature on the opposition of *eros* and *agapé* since the days of the early Christians.[29] In Freud, it could not be more blatant. ("Love is nothing but lust, plus the ordeal of civility.") But the more general misunderstanding here is a variation on the theme that any activity that is motivated even in part by the anticipation of pleasure is selfish and therefore cannot be a virtue. Yet it is the nature of the virtues, as Aristotle insistently pointed out, that they are neither selfish nor selfless, though to be sure they are essential to our "flourishing." What's more, if I truly have a virtue (rather than just acting *as if* I have one), I enjoy its exercise. If I am generous, I enjoy giving. If I am truly witty, I enjoy being witty. And presumably if I am courageous, I even enjoy being courageous, despite the fear that Aristotle insists is an essential part of that virtue. (Thinking about doing something brave, bungee-jumping, for example, one can readily see how fear and exhilaration might happily join hands). This, too, is an important insight. Exercising one's virtue is neither selfish nor selfless but it is enjoyable. But then the idea of *eros* as a virtue makes perfectly good sense, too, and it is not undermined by the accusation that it is either pleasurable or selfish. In erotic love, one's beloved is there to be loved, and loving her is a pleasure, and that does not makes the love any less virtuous. Indeed, it would not be unreasonable to suggest that the experience of love is pleasurable in part because it is a virtue, and what one experiences is one's (morally) good feelings towards the beloved.

It remains to be seen, however, whether *eros* is best defined as a mode of de-

28. Kant, *Lectures on Ethics,* trans. L. Infield (Indianapolis, Hackett, 1963), 164.
29. Notably, Andres Nygren, *Eros and Agape,* but similar arguments persist in contemporary analytic literature, for instance, in George Nakhnikian, "Love in Human Reason," *Midwest Studies in Philosophy,* 3:286–317, where he argues against Aristotle's third and preferred mode of friendship on the grounds that it is, despite Aristotle's insistence to the contrary, still motivated by self-interest.

sire, even granted that it is a mistake to think of it as a selfish desire. To be sure, it does include sexual desire, but erotic desire is not just sexual. It also includes such general physical desires as to "be with," such personal desires as "to be appreciated" and "to be happily together," such inspirational desires as "to be the best for you," and such "altruistic" desires as "to do anything I can for you." Nevertheless, I agree with Velleman that this alone will not serve as an adequate analysis of love. *Eros* is not just a matter of desire.

Against the Conative Theory of Love

> In the soul . . . a thirst for mastery; in the mind sympathy; in the body, nothing but a delicately hidden desire to possess, after many mysteries.
>
> La Rochefoucauld, *Maxims*

Velleman takes the argument against Freud a giant step further. He takes Freud's crude drive theory as a model that has been pursued by most (analytic) philosophers since. The model (which he calls "conative") is that love is essentially characterized by desire. In this, "they are in unexpected agreement with Freud" even though they have "de-emphasized the sexual" (351). Most (analytic) philosophers, Velleman says, merely defend "aim-inhibited versions of Freud" (354). That is, they defend the idea of love being a desire or a set of desires but politely leave sexual desire out of it. But they nevertheless define and understand love in terms of an aim. Velleman, rejecting this, says that love is not a matter of desire or a "pro-attitude toward a result." I think he is right. Velleman accepts the obvious fact that love is accompanied by desires (and I presume that he would accept the equally obvious fact that erotic love is accompanied by sexual desires). He quotes a wide variety of philosophers on love as desire, but I will quote only one, Harry Frankfurt (whom Velleman credits with suggesting the central thesis of his essay). Frankfurt writes, "What I have in mind in speaking of love is, roughly and only in part, a concern specifically for the well-being or flourishing of the beloved object that is more or less disinterested and that is more or less constrained."[30] I think that we should take seriously the qualification "only in part," but in general, I have to agree with Velleman and not with Frankfurt. I think the emphasis on *caring* has been overdone in recent philosophical discussions of love (and in virtue ethics more generally).

30. Harry Frankfurt, "On Caring," in *Necessity, Volition, and Love* (Cambridge: Cambridge University Press, 1999), 168.

Velleman writes, convincingly, "when I think of other people I love [besides my children]—parents, brothers, friends, former teachers and students—I do not think of myself as an agent of their interests," and, "at the thought of a close friend, my heart doesn't fill with an urge to do something for him, though it may indeed fill with love." This metaphorical *bon mot* is a good example of Velleman's occasional but insightful use of phenomenology. I am not quite sure that I would describe my thinking of my wife as "my heart filling with love," mainly because I am deeply suspicious of "heart" imagery, but Velleman is making an excellent point, I think, about the centrality of a certain kind of experience—as opposed to having certain kinds of desires. But I do not think that any emotion concepts, especially "love," can be precisely circumscribed by necessary and sufficient conditions (this is why I insist on emphasizing Frankfurt's qualifying phrase "only in part"). However, I do agree that such desires concerning the well-being of the beloved, while much more central to love than Velleman is willing to allow, do not form the conceptual core of that emotion.

I have written at some length about what I take to be the nature of love.[31] To be sure, it involves a great many desires, including those Velleman dismisses as inessential, such as wanting to act upon or interact with the beloved. But I think that what lies at the core of love is—as Velleman says—a "way of seeing," that is, a way of orienting and engaging oneself in the world. But I think that we mean very different things by this phrase. I agree with him that the various desires of love follow from this "way of seeing" and are not themselves fundamental—though again I want to be very cautious in making claims about what is essential to an emotion and what is not. In brief, I follow Aristophanes in Plato's *Symposium* in suggesting (without the mythological absurdities) that love involves seeing ourselves as in some sense "one" with our beloved. Thus the "seeing clearly" is not just an appreciation of the beloved (much less just an appreciation of the beloved as a Kantian end-in-itself) but a "seeing clearly" that is defined by the particularities of our relationship and thus a seeing of self as well as a seeing of the other.

To put it somewhat differently, "reasons for love" are not just features of the other person, whether his or her golden hair and bright blue eyes or his or her Kantian Will.[32] They also include "Aristophanic" reasons, reasons that are de-

---

31. Robert C. Solomon, *About Love* (Lanham, MD: Rowman and Littlefield, 2001).

32. I have discussed reasons for love in my recent "Reasons for Love," *Journal of the Theory of Social Behavior* 3.2: 1–28. Please note that attributions to epigraphs in this paper include: Aristotle, *Nicomachean Ethics*, Bk2, chap. 5, Ross translation; A. Schopenhauer, *World as Will and Representation*, quoted in *Sexual Love and Western Morality*, ed. D. Verene (New York: Harper and Row), translation by E. Payne; La

termined not by features of the beloved but features of the relationship, for instance, time spent together and experience shared. This is why one's beloved—to use an ugly legal term—is "non-fungible," irreplaceable, not because he or she is irreplaceable in any mysterious way (e.g. as a Kantian end-in-itself) but because of the particularities and peculiarities of the relationship. Velleman may well disagree with any such Aristophanic account, but I agree with him that love is defined by its object, not by its aims.

Ethics and Particularity

> One more word against Kant as a moralist. A virtue must be our own invention, our most necessary self-expression. The fundamental laws of self-preservation and growth demand the opposite—that everyone invent his own virtue, his own categorical imperative.
>
> Friedrich Nietzsche, *The Anti-Christ*

It is one of the charms of Velleman's account of Kant that it appears to put the "heart" back into him. Velleman's Kant embraces the passions, including compassion and love. Indeed, love is presented to us as a moral emotion. Although he does not focus on *eros,* he tries to prove that love and morality are compatible because love is ultimately not so "partial" as we have been led to believe. What we love in the beloved is the person as an "end in itself," but this is a feature of all rational beings and so not at all a distinguishing feature of the beloved. Nevertheless, one can get hold of this evasive Kantian "true self" only by way of the more manifest (empirical) features of the individual, and so Velleman suggests that "the immediate object of love . . . is the manifest person, embodied in flesh and blood and accessible to the senses." I think that Velleman is struggling with some very important conflicting intuitions here, and I find his purported Kantian solution ingenious, quite independently of my deep doubts about it. It is a conflict that goes back to Plato (at least), a conflict between the idea that what we love about a person is his or her distinguishing features (particularly his or her charms and virtues) and the idea that all such features are ultimately superficial and what we really love is the person him or herself. Given the contrast between a narrow obsession (say, a sexual fetish) and an appreciation of "the whole person," we can easily understand why one might want to say that it is not just for the value of those features that one loves but rather for the value of the beloved himself or herself. What's more, if we were better peo-

---

Rochefoucauld, *Maxims,* trans. J. Heayd (Boston and New York: Houghton Mifflin, 1917); and F. Nietzsche, *Anti-Christ,* sec. 11, trans. W. Kaufmann (New York: Random House, 1954).

ple, we *could have* fallen in love with anyone, since everyone is, in the Kantian sense, an end in himself or herself.

I take it that what Velleman is trying to do is to work his way through this thicket of conflicting intuitions and ideas and provide us with a single picture that takes adequate account of both the claim that we love persons because of their features and for themselves and the idea that we do in fact love one person but we could (ideally) have loved anyone else. Velleman's Kantian account does so, but only, I think, at a cost that many people would be unwilling to pay. Velleman interprets love as a special sense of "seeing clearly," a phrase he borrows from Iris Murdoch, which he thinks fits well into Kant's moral philosophy. What we see clearly in love is not the beloved in his or her particularity, our vision distorted by "overvaluation and transference." What we see is the beloved as an "end in itself," which in Kant's unusual usage (as in the second formulation of the categorical imperative) refers to the person not in his or her particulars but with regard to what Kant calls the "humanity" in that person. But whatever we might say about Kant and morality (and I have both Nietzschean and Hegelian doubts about Kant's universal notions and morality), love is not this at all but rather a matter of particulars,—the particular love of a particular person for another particular person and the particular (and often peculiar) relationship that embodies that love.

Murdoch, a Platonist, seems to want it both ways. Going back to Plato's *Symposium,* we can readily appreciate just how this might be. Socrates claims that love is seeing the (Form of) beauty in or through the beloved without thereby denying the relevance of his or her particular virtues. On the one hand, we see something objective "in" the person, but on the other hand it is the particular person we love in order to do so. Kant, it seems to me, has closed off this peculiar form of compromise. In so far as what we see clearly is the humanity in the other person, I would argue that we do not love him or her, but humanity. It is like some medieval notions of "Platonic" love: one sees God clearly through the other person, but the particularities of the person, in particular, his or her fleshy bits, are rendered irrelevant. I want to argue the contrary, that it is the peculiarities of a person that we love, not what is universal about them. This is not to deny that one of the reasons I love my beloved is because she is human (and if I were to find out that she is not human, but an alien or a robot, I might well no longer love her). Nor is it to deny that most of the things I love in my beloved can be described in general terms and found in other people as well. But it is her particularities, not her universal features (for instance, her rational Will) that I love.

In the Kantian paradigm, by contrast, it is the universal—humanity (and not *her* humanity) that I love. Here Kant should be compared with New Testament ethics, where *agape* at least can be argued to be universal (or, one might also say, "indiscriminate") love, and not love for any particular person. But on many alternative interpretations Christian love, as love, is emphatically the love of particulars—even if of every particular and not just of the universal (God, humanity) as such. Love, by contrast, is "pathological." It is necessarily involves "overvaluation and transference." It is the elevation—and not just by virtue of sexual desire—of one otherwise ordinary person to extraordinary heights with extraordinary privileges. The idea of a categorical imperative (even on the second formulation) in such instances is laughable. The very distinction between using a person as means and treating them as ends in themselves disintegrates as we try to apply it. (This is the force of the Aristophanic vision: we conceive of the other person's interests *as* our own.) But the virtue of love is and ought to be entirely preferential and personal. The lover who gives special preference to his love (though not, of course, in a bureaucratic or departmental position of authority) is virtuous. A lover who insisted on treating everyone including his or her lover the same (except in such circumstances) would strike us as utterly repulsive. The lover who just appreciates the humanity in his or her lover—as presumably she or he should in everyone else as well, just isn't a lover, whatever else he or she might be.

If "seeing clearly" means seeing what is universal in a person, his or her intrinsic worth, what is side-lined and diminished in such an analysis are all of those particulars that not only guide our way into love but enhance it all the way along—by way of "crystallization" and new ways of appreciating and loving the beloved. What the Kantian "sees clearly" in the other is an abstract ideal, an empty formal self that is empirically vacuous. We do not experience such a self, even in ourselves. We reason to it, by means of various Cartesian and Kantian devices. And, as for the beloved, we do not have even that transcendental advantage. The self supposedly loved is no self at all. Indeed, it seems to me far more insightful and phenomenologically accurate to say that what I really love about my wife is her distinctive Irish nose, not her self-in-itself. Quite frankly, I do not understand the latter reference at all, except as an awkward way of pointing out that I really do not love her nose, which is also, in a different sense, an abstraction, but I rather love her nose *because it is hers*. But that need on the part of the lover to keep expanding his or her perception and appreciation of the beloved remains firmly concrete and empirical.

Velleman complains about the "overvaluation and transference" that distorts perception in erotic love. But "seeing clearly" surely cannot mean "seeing objectively" or "seeing with scientific accuracy." It has been one of the most common accusations against the emotions, and against love in particular, that they confuse or distort our experience (Leibniz and Malebranche called them "confused perceptions"). But if what is in question here is the infamous resistance of emotions to canons of consistency, their alleged lack of "common sense" and tendency to bias perception and judgment, their apparent tolerance of contradiction (which Freud made one of the hallmarks of "the Unconscious"), and their refusal to conform to obvious considerations of objectivity, then one should ask whether it is not just such features that constitutes what is virtuous about love. In love, one learns to see a possibly ordinary human being as exceptional, with exceptional charms and virtues. Stendhal famously called this "crystallization" after the phenomenon of a twig collecting salt crystals in a damp cave. (It is a matter of some dispute whether Stendhal intended this to refer to merely imagining virtues or to seeing clearly real virtues, but I expect that he would have rightly insisted that from the point of view of the lover this difference is of no importance or perhaps it is no difference at all.) I would say, it is seeing clearly virtues that other people, and very likely oneself before falling in love, have simply ignored or do not see.

A homely lover looks lovingly at his equally plain beloved and declares, "you are the most beautiful woman in the world." Is he mistaken? I would say not. It is not that love is blind. The lover might rightly claim to see much more than we do, or more deeply. Impolitely pressed, our enraptured lover may resentfully concede the point, perhaps doing a phenomenological retreat to, "Well, she's the most beautiful woman in the world to me!" Beauty is in the eye of the beholder, it is said, but is this a matter of misperception? Or is it rather one of the virtues of love that it allows us to see clearly what is ordinary as very special?

Love is "seeing clearly" just those particulars that make the beloved such a special person *to me*. And the more such particulars I appreciate, the richer my love becomes. But at no point should I lose sight of the fact that they *are* particulars, albeit particulars that attach to the beloved and to our relationship. That is, at no point should I indulge in the philosophical fantasy that the person I love is beyond or "behind" the particulars, a stripped down end-in-itself, a self denuded of those delightful sensuous properties and eccentricities that make our love what it is. But do I have an argument against Velleman's Kantian fantasy, the fantasy of the beloved as incomparable and priceless? No, and I would not know how to go on constructing such an argument. But when I consult my own experience and intuitions about love—not those I have nurtured as a philosopher but those I have lived through as a (not always successful) lover, I find my phenomenology is quite opposed to any such vision. Love for me is an Aristophanic sense of togetherness, punctuated by pleasure and continuously energized by the myriad desires that swim along with our love like a school of dolphins off to port. Erotic love is a virtue because, once we have dismissed such cruder kin as lust and "mere" sexual desire, it necessarily involves and not just motivates long-term care and passionate benevolence toward another person. Erotic love is a virtue, because it is exciting—an unappreciated source of virtue in itself—and it inspires noble behavior. And if I were to bring Kant to my side I would refer back to the pre-critical Kant, the Kant of the inclinations, and I would say that erotic love is a moral virtue simply because it is—or at least it can be—*beautiful,* in not only a phenomenological and aesthetic sense but a moral sense as well.

CHAPTER 5

Aristotle on the Moral Relevance of Self-Respect

DANIEL RUSSELL

Everyone agrees that self-respect is important. Without it, people tend to make a mess of their lives, or nothing of them at all. It is a character trait that we try to instill in our children so that they may become strong, productive, and happy adults.[1] But when we ask whether self-respect is of *moral* importance—whether self-respect is a morally good trait of persons, whether its absence can constitute a kind of moral failure, and so on—we find less agreement. Some philosophers hold that a person's actions and attitudes are open to moral assessment only insofar as they affect other persons.[2] From such a perspective, if self-respect concerns only my treatment of myself, then self-respect cannot be morally relevant, even if it is some other sort of good. In fact, on such a view self-respect may be potentially problematic, since acting from respect for oneself may be in tension with acting out of respect for others.[3]

1. Indeed, Rawls has argued famously that self-respect is so crucial to the human good that social institutions should be arranged so that they ensure the social bases of self-respect. See John Rawls, *A Theory of Justice* (Cambridge: Harvard University Press, 1971), secs. 29, 67. Whether or not the welfare state has such an effect, I think Rawls must be right about how important self-respect is in any good human life.

2. An extreme form of this view, as Telfer describes it, is that morality is "by definition interpersonal"; Elizabeth Telfer, "Self-Respect," *Philosophical Quarterly* 18 (1968): 116. Recently, Milo has claimed that moral truths are "truths about an ideal social order . . . truths about what norms and standards hypothetical contractors would have reason to choose" to govern their interaction, and which are thus necessarily interpersonal. Ronald Milo, "Contractarian Constructivism," *Journal of Philosophy* 92 (1995): 185, 186. And Paul and Elder assert that "The proper role of ethical reasoning is to highlight acts of two kinds: those which enhance the well-being of others—that warrant our praise—and those that harm or diminish the well-being of others—and thus warrant our criticism." Richard Paul and Linda Elder, *The Miniature Guide to Understanding the Foundations of Ethical Reasoning* (Dillon Beach, Calif.: The Foundation for Critical Thinking, 2003), 2.

3. See Telfer, "Self-Respect," 121.

It is also possible, however, to maintain that morality is interpersonal while denying that self-respect concerns only treatment of oneself. Perhaps a lack of self-respect is morally significant because it undermines a person's ability to develop the right kinds of regard for others. Perhaps a lack of self-respect belies a lack of respect for persons, since it shows a lack of respect for personhood in oneself.[4] Still, such positions seem to imply that self-respect has no *particular* moral value of its own, and no *special* role to play, aside from its connections to certain other-regarding concerns from which it borrows whatever moral relevance it might turn out to have.

But surely we must ask whether self-respect has any moral relevance *independent* of other-regarding concerns. How might we argue that self-respect is also morally relevant strictly in its own right? And how might we show what is of special moral relevance about *self*-respect, aside from its being merely one form of respect for persons in general? Since in virtue ethics moral reflection begins with concerns about what sorts of character make a person morally good, we should be able to look to virtue ethics for an account of self-respect that does not require some link to other-regarding or agent-neutral considerations whose moral relevance is what really turns the gears. And that is also, I believe, the kind of answer we should want.[5]

I believe too that we can find the basic outline of such an answer in the ancient virtue ethicists, and particularly in Aristotle's *Nicomachean Ethics* (*NE*).[6] I maintain that self-respect enters Aristotelian virtue ethics, first, as a form of *stability* and *strength* of character, as is especially apparent in the virtue of courage: to respect oneself is part of what it is to act as the courageous person would, and is in fact a form of moral fortitude. Second, self-respect is a form of the *sterling, noble quality* of good character, that is, good character's quality of being not merely innocent of any shabby or contemptible behavior, but indeed *above* any shabby or contemptible behavior. This fact about self-respect is apparent, I argue, in the Aristotelian virtue of pride. And third, self-respect is also a form of *maturity of character,* and as such is the key both to moral development and to love of self and others. Self-respect is the better part of good character—*morally*

---

4. As Jean Hampton once put the point to me in conversation, if a person really does respect others as persons, then why shouldn't she respect herself as a person, since she is also a person as much as they? A similar point can be seen in Christine Korsgaard's discussion of Kant's formula of humanity in *Creating the Kingdom of Ends* (Cambridge: Cambridge University Press, 1996), chapter 4. Indeed, Thomas Hill, "Servility and Self-Respect," *Monist* 57 (1973): 104 suggests that a lack of self-respect threatens one's very capacity for respecting others.

5. A virtue theoretical account of self-respect does not, however, require that self-respect be one of the virtues, and in fact I do not think that it is.

6. In this paper I follow the translation of the *NE* by David Ross, *Aristotle: The Nicomachean Ethics,* revised by J. L. Ackrill and J. O. Urmson (Oxford: Oxford World's Classics, 1980).

good character—and is therefore of great moral relevance in its own right. I cannot hope in one paper to effect a very thorough shift in those who staunchly deny the thesis that self-regarding behavior can be morally relevant in its own right, but I do hope to make that thesis much harder to deny.

Let me begin by highlighting several features of self-respect that will be especially helpful for understanding my argument. First, while self-respect does not seem to be a distinct virtue, self-respect is clearly a distinct character trait, a character trait whose presence or absence is one of the things that make a person the sort of person she is. It makes sense to speak of acting as the self-respecting person would. When a self-respecting person defers to others or makes sacrifices, say, she does so *as* a self-respecting person would: on the right sorts of occasions, in the right sorts of ways, for the right sorts of reasons—because doing so would be wise, and not because she thinks that her judgment or her interests are "only hers" and so not very important, or because she is too feeble to commit to them.

Second, self-respect is a deep and firm commitment to oneself—to one's interests and goals, to one's judgment and convictions, and to one's progress and development. It is characteristic of self-respecting persons to be true to their own judgment, including the judgment that their interests are worth taking seriously, to have the courage of their convictions, and to stand up for themselves. This also means that self-respect is more than "feeling good" about oneself.[7]

And third, such people are not merely true to their values, whatever they are, but are committed to having their values be worthy of them, and are committed to themselves as being worth the effort it takes to rise to embrace worthwhile values. This also means that self-respect is not just *any* commitment to oneself, but a reflective and rational commitment to oneself as valuable and *worthy* of respect, and thus worthy of values one can respect. Fatuousness, stubbornness, and naïve selfishness, for instance, will not be forms of self-respect. It makes sense to tell people that they *ought* to respect themselves.

What, more precisely, is this sort of commitment to oneself? For one thing, it is to live by convictions that I have made *mine*. I do not do so when my convictions are lacking in the emotional or intellectual depth necessary for them to regulate in my psyche as a whole. Making my convictions mine may not require that I give philosophical arguments for them, but it will require a mature level of reflection about what makes my convictions worth having. And since such regulative convictions are so great a part of me, they will also require a mature level of reflection about who I am, and am to be.

---

7. Feeling good about oneself is more a matter of self-*esteem*, I think, than of self-respect. In any case, it is worth noting that I am concerned only with self-respect as a motivating and reason-giving feature of a person, what Robin Dillon calls "conative self-respect" ("How to Lose Your Self-Respect," *American Philosophical Quarterly* 29 [1992]), as opposed to, say, a way of thinking or feeling about oneself.

It is important to note, however, that living as the self-respecting person does by convictions of one's own does not mean having convictions that are all about oneself, as opposed to having any "selfless" convictions. Nor does it mean having convictions that are wholly one's own inventions. What makes my convictions mine is my seeing for myself that they are worth my having, my understanding what makes them worth my having them, and their acquiring a stable emotional and intellectual hold within me. Consequently, we cannot always tell whether a conviction is that of a self-respecting or self-abasing person just by its content or origin. Such status will depend rather on how one's conviction fits into a larger body of practical reasoning about oneself and one's values.

Note also that commitment to some ideal cannot *substitute* for commitment to oneself, as if we could have commitments that we have made our own, without committing to ourselves. In order to make an ideal *mine*, I must find myself to be worthy of that ideal, and I must find it to be worthy of me. Without a commitment to an ideal *as* one's own—as an ideal in which one has taken a great personal stake—one does not have real commitment. We must not suppose that we can commit to ideals without committing to those ideals *as our own.*[8] A person's ideals and values do so much to make her the person that she is that we cannot prize apart her commitments to those ideals from her commitment to that person.

These observations also suggest that self-respect is a *global* trait of one's character as a whole. It will not be one character trait among many, but a trait of the working of the practical psyche as a whole as it reflects on itself and its reasons. Consequently, self-respect must change and develop as the agent does, in the content of one's commitment to oneself as well as in the depth and seriousness with which one commits. And the maturing of self-respect will be necessary for coming to hold values that effectively regulate one's behavior,[9] that form a coherent and mutually supporting whole, and that can have the strength of practical intelligence backing them.

Self-respect is also *holistic,* since I must approach the ideals I might adopt against the background of my self as a whole. Determining my commitments is much of the task of figuring out who I am, and I cannot approach my com-

8. For that reason, "Self-respect," as Rawls says (*A Theory of Justice,* 178), "is not so much a part of any rational plan of life as the sense that one's plan is worth carrying out."

9. As Aristotle notes, virtue regulates behavior because it is not bare knowledge or disposition, but is concerned with actions and passions (II.3, 1104b13–14), pleasures and pains (see II.3, esp. 1104b3–13, 29–1105a16), and motivations (see II.4, 1105a26–b5); in fact, Aristotle seems to treat someone's values not as bare judgments but as the integration of the psyche with respect to what she values (see VI.13, 1144b14–1145a6).

mitments piecemeal if I am to make them my own. For *I* am not piecemeal, but a whole consisting of closely interconnected beliefs, desires, skills, attitudes, and emotions, and it is for such a whole that I must choose and embrace certain convictions and reject others. Making convictions of one's own is a task of constructing the basic commitments of a whole self that give it its particular structure. Making a value one's own is to embrace corresponding ways of thinking, ways of being pleased and pained, ways of emotional response, ways of prioritizing, ways of planning and deliberating. This is what it is to commit to one's judgments, interests, and values, as the self-respecting person does.[10] One's values cannot play such roles if confined to its own corner of a person's psyche, leaving one free to move on and choose, piecemeal, which value to adopt next.[11] Here we see how from a primarily "formal" account of self-respect—as a character trait that plays such-and-such a role in a person's psyche—we might begin moving towards a more "substantive" one. For it is clear that self-respect will not be a part of just any character, regardless of its content; tragically, some person's characters are what they are precisely because of a lack of self-respect. Self-respect itself is not a purely formal trait, but like so many of our character traits, it is a dimension of the agent's good: self-respect can flourish, succeed, and hit the mark—or wither, languish, and fall short—as the kind of thing that it is. We see its success in people of virtue. For self-respect and virtue shape each other: one must start with some form of self-respect in order to develop as a person of virtue, and as a person so develops, the self that he respects changes into a person that is more and more worthy of his own respect, and anchored more and more stably in his commitment to the person he has become and is becoming. And we see self-respect fail and suffer in vicious people, in whom commitment to oneself devolves into mere selfishness or vanity, in turn giving them that much less to respect in themselves. And so as self-respect thrives or languishes, it shapes not only the *form* of one's character—what patterns and connections hold among dimensions of the psyche, say—but also its *substance*. And as our account of self-respect unfolds, it will become increasingly apparent that self-respect can thrive as the sort of thing it is only when it is a commitment to personal values of a virtuous kind.

Surely I have not said all that should be said by way of introducing self-respect. But starting with the idea that self-respect is a character trait consisting in rational commitment to oneself, and thriving as the kind of thing it is only

10. We shall see below that this fact about self-respect obviates worries that Aristotle lacks a distinct word for self-respect.

11. Notice that this observation about the nature of persons should have significant implications for the unity and reciprocity of the virtues. But it does not, we should note, *presuppose* some particular conception of the unity or reciprocity of the virtues.

when it is a rational commitment self worthy of respect, we can examine a number of roles that self-respect plays in the morally good character. I shall examine three ways in which self-respect can thrive: first, as a form of the strength of morally good character, which we see in the role of self-respect within the virtue of courage; second, as a form of the noble quality of morally good character, which we see in the virtue of pride; and third, as the basis of genuine self-love.

Aristotle begins his discussion of the virtue of courage in *NE* III.6–9 by classifying courage as a mean with respect to fear and confidence (III.6, 1115a6–9; III.7, 1116a10–15; II.7, 1107a33–b4), and opposed to recklessness on the one hand and cowardice on the other (III.7, 1115b24–1116a9). What is it to find the mean with respect to an emotion like fear? The so-called doctrine of the mean identifies the mean with respect to an emotion as having the emotion in the right way, about the right things, on the right occasions, for the right reasons, and so on (II.6, 1106b18–23).[12]

Consequently, it is not helpful to think of courage in strictly quantitative terms, as if it were a matter of not having "too much" fear, say; indeed, for Aristotle the emotions are not just "feelings" that one might have in greater or lesser quantities, but attitudes with complex cognitive structures,[13] and fear, in particular, is an attitude towards things that are fearsome, as being worth fearing (III.6, 1115a10 ff). Having "too much" fear, then, is in fact a matter of taking things to be worth fearing that are not worth fearing, or not worth fearing on the occasion in question, or not worth fearing to the degree that one thinks they are, and so on. Thus while Aristotle recognizes that people fear all kinds of things (III.7, 1115b7–13), his main interest is not in what people happen to be afraid of, but in things that really are fearful, that is, worth fearing (see III.7, 1115b13–24), and these he says are evils that arise from vice and depend on oneself, such as disgrace—and what is disgraceful is not simply what one happens to find embarrassing, but something that really is a disgrace for a person, belying bad character (see III.6, 1115a10–19). So when Aristotle says that it is of things of this sort that the courageous person will be afraid, he is making not the trite observation that even the courageous person is afraid sometimes, but the interesting observation that courageous people have the right sorts of values, and their emotions of fear and confidence properly track those values. That is why courage is a matter of having fear and confidence about the right things,

---

12. Aristotle limits this analysis, of course, to those emotions that do admit of a mean in the first place, as e.g. spite, shamelessness, and envy do not (II.6, 1107a8–26).

13. See the discussion of emotion in *Rhetoric* II.1–11. For this reason, it is also important to distinguish the emotion of fear from phobia, neurosis, panic, and the like.

at the right times, for the right reasons, and in the right manner, where "right" is determined by proper reasoning about what counts as doing good in the case at hand (see III.7, 1115b11–13, 1116a10–15).

These observations about the emotions of fear and confidence allow Aristotle to demarcate the virtue of courage from other character traits that are concerned with fear and confidence but are not virtues (see III.6, 1115a10–22; III.7, 1115b24–33; III.8). Rash or reckless people, he observes, are sometimes called courageous, since they are bold and charge ahead into things that frighten most people, but Aristotle says such people are not really courageous, because such people are bold not in spite of the danger to themselves, but rather because of insensitivity to that danger. Their boldness and confidence do not come from having correct attitudes about what things are worth fighting, suffering, or dying for. Instead, they are bold and confident about the wrong things and for the wrong reasons, and as a result they don't always stand their ground, and cannot be counted on to stand and fight, suffer, or die for something when it is worth fighting, suffering, or dying for; that is why they cannot really be courageous (III.7, 1115b24–28).

Likewise, swaggering people try not so much to be courageous as to seem so, and so they too cannot be counted on to stand up to what is really fearful, or to fight for what is worth fighting for (III.7, 1115b28–33). Even a dutiful soldier is courageous not as such, but only if he is motivated by what really is good or bad, that is, only if he despises doing the disgraceful or ignoble (III.8, 1116a27–b3). Furthermore, the skill that enables certain experts to face dangers as part of their jobs does not by itself make them courageous; rather, what makes the difference is one's resolve to stand up for what is worth standing up for (III.8, 1116b3–23).[14] And finally, passionate people are not courageous either, despite their bold charging, since being "driven" to do something isn't the same as going for it as good and honorable (III.8, 1116b23–1117a9). These people all superficially resemble the courageous, but are not courageous in fact: what separates them from the courageous is their failure to resolve to fight evils *as* evils. Courageous action, in the proper sense, comes from properly discerning what is worth what: what is worth fighting for, what is worth dying for, and what is worse than death or injury.

One's reasons for facing a danger make all the difference as to whether one faces the danger as a courageous person does. And for Aristotle, facing danger as a courageous person does means (among other things) facing the danger because one decides, in accordance with right reason, that doing so is the right thing to do, and that that makes the risk worth taking. Here the faux courageous

14. See also the discussion of sanguine people at NE III.8, 1117a9–22.

display two defects. One is that, as we see in the reckless, their behavior does not take their own interests into account in the right way. This suggests that for Aristotle a self-deprecating person could not be a courageous person, even if she were to go boldly where others fear to tread. The reason is that she would not be going boldly *as the courageous person would:* her action does not issue from a firm and stable character that reliably places the proper sort of weight on her own interests. This seems to me the right kind of result: having a blind spot about one's own value is a defect in one's understanding of values,[15] and is therefore incompatible with the possession of practical wisdom (*phronēsis*). Such a person, then, will not act from practical wisdom, and thus will not act as the virtuous person acts.[16]

But an even deeper defect in the faux courageous is that they do not act on the right kinds of reasons. This is because moral fortitude is a crucial dimension of the courageous person. According to Aristotle, the courageous act from moral fortitude or what we may call the "courage of their convictions." What the courageous do, and the faux courageous do not, is act from a firm, stable, and tenacious commitment to stand up for the right kinds of reasons (see esp. III.8). This fortitude is very different from being stubborn or sanguine, since it is based in firm and *rational* commitment. That is a matter of knowing what can be accepted at what price, and what cannot be accepted at any price. That is why Aristotle takes such pains to wean us away from the idea that courage is a "soldier's virtue," starting as he does with the notion that what courageous people fear are disgrace and, in general, what arises from bad character (III.6).[17] He is much more interested in courage as we find it in people who respect their judgment, who have the strength to stand up for what is right, who refuse to be intimidated or to play along sheepishly—in short, people of strong conviction and the character to stand behind their conviction. And as such, it is clear that this moral fortitude is no different from that trait that we have been discussing as self-respect.

It seems independently plausible to think of self-respect as a form of moral

---

15. Dillon in "How to Lose Your Self-Respect" (135) claims that self-respect is respect for something with moral worth, and a failure to recognize such worth "signifies a kind of moral corruption."

16. And this point generalizes: since practical wisdom is the basis of every virtue, for Aristotle (VI.12–13), such a blind spot is incompatible with every virtue; so it turns out that, for Aristotle, a person deficient in self-respect cannot have any of the virtues at all—a bold view indeed (and bolder than the view I shall try to defend here).

17. Of course, Aristotle does remark that courage is often associated with facing death and danger nobly in battle (III.6, 1115a29–35), but I think he notes this not to say what courage is primarily about. He does, after all, go on to say that it is about many different kinds of things as well, 1115a35–b6, and makes a point of remarking about soldiers who face danger out of duty and not out of courage, at III.8, 1116a27–b3. Rather, I think that Aristotle means only to show that his account of courage can make sense of the common association of courage with persevering in battle.

fortitude. Consider just how deep a commitment to oneself, and thus how much self-respect, must make up the courage of one's convictions. Such commitments can require one to end relationships, face dangers, put others in danger, lose jobs, lose careers, postpone or forgo plans. Under such pressures, people often tend to seek compromise and to rationalize. And sometimes compromising is the thing to do, perhaps even the *virtuous* thing to do. But to compromise *as* a virtuous person would is to compromise against the backdrop of a character that would refuse to compromise if it were *not* the virtuous thing to do. And self-respect is the better part of that power of good character, because being the sort of person who can put an end to those thoughts is being a person with a deep commitment to oneself: such a commitment to myself is a commitment that I really will think carefully—deeply, painstakingly—about in terms of what a situation demands of me; that I will do what I decide I must do; and that while doing so has a cost, betraying myself by doing wrong is simply unacceptable. Once I have made that betrayal, I have too little of myself left, and too little left of myself to give.

And here it is important to remember that self-respect is not a purely formal trait. It would be a mistake to suppose that while the faux courageous have different values from those of the genuinely courageous, they have just as much respect for themselves and their values, as the genuinely courageous do. Since Aristotle believes that there are facts about value that right reason can discern (see, e.g., VI.5, 1140b20–21), and since self-respect requires a self that one recognizes as *worthy* of respect, the faux courageous can respect themselves only so long as they remain unreflective enough that they do not realize how inadequate their values are, and how little such people actually stand for. But in that case, they cannot respect themselves as much as the courageous do, if they can respect themselves at all. The more they come to respect themselves, then, the more reflective they will have had to become, and thus the less they will want to cling to their prior values, in virtue of which they fell short of real courage. Self-respect and shabby values, then, tend to pull against each other under the pressures of rational reflection. By contrast, self-respect tends to strengthen, and be strengthened by, values that can hold up under rational reflection, and this is what makes self-respect a form of substantive moral fortitude—not just standing up, but standing up for the *right*.

When it comes down to it, then, the moral fortitude that one needs to reach down and find within oneself in the moment of truth is a commitment to one's judgment as trustworthy, as worth committing to even at great cost, and as binding upon what one really can consider an option. And so the courage of my convictions is also made up of an enormous trust in myself. Since courage is a virtue, this trust must be a well-founded trust, and such trust can only come from having been the sort of person who has already invested enough in himself to know that he is trustworthy in the judgments he makes. This is, I think, another reason for thinking that Aristotle is right when he says that virtue is found mainly among those advanced in years and experience (I.3, 1094b27–1095a11): doing the right thing, as the virtuous person would do it, requires one to be ready to judge for oneself and to trust oneself, and that requires the sort of preparation that only a long pattern of commitment to one's judgment can bring. It also explains why, as Aristotle thinks, moral development is a very social activity: part of being committed to myself and my judgment when I am young and relatively inexperienced, is being committed to determining when the best I can do is to seek the guidance of people wiser than I. Consequently, much of the difference between virtuous and non-virtuous persons, and between persons at different stages of development in virtue, consists in their commitment to themselves and to their judgment, and so much of the difference in character comes down to differences in respect for themselves.

Like every virtue, courage has many aspects and facets, and in this section I have argued that self-respect is the aspect of courage that is its strong regard for the agent's interests and considered convictions, and the aspect that is the moral fortitude of the courageous person. We should take a closer look now at two points that have emerged in our discussion of self-respect. One is the idea that self-respect, like courage, involves knowing what is worth what—including knowing what things are simply unacceptable at any cost, and beneath oneself—and this suggests that self-respect is that feature of a virtuous character that is its nobility, its sense of dignity and worth, its sterling quality. As I shall argue, this is an important aspect of pride. Another is the idea that the self-respecting person is sufficiently committed to herself to develop and stand by serious ideals, and so self-respect is a form of moral maturity. I take up these two ideas in turn.

It strikes some people as odd to talk of pride as a virtue, much less a *moral* virtue. Some classify it among personality traits (alongside having a good sense of humor, or a way with words, say) rather than character traits, or among social virtues or a gentleman's graces (alongside a knack for putting people at ease, or a grand and graceful air, say), while others even think of it as a vice or one of the deadly sins (alongside avarice, sloth, etc.). And we often do use the term "pride" to talk about these sorts of traits. But I think that *Aristotelian* pride is clearly a moral virtue.[18] Pride, of the sort that concerns Aristotle, is a matter of

---

18. Aristotle's discussion of the virtue of pride in *NE* IV.3 (see also *Eudemian Ethics* [*EE*] III.5) has been the center of much controversy for two main reasons. One, some argue that pride for Aristotle is a "large-scale" virtue—i.e. a virtue available only to those with extraordinary means and spheres of action—a view that presents serious challenges for the reciprocity of the virtues that Aristotle maintains

knowing what things are worthy of oneself and what things are beneath one-self. It is not vanity or snobbishness or haughtiness, but a sense of one's own dig-nity and of what things are appropriate to it. This is clear in Aristotle's insistence that pride is not simply a matter of thinking very well of oneself, but of *being* a worthy person and appropriately aware of one's worth (IV.3, 1123a34–b15). And that fact about pride makes pride a moral virtue, since pride consists in know-ing that the only things worth your doing are good and honorable things, and that doing evil or base things is simply not an option: "it would be most unbe-coming," Aristotle says, "for a proud man to fly from danger, swinging his arms side to side, or to wrong another; for to what end should he do disgraceful things, he to whom nothing is great?" (IV.3, 1123b31–32). Pride is the differ-ence between someone who avoids doing bad and someone who despises do-ing bad.

Pride, for Aristotle, has many aspects, but its most important aspect, I think, is that it is the impeccability of the virtuous person's character, and in this re-spect it is identical to the virtuous person's respect for herself: pride consists in the virtuous person's trait of acting only in ways that are worthy of her dignity. Now Aristotle was of course aware that pride is often regarded as a social grace, and even a mark of social class, and indeed he begins his discussion of pride with certain garden-variety ideas about pride: that pride is associated with prominent people, with wealthy people, with people who occupy important positions, and so on. But the point that he takes away from common ideas about pride is sim-ply that pride concerns one's "distinctions" or "honors" (*timai*, 1123b20–24), which we bestow on the basis of a person's goodness, and in that case, the *truly* proud person—the person who is proud in the real and proper sense of the term— must be truly good (*hōs alēthōs . . . agathon*, 1123b29; cf. 1124a25). In-terestingly, at this point in the discussion socially bestowed distinctions *per se* rapidly fade in importance, as do the external achievements of wealth and of-fice to which such distinctions are commonly attached. Such social position is "a little thing" to the truly proud person,[19] Aristotle says (*mikron*, 1124a16–19). What comes to the fore instead is the virtuous character that is the real basis of

---

in VI.13. See Terence Irwin, "Disunity in the Aristotelian Virtues," *Oxford Studies in Ancient Philosophy*, Supplement (1988), and Stephen Gardiner, "Aristotle's Basic and Nonbasic Virtues," *Oxford Studies in An-cient Philosophy* 20 (2001). And two, some argue that pride as Aristotle understands it is not a moral virtue, but rather a mere social grace (*vel sim.*), or even a sort of priggishness. See W. F. R. Hardie, "'Magnanim-ity' in Aristotle's Ethics," *Phronesis* 78 (1978): 65 and references. In this section I argue that Aristotle in fact pulls away from popular understandings of pride as a large-scale virtue, and instead conceives of pride as not only a moral virtue, but indeed as a central moral virtue. I have benefited here from conversations with Steve Gardiner and Christine Swanton, who themselves disagree with my view concerning pride.

19. See Aristotle's claim at *EE* III.5, 1232a32–39 that the proud person is the best at judging great and little goods correctly.

any truly *meaningful* distinction or honor. And interestingly, Aristotle says one needs such a proud character in order to handle one's circumstances appropriately (*emmelōs*, 1124a31), whether they are favorable *or the opposite*: the proud person, Aristotle says, will deal reasonably with wealth, political power, and good fortune in general, just as he will deal reasonably with all bad fortune and "whatever may befall him," staying on an even keel whether his fortune be good or bad (1123a12–16). Pride turns out to be less properly a trait of wealthy, powerful, important people than it is a trait of people of strong character and well-reasoned priorities, who recognize that one's public distinctions or honors are not nearly so important as the virtues on which true honor is based, and which are equally necessary for doing well, whatever one's lot.

Thus, so far from merely embodying common ideas about pride as the socialite's virtue, Aristotle endeavors to wean us away from these sorts of ideas and to define a true sort of pride belonging to persons who are truly good (*agathos*, 1123b29), and who are not only virtuous, but indeed outstanding and exemplary in the virtues (1123b30). It is utterly ridiculous, Aristotle says, to think of the truly proud person in any other terms (1123b31–34), and this is why it is impossible for such a person to be a coward, to treat anyone unjustly, to treat other people as beneath himself, to be reckless, to talk badly about others behind their back, to brag about himself, to say what people want to hear rather than what he thinks is the truth, to think it is the business of others to bail him out, to hold a grudge, to be petulant or acquisitive, to sell out to other people's wishes, and so on (1123a29–1125a16). Aristotle builds up a rich image of the sort of person he takes the truly proud person to be, a person of true dignity, able to deal with shifting circumstances and reversals of fortune, ever mindful of the needs of others, and with such a sterling character that the very idea of his stooping to wrongdoing is simply unthinkable. Indeed, pride seems to me, and I think to Aristotle—who calls pride a "crown" of the virtues (IV.3, 1124a1–3)—to be a *central* moral virtue.

It is for this reason that true pride does not involve the thought that helping the needy, say, is "beneath me"; on the contrary, pride as Aristotle understands it recognizes that what is beneath me is the very act of refusing to help the needy—only a callous prig would think *that* is beneath him, or would help only amidst a flourish of trumpets. For Aristotle, the truly proud person is keen to lend a helping hand, without lording over the people who receive his help (IV.3, 1124b18–23). Aristotle also recognizes the difference between being disdainful and being a prig: only a virtuous person can be disdainful in the right sort of way (1124b5–6), that is, disdainful of one's circumstances—one's good or bad fortune—and of the goods and evils that motivate people to do wrong or hesitate to do right; money, power, honor (1124a12–19), reputation (1124b26–31;

cp. *EE* III.5, 1232b4–28), and even safety and life itself (*NE* 1124b6–9) simply do not mean as much to him as his character that makes his life worthwhile. Those who are improperly—although frequently—called proud are instead disdainful of other *people,* thinking themselves above them (1124a26–b6; cf. 1124b17–23). As we have seen, for Aristotle what is truly disgraceful is not what would happen to embarrass someone, but what it is really worth being embarrassed about—and that is being a morally shabby person (see also 1123b34–1124a1). Having a strong sense of my dignity and value as a rational agent, then, is to recognize that having bad priorities, values, and attitudes, doing bad things, being indifferent about doing good things, making other people feel lowly—*those* are the things that are beneath me.

What has pride to do with self-respect? The connection for Aristotle is, I think, much the same as it is for Epictetus, who relates the following mock conversation:

"Go and salute Mr. So-and-so." "All right, I salute him." "How?" "Not in an abject fashion." "But you were shut out." "That's because I haven't learned how to enter through the window. And when I find the door shut against me, I must either go away or enter through the window." "But speak with the man too!" "I did so." "How?" "Not in an abject fashion." "But you did not succeed."—Now surely that was not your business, but his. So why do you encroach on what concerns someone else? If you always remember what is yours and what concerns someone else, you will never be disturbed.[20]

Notice that the imagined person who has gone to visit a potential patron understands the ultimate goal of his activity quite differently from the one who chides him for being turned away. The latter thinks that the ultimate goal is to gain admittance to the patron's company and good favor. But the man who made this "unsuccessful" visit notes that if the goal were to get into the house, it would be enough just to go in through the window. What is *not an option,* though, is debasing himself in order to gain admittance, because getting in is not the most important goal. One may go in by the door, and one may even go in by the window, but one must never go in by debasing oneself. As the man who was turned away sees it, the ultimate goal of this exercise is not to gain admittance—although, of course, he would rather do that, other things being equal—but to act well and in a matter that befits a noble person, whether he gets in or not. Epictetus' point is that acting well is itself the real goal, in the end, of this exercise, as it is of *every* exercise.

20. Epictetus, *Discourses* II.6.6–8, translated by Brad Inwood and Lloyd Gerson, *Hellenistic Philosophy,* 2nd edition (Indianapolis: Hackett Publishing, 1997), sec. II-98.

As Epictetus shows, acting as the virtuous person acts is (among other things) acting in a dignified, self-respecting way—in a way that views falling short of one's convictions, and one's dignity, as simply not an option—and acting in that way involves putting more value on character than on circumstances. The strength that comes from proper self-respect is a strength of character that enables one to stand up for what is right and abide by one's convictions, because self-respect realizes that acting well, in a manner worthy of a rational person, is always within one's reach, and that nothing is worth acting badly.[21] The self-respect of the virtuous person, then, is her nobility, her impeccability, and the sterling quality of her character, and thus the foundation of her virtue of pride.[22]

This Stoic idea hearkens back to Aristotle's claim (see II.4, 1105a17–33, b5–12) that a virtuous act is one that is done *as* a virtuous person would do it; in this case, acting as the virtuous person acts means acting in ways that one recognizes are worthy of a rational agent. This goes beyond doing the right thing for the right reason, to include the recognition that one is worthy of nothing less. To recognize that worth in oneself is part of what it is to act as the virtuous person acts. This is an intriguing idea. Used as we are to classifying pride and self-respect as purely self-regarding traits—and to thinking of self-regarding traits as outside the realm of ethical goodness—we do not typically think of self-respect and pride as fundamental to *every* good action and trait.[23] Truly to respect oneself is to recognize that one is worthy of nothing less than fine behavior and noble character. That recognition is the basis of true pride, and from pride flow all noble actions. Our interests have weight, and we cannot have the virtues without registering that value.[24]

21. On the disdainfulness of the proud person in Aristotle's ethics, see IV.3, 1124a13–20; see also *EE* III.5, 1232b4–13.

22. I do not think, however, that self-respect is the same thing as pride for Aristotle. For one thing, in discussing pride Aristotle gives a nod to the popular idea that goods of fortune make some contribution to pride (IV.3, 1124a20ff); although Aristotle goes on to downplay this idea, and to concentrate on the personal goodness it takes to be rich in external goods without becoming a prig, still the fact that he considers this popular idea an intelligible one with respect to pride strongly suggests that he is working with a different concept than self-respect. For another, pride is concerned with a narrower range of goods—distinctions or honors, for the most part (IV.3, 1123b15–24, 1124a4–5, 1125a34–35)—than self-respect seems to be. Rather, self-respect on my view is concerned not with a particular set of goods, but with oneself in relation to goodness quite generally. Notice, however, that Aristotle does suggest a form of pride that is similarly global, at *EE* III.5, 1232b17–27. I have benefited here from conversations with Rosalind Hursthouse.

23. Here Aristotle would seem to agree with Kant's view that every immoral act constitutes a failure to respect oneself; for this Kantian view, see Stephen J. Massey, "Kant on Self-Respect," *Journal of the History of Philosophy* 21 (1983), esp. 64–69; see also Hill, "Servility and Self-Respect," 97–102; and Korsgaard, *The Sources of Normativity* (Cambridge: Cambridge University Press, 1996), 100ff.

24. This is also clear in Aristotle's account of anger. Like the other emotions, anger is not so much a feeling as it is an attitude, in particular an attitude about actions done in relation to oneself insofar as those actions fall below what one sees oneself as worthy of (see *Rhetoric* II.2–3; and *NE* IV.5). Anger,

It is self-respect, then, that accounts for the strength, and the grandness, of the virtuous character, the grandness that is the most important aspect of pride as a moral virtue. Hence self-respect is located deeply within the proper assessment of character, as it is part of a strong and stable character from which good action flows. Such a character refuses anything less as unworthy of itself, and such a character is morally relevant in its own right. So too, therefore, is self-respect.

So far I have examined ways in which self-respect forms part of a good character in Aristotle's ethics, and ways in which the lack of self-respect is tied to bad character. But we can also say something about self-respect in people whose characters are still developing.[25] In this final section I argue that self-respect is itself a form of moral maturity. I argue first that self-respect is a crucial basis of moral development, and second that self-respect is a crucial basis of one's developed capacity for loving oneself and others.

Aristotle rightly notes that our moral lives require frequent innovation and improvisation, as many other practical skills do. Matters of conduct, Aristotle says, require a person to consider each case and determine what is appropriate to it, somewhat as medical practice and or navigation do (I.3, 1094b11–27; II.2, 1103b34–1104a10). Consequently, doing well is not simply a matter of doing the right kind of action, but also of being the right kind of *agent,* since an action will be justly or temperately done only if it is done by a just and temperate person (II.4, 1105a26–30). Here Aristotle notes that as people learning a language may produce competent utterances, but not as competent speakers do—not, that is, on the basis of a firm skill, knowledge, and understanding of the language—likewise, people learning to be just or temperate may produce competent actions within those spheres, but they do not do so as just and temperate people do (see II.4, 1105a17–26, with 1105b5–12). In particular, Aristotle says that virtuous action must be done from knowledge, from a choice of

then, seems very closely tied to pride: I become angry when I think that other people have acted in ways that are beneath what I am worth, and thus I am a person who manages my anger in a virtuous way only if I have a healthy sense of what I am worth, that is, if I have the virtue of pride. If my estimation of my worth is unrealistically high, then I will be not proud but fatuous, and will respond angrily when anger is inappropriate, i.e. be an irascible person; and if my estimation of my worth is unrealistically low, then I will be not proud but servile, and will not respond angrily when anger is appropriate. (Note Aristotle's assumption that there *are* appropriate occasions for anger, an assumption that, as Seneca would later point out, is hardly beyond question).

25. I have especially in mind young people whose characters are still forming. Another sort of development is that from worse character to better (people trying to "turn their lives around"). I shall not discuss the latter sort of development here, since Aristotle has (interestingly) very little that is optimistic to say about turning one's life around. But I think that my comments will apply also to people who are turning their lives around, should we be more optimistic about such a prospect than Aristotle was.

such action for its own sake, and from a firm and stable character. And self-respect, I argue, is an important part of the development of each of these three characteristics of the virtuous agent.

The last of these—a good character that is firm and stable—we can discuss first, as the necessity of self-respect for the development of such character follows from what we have already said about the global and holistic nature of self-respect, and from its necessity for making one's commitments one's own. For moral maturity must obtain within a person as a *whole*. If I believe that injustice is evil, but am not emotionally repulsed by injustice, then I suffer from serious moral immaturity, since I do not understand with my whole self that injustice is evil. I may "know," because I've been told, that injustice is evil, but I also need to "own" that conviction for myself—to "know it in my bones";[26] and so part of living up to my convictions is grasping them as they must be grasped by the kind of being that I am, a being that is both rational and passionate. The virtuous person, then, is not merely committed to values one by one, but is committed to being a whole person defined in part by the well-reasoned values she has. Aristotle's virtuous person is a self-respecting person, and necessarily so, since the unity of her character is the shape that her commitment to herself as a whole takes within her psyche.[27]

As to the first characteristic, self-respect is essential for the development of the kinds of knowledge, or skills, that are appropriate to virtue. It is difficult to know the right thing to do, and it takes special effort and development to attain the kind of discernment that is needed (II.9, 1109a20–30, 1109b14–26). And it takes all the more effort and development since virtue requires "a reasoned and true state of capacity to act with regard to human goods" (VI.5, 1140b20–21),[28] that is, practical wisdom. Consequently, in order to become a virtuous person one must take oneself to be worth the trouble of developing convictions in accordance with the truth.

The knowledge that one needs in order to act as a virtuous person clearly includes knowledge about values, and about what is appropriate and inappropriate. Since Aristotle understands this knowledge to be a kind of practical skill (see I.3, 1094b27–1095a13; II.4, 1105b12–18), this knowledge will require a deep personal commitment to those values, and thus a deep commitment to

---

26. I owe the phrase to David Schmidtz.

27. So much, then, for worries we might have had that Aristotle has distinct no word for self-respect.

28. It is important to note, however, that the requirement that practical wisdom be *reasoned* seems to be different from, and weaker than, the requirement that it be *true*. In my comments I shall require no more than the former. I have benefited from discussions with Rhonda Smith and Anne Tarver on this point.

oneself. So much should be clear from what I have said already. At present, however, I wish to explore another aspect of the virtuous person's knowledge, and that is a more ground-level skill of knowing *what to do*.

In a normal adult there are some failings for which ignorance is simply not a good enough excuse—there are, as Rosalind Hursthouse and Philippa Foot have each argued, certain practical skills and values that we think any decent adult, who has had the sorts of experiences and opportunities that a normal adult life affords, really can be expected to have.[29] We can call the sort of ignorance that falls short of this norm "cluelessness." In a normal adult, cluelessness can often be attributed simply to not developing serious values and hence not doing what is needed to live up to those serious values. Therefore, cluelessness becomes a serious *moral* failing.[30] One does not succeed morally merely by resolving to.

Notice that the lack of self-respect can produce immature and culpably ignorant adults, and often cluelessness will be one way that a failure in self-respect will manifest itself. Cluelessness typically results, after all, from a failure to invest in oneself: it is a failure to develop the basic skills that one needs to live in accordance with one's convictions. If I really do put a value on the things I say I do, then I simply must invest in finding what it takes to live by them. If I do not, then perhaps I do not take those values very seriously after all, or I do not think that I am worth investing in, or (which may be the same thing) I think that my values—being, after all, merely mine—are not important enough to invest in. If I fail to develop for such reasons, then my moral immaturity—my failure to develop good character and practical wisdom—will be the shape that my failure to respect myself will take in my life. This failure leaves me unable to cope with the challenges of my moral life, much less to respond to them as the virtuous person would.

<hr />

29. See Rosalind Hursthouse, *On Virtue Ethics* (Oxford: Oxford University Press, 1999), 148–149, 118; Philippa Foot, *Virtues and Vices and Other Essays in Moral Philosophy* (Berkeley: University of California Press, 1978), 165–166. Steve Gardiner reminds me of Elizabeth Bennet's chiding Mr. Darcy in Jane Austen's *Pride and Prejudice* for the rather odd behavior he had displayed at a ball, to which he responds, "I certainly have not the talent which some people possess . . . of conversing easily with those I have never seen before. I cannot catch their tone of conversation, or appear interested in their concerns, as I often see done." Elizabeth, seated at the piano, retorts, "My fingers . . . do not move over this instrument in the masterly manner which I see so many women's do. They have not the same force or rapidity, and do not produce the same expression. But then I have always supposed it to be my own fault—because I would not take the trouble of practising. It is not that I do not believe *my* fingers as capable as any other woman's of superior execution."

30. This explains, I think, why Aristotle makes the otherwise rather striking claim that the possession of practical wisdom implies the possession of cleverness at finding the best means to a given end (VI.12, 1144a23–29), and why he makes a special point of highlighting this feature of practical wisdom in contrast to "philosophic" wisdom (VI.7, 1141b2–12).

Conversely, moral maturity is the shape that self-respect takes in a person's life in practice. A morally mature person takes responsibility for himself, and that means seeing what needs to be done, and stepping up and doing it. Of course, a mature person may not always have the means to do so, and may not be able to do so without relying on others for help and support.[31] But what is certain is that one will never be able to act as a morally mature person unless she prepares herself to do so. This preparation must include, on one level, a strong commitment to one's sincerely held convictions, but on another an investment in acquiring the skills necessary for living up to those convictions. Since that is an investment in oneself, it requires a commitment to oneself as worth the effort and sacrifice.

The second feature of moral maturity that Aristotle identifies is related to the first: living up to one's values for their own sake. Self-respect makes real, effective commitment to values possible, and that is what draws the line between hypocrisy and integrity; and without integrity we lose the ability to look our children in the eye, to stand for something before others, to go on as the people we are committed to being. Without respecting her own moral conviction, a person may stand to lose everything that makes her life the one she finds worth living. She may stand to lose her whole ability to take responsibility for herself in those projects that define her as the moral being she is. She may stand to lose her very identity. To fail to live up to one's values for their own sakes, is to fail to live up to oneself. And that none of us can afford.

Do such thoughts make us selfish? To be sure, people should love their fellow man, and defend their cause for that reason, not because of concern for themselves. But treating others well out of self-respect is not an alternative to doing so out of respect for others. Consider Atticus Finch's unpopular decision to defend Tom Robinson in Harper Lee's *To Kill a Mockingbird*. Atticus does so, he tells his daughter, because if he did not, he would betray everything he believes in, and could not even have the authority to correct his children. But he does not remain true to himself *instead* of acting out of good will for Tom. It is because his good will for Tom is part of who he is that being true to himself requires him to do this unpopular act; Atticus is a man of good will, and so it is to himself *as* a man of good will that he must be true. A person's good will is not one thing and his commitment to himself as a person of good will another, as if one could commit to good will as a reason for acting without committing

---

31. As Schmidtz has argued, being responsible is a matter of taking responsibility for oneself, but not necessarily of doing so all *by* oneself, without help and support; see David Schmidtz and Robert Goodin, *Social Welfare and Individual Responsibility* (Cambridge: Cambridge University Press, 1998), 7–9.

to himself as someone whose reasons for acting are worth taking seriously. Self-respect, then, is the difference between a world in which good will has a real role to play, and a world in which it is only a sentimental notion. It is the difference between a world in which morally mature persons do what must be done—leading, serving, setting an example, getting jobs done—and a world in which they wonder whether someone else might be available. Consequently, it is self-respect that makes it possible for a person to act "on principle" in the first place, and thus to choose so to act for its own sake.

Notice a consequence of this fact about self-respect and acting on principle: the line between respecting oneself and respecting others no longer seems very sharp. In practice, there seems to be little difference between Atticus' acting out of respect for himself and acting out of respect for Tom, where Atticus has made a commitment to the worth of people like Tom a commitment of his own. Not only is the action the same in both cases, but indeed the *reason* for the action seems the same. There is nothing virtuous—and nothing respectful of others—about doing "the right thing" out of vanity, say, or self-satisfaction and *noblesse oblige,* or in the grips of fear of conscience, or to save one's skin. But contrast such motives with acting from self-respect, which makes it possible to do what respecting someone else requires. And one's respect for others, if it is genuine, will be a central value within oneself to which one must be true. Self-respect, then, is a crucial basis for developing the moral maturity that acting as a virtuous person demands.

And self-respect is also a form of the moral maturity necessary for loving oneself and others. Self-love, for Aristotle, is a part of moral character that enables a person to include other people in her life in the right ways, and I think that on Aristotle's view self-respect turns out to be the maturity that makes a character capable of self-love, and therefore also of loving others.

According to Aristotle, only those who love themselves are really capable of loving other people (see IX.4), because a real friend is a "second self," that is, one with whom one shares one's life. To have a real friend, Aristotle says, is to extend to another person one's love for oneself: one's valuing and doing what is good for the sake of oneself, of valuing and wishing the preservation of what is best in oneself, of being at peace with oneself and appreciating one's own company, of being integrated in one's thoughts and desires, and of being consistent in what brings one delight and grief (IX.4, 1166a1–b2).[32] Note that, on this

---

32. People with bad characters, Aristotle says, do not stand in this loving relation to themselves—they "love themselves" only in the pejorative sense of being greedy or fatuous (IX.8, 1168b15–25)—and so they have no love that can grow to include others whom they value genuinely for their own sake (IX.4, 1166b2–29).

view, I can love another person only if I bring to the relationship the love that I already have for myself.[33] I think that Aristotle is right about that: if I have not invested enough in myself to develop my values reflectively and under mature scrutiny, or if I have not invested enough in myself to know what it means to live up to those values—if I have not taken myself to be worth the trouble—then I shall not be in harmony with myself, in Aristotle's sense, and thus I will not yet be capable of expanding my life to include others in the right way, as second selves. If I am not in harmony with myself as to what pleases and what grieves me, then how can anyone else be in harmony with me as to those things? Or if my values are only pallid and thin, how can I offer anything for another to be in real harmony with me about?

Clearly, self-respect is a kind of harmony with oneself, and is much of what makes one who one is. Consequently, a person will have to bring her respect for herself to the table in order to form real friendships. Self-respect is a form of moral maturity that is central to the character of the loving person, and that is the sort of character one needs to live well. Self-respect, then, is an essential aspect of the human good, and so self-respect is morally relevant in its own right, because good human character is.

Notice that our observations about moral maturity reveal that while self-respect is, of course, a case of respecting a person, it is not just that. A person's life, how well one lives one's life, what sort of person one becomes—these things must have moral value, if anything does. And self-respect has a very special, defining role of its own to play in every good human life.

Self-respect is a form of stability of character, visible in the characteristic behavior and moral fortitude of the virtuous person. It is a form of nobility of character. And self-respect is a form of moral maturity, the key to moral development and the capacity for real love.[34] I do not pretend to have swayed those who insist that morality is necessarily interpersonal,[35] but I do hope I

---

33. To put the point colloquially, we don't go out and find love, we go out and spread love around. On this point, I find Keith Lehrer, chapter 5 in *Self-Trust* (Oxford: Oxford University Press, 1997) to be particularly instructive in arguing that autonomous love for another is an extension of one's commitment to oneself.

34. One potentially serious complication for the view I have attributed to Aristotle is the fact that Aristotle clearly denies the possibility of treating oneself unjustly, or of voluntarily mistreating oneself in any way (see V.9, 11). Although I cannot pursue the issue here, my own view is that Aristotle has several independent reasons—as do we—to jettison the ideas that lead him to this conclusion.

35. Nor do I pretend to have swayed those who, like Rawls (and Kant before him), believe that only those features of persons are morally relevant that are features of them purely *qua* rational agents, where these are taken as separate from such contingent or "empirical" facts about them as their skills, their talents, and indeed their very characters which, Rawls argues, are ultimately due to the outcomes of the natural and social lottery (see Rawls, *A Theory of Justice,* esp. secs. 12, 48). I do, however, believe that such

have shown how much sense it makes to think that moral relevance starts with the state of one's soul and extends outward. Nowhere is that thesis more compelling than in the distinctive account of self-respect that Aristotelian virtue ethics has to offer.[36]

---

a view is fraught with deep independent problems, and in appreciating these problems I am especially indebted to the work of Mark LeBar. But of course I cannot pursue the issue here.

36. I thank Julia Annas, Mark LeBar, and Rhonda Smith for their contributions to my thought on this subject, and for their comments on earlier versions of this paper. Thanks also to audiences at Wichita State University, especially Debby Soles and Anne Tarver, and at the "Virtue Ethics: Old and New" conference, especially Steve Gardiner, Grant Gillett, Rosalind Hursthouse, and Christine Swanton. Finally, I owe thanks to the anonymous reader for Cornell, and the deepest thanks to Steve Gardiner for his helpful and thoughtful suggestions on several drafts of this paper.

PART 3

THE NATURE OF VIRTUE
RECONSIDERED

CHAPTER 6

Negative Virtues: Zhuangzi's Wuwei

KATHLEEN MARIE HIGGINS

Recent Western ethical discussion has understood virtue almost exclusively in terms of the active exercise of an agent's powers. Although the virtues identified in this fashion include many active capacities of importance for ethics, they do not comprise the whole domain of virtue. Owing to the emphasis on activity in many Western discussions of virtue, the contemporary field of virtue ethics has tended to ignore a category of virtues that plays a prominent role in certain schools of Asian thought. I will call this category of virtues "negative virtues,"[1] virtues characterized by one's abstaining from certain activities or states of mind. In particular, such virtues are often described in terms of the avoidance of certain intra-psychic activities, such as reflection and obsessional thought. What is virtuous in a negative virtue is typically a matter of psychological orientation. One is negatively virtuous as consequence of cultivating inner stillness and relinquishing efforts to control one's situation (both of which appear, from a typical Western point of view, to be "doing nothing.") If Western virtue largely concerns ideals for pursuing projects or courses of action, such negative virtues are virtues of abandoning projects.[2]

In labeling such virtues "negative," I have in mind a comparison between such

---

1. My usage, if not my attitude, is similar to that of Nietzsche when he remarks, "I do not like negative virtues—virtues whose very essence it is to negate and deny oneself something." Friedrich Nietzsche, *The Gay Science, with a Prelude in Rhymes and an Appendix of Songs,* trans. and ed. Walter Kaufmann (New York: Random House, 1974), 244.

2. I do not mean to suggest that such emphases are unprecedented in Western thought. See note 3 below. Nevertheless, Western ethical thought is predominantly more concerned with active virtues than with the kind of negative virtue that I will be discussing in connection with Zhuangzi.

virtues and negative space in art. During a rest in music, the tendencies of the music just preceding it are resonantly evident. In the visual arts negative space provides a particularly effective field of display for the tendencies of environing elements. Similarly, negative virtue provides the space for the operation of desirable tendencies, which might be checked or hindered by an agent's assertiveness.

Negative virtues are structured differently than those virtues properly characterized as "dispositions" to behave in certain ways, or as "action-guiding." However, not every case of refraining from activity is evidence of negative virtue in my sense. Avoidance of a vicious action, in the external sense of not committing it, is neither necessarily negative in the relevant sense nor necessarily virtuous. One may avoid an action because one has no occasion to perpetrate it. I am not virtuous for having avoided assassinating the Queen of England if I have never been in a position to do so. One may also, as Kant and Nietzsche both remind us, externally conform to moral codes from many motives, some of which are far from virtuous.

Nor do I mean to include among negative virtues all virtues that *can* be defined in negative terms as well as positive ones. One might describe Socrates' definition of justice in the *Republic* as either minding one's own business or as not interfering in others' business. The second paraphrase does not establish that justice is a negative virtue. An element of moderation or self-restraint alone is also insufficient to establish a negative virtue. One may avoid excess yet nevertheless be quite assertive in one's activity. One may also stifle one's action while being energetically disposed to control one's situation or to act as soon as conditions are more favorable.

The paradigm cases I have in mind for negative virtues come from certain Asian traditions.[3] One example is the virtue developed through karma-yoga, as

3. Although I am taking virtues from Asian traditions as paradigm cases, I acknowledge that some Western accounts of virtues are comparable. Nietzsche's stated dislike of negative virtues notwithstanding, his descriptions of virtues sometimes resemble Daoist accounts of virtues. For example, his Zarathustra urges that one should avoid constraining one's virtues by naming them. Nietzsche similarly insists that in order to become what one is (his ideal), one must not have a conscious conception of what one is. He also praises solitude as a virtue. However, Nietzsche denies that Schopenhauerian resignation is virtuous, and he certainly encourages willful activity. So he is hardly a Western Daoist.

The specifically "feminine" virtue commonly advocated for women in the eighteenth century bears some relationship to Daoist emphasis on receptivity and assuming the role of "the female." However, Daoist references to such virtue are not tied to the gender of the person involved; the role of the female is advocated for everyone. Given the dearth of contemporary Western discussions of receptivity as a virtue, perhaps we can assume that what was viewed as masculine virtue in the eighteenth century has become the entire class under discussion, with "virtue" returning to its etymological root (*vir*, meaning "man").

Western mystical traditions, as well as other religious schools of thought, also value the negative virtue of surrendering oneself. The very term "Islam" refers to such surrender to God; and Kierkegaard's leap

articulated in the *Bhagavad Gita*. Such virtue involves relinquishing the sense of one's actions being one's own. Although one continues to fulfill one's positive duties, one no longer identifies oneself as the doer of these actions. Nor does one view oneself as entitled to the fruits of one's actions. The *Bhagavad Gita* suggests that one subsume one's own will into that of the ground of being, identifying oneself as a vessel of that ground. By surrendering a sense of oneself as a separate agent or doer, one ceases to accumulate personal karma and the accompanying need to work through karmic tendencies. The virtue of "nondoership" would count as a negative virtue in my sense.

Another paradigm case is the one on which I will focus. This is the case of the Daoist virtue *wuwei*, non-action or non-assertive action.[4] In order to elucidate this concept I will emphasize the writings attributed to Zhuangzi (Chuang Tzu),[5] a Daoist thinker of the fourth century B.C.E., who uses particularly striking images to clarify the Daoist ethical ideal and the virtues necessary to it.

Zhuangzi's conception of virtue depends upon the metaphysical presupposi-

---

of faith also involves giving up one's self-reliance in favor of *reliance* on God. Aquinas' category of "infused virtue," virtue that cannot be acquired by effort but can only be infused by God, resembles Daoist *wuwei* in tying virtue to lack of effort and attunement to a larger power.

One might note that even Aristotle, for all his emphasis on activity, describes the magnanimous man as being calm and unwilling to concern himself with petty matters. However, Aristotle's analysis of virtue as inherently active contrasts significantly with the Daoist perspective. Perhaps the Skeptics and Stoics are the Western schools of thought that come closest to advocating Daoist-style negative virtue. The Skeptical virtue of withholding assent and the Stoic virtue of detachment from unstable things in the world as a means for attaining the goal of *ataraxia* ("freedom from disturbance," as Martha Nussbaum translates it) both resemble Daoist virtue in certain respects. For discussion of the relationship between Zhuangzi and ancient skepticism, see Paul Kjellberg, "Sextus Empiricus, Zhuangzi, and Xunzi on 'Why Be Skeptical?'" in *Essays on Skepticism, Relativism, and Ethics in the Zhuangzi,* ed. Paul Kjellberg and P. J. Ivanhoe (Albany: State University of New York Press, 1996), 1–25. Zhuangzi and Epictetus, describing the method for coming to grips with the death of a loved one, similarly encourage one to focus on the naturalness of death. A basis for comparison that might be fruitfully explored is the common tendency of these schools to consider a transformation of one's mode of perception to be crucial to attaining the ethical goal. The Stoic emphasis on reason as the means for rectifying one's perception is, however, in striking contrast with the Daoist insistence that reason can interfere with perception.

4. The notion of *wuwei* appears in the work of most major ancient Chinese philosophers. For a survey of the use of this term by various schools, see Edward G. Slingerland, *Effortless Action: Wuwei as Conceptual Metaphor and Spiritual Idea in Early China* (Oxford: Oxford University Press, 2003). For discussions of Mencius' use of the concept, see Roger T. Ames, chapter 1 in *The Art of Rulership: A Study in Ancient Chinese Political Thought* (Honolulu: University of Hawaii Press, 1983); and Henry G. Skaja, "How to Interpret Chapter 16 of the *Zhuangzi*: 'Repairers of Nature (*Shan Xing*),'" in *Wandering at Ease in the Zhuangzi,* ed. Roger T. Ames (Albany: State University of New York Press, 1998), 112–113.

5. Zhuangzi is credited with a text of thirty-three chapters. Although scholars now think that he was the actual author of only seven of these chapters, I will follow convention in referring to the entirety of the text as Zhuangzi's. The *Zhuangzi* (that is, the text attributed to Zhuangzi) is noteworthy for its outlandish stories and its startling heroes.

tion that the world is essentially in flux. The flow of reality is called the *Dao* (the Way). The good life requires that one recognize one's own participation in the flow of things and attune one's course of action to the prevailing flow of energy within the *Dao*. Crucial to this attunement is accurate perception. Any outlook that distorts the dynamic character of reality or the energies active within it is a potential hindrance to perceiving one's situation as it is. Accordingly, language, which categorizes in accordance with fixed terms, always threatens to distract one from reality, or worse, to lead one to imagine that fixed formulations capture reality's nature. The *Dao De Jing*, or *Laozi* (*Lao Tzu*), another central text of Daoism, opens with the caveat, "The Way (*Dao*) that can be spoken of is not the constant Way (*Dao*)."

Zhuangzi presupposes that we can have knowledge of the world, but that it is always perspectival. His character Wang Ni makes comments reminiscent of Xenophon.

> "Men claim that Mao-ch'iang and Lady Li were beautiful, but if fish saw them they would dive to the bottom of the stream, if birds saw them they would fly away, and if deer saw them they would break into a run. Of these four, which knows how to fix the standard of beauty for the world?"[6]

Our knowledge of the world is always from a point of view. Nevertheless, we can have a kind of objectivity, gained through mirroring the environment without imposing preconceived judgments or categories on it.[7] David H. Hall and Roger T. Ames stress that this mirroring occurs "at the moment," without reference to one's memories or anticipations.[8]

This condition of mirroring depends on the non-assertive virtue *wuwei*, a term used to characterize the stance of the Daoist exemplary person. *Wuwei* can be rendered as "no action" or "non-action," but Hall and Ames contend that this is unfortunate. They instead prefer the translation "non-assertive action," emphasizing that *wuwei* does not stop all activity, but only action in which the

6. Chuang Tzu, "Discussion on Making All Things Equal (Section 2)," in *The Complete Works of Chuang Tzu,* trans. Burton Watson (New York: Columbia University Press, 1968), 46. Burton Watson uses a different transliteration scheme than the one I use in the body of the text. Watson employs the older Wade-Giles scheme, which was devised in the West and remains in common use in Taiwanese publications of English translations of Chinese texts. I use the pinyin scheme, devised in the People's Republic of China and now in widespread use in the United States. In pinyin, "Chuang Tzu" is "Zhuangzi," and "Mao-ch'iang" is "Maoqiang."

7. Nietzsche's comment on perspectival objectivity in Friedrich Nietzsche, *On the Genealogy of Morals,* in *On the Genealogy of Morals and Ecce Homo,* trans. Walter Kaufmann and R. J. Hollingdale, ed. Walter Kaufmann (New York: Random House, 1967), 3:12, 119.

8. David L. Hall and Roger T. Ames, *Thinking from the Han: Self, Truth, and Transcendence in Chinese and Western Culture* (Albany: State University of New York Press, 1998), 51.

agent attempts to direct the course of the world (in accordance with preconceived expectations and habits) instead of flowing with it.[9]

Henry G. Skaja characterizes *wuwei* as "non-interference in the naturally integral, spontaneous, and harmonious process of life/growth (*sheng*)."[10] Skaja's
interpretation emphasizes the interrelation between *wuwei* and a positive characterization of the optimal mode of operation. The consequence of being *wuwei*
is that one's actions are *ziran*, that is, spontaneous. A. C. Graham translates *wuwei*
as "doing nothing." "Man takes pride in distinguishing himself from nature by
his purposive action; Lao-tzu by a classic reversal describes the behavior of the
sage as Doing Nothing."[11]

François Jullien points out, perhaps surprisingly, that such "doing nothing" is
the key to efficacy in human experience.

> In China, "practical reason" . . . lies in adapting to the propensity at work so as to
> be carried along by it and exploit it. No initial alternative between good and evil
> is involved, since the status of both is ontological. It is simply a matter of either
> "going along with" the propensity and thereby profiting from it or "going against
> it" and being ruined. For what is valid for the general is as *also* valid for the sage. . . .
> Far from seeking to reconstruct the world on the basis of some order or another,
> attempting to impose his own designs on it and force the course of things, all he
> does is respond and react to whatever reality prompts within him. And this he does
> not do partially or at particular moments, when it is in his interest to do so, but in
> all situations and continuously. In this way his power to change reality is checked
> by no obstacles or limits. He does not "act," does nothing himself (on his own ini-
> tiative), and the degree of the efficacy of this behavior is determined by the extent
> to which he refrains from trying to manage things.[12]

Zhuangzi illustrates the efficacy of *wuwei* through his story of Cook Ding, who
describes his expertise in butchering an ox.

> "What I care about is the Way, which goes beyond skill. When I first began cut-
> ting up oxen, all I could see was the ox itself. After three years I no longer saw the
> whole ox. And now—now I go at it by spirit and don't look with my eyes. Per-

9. Hall and Ames, *Thinking from the Han*, 52. Andy Young, similarly, proposes "effortless effort" or
"creative quietude" as translations. See Andy Young, "Teaching *Wu Wei* Using Modeling Clay," *Teaching
Philosophy* 19:2 (June 1996): 167.

10. Henry G. Skaja, "How to Interpret Chapter 16 of the *Zhuangzi*," 107.

11. A. C. Graham, *Disputers of the Dao: Philosophical Argument in Ancient China* (La Salle, IL: Open
Court, 1989), 232.

12. François Jullien, *The Propensity of Things: Toward a History of Efficacy in China*, trans. Janet Lloyd
(New York: Zone Books, 1995), 263–264.

ception and understanding have come to a stop and spirit moves where it wants. I go along with the natural makeup, strike in the big hollows, guide the knife through the big openings, and follow things as they are. So I never touch the smallest ligament or tendon, much less a main joint."[13]

Cook Ding claims that he is so successful in not forcing his knife that he has never had to sharpen it in the nineteen years he has had it (nineteen years being a standard way of a referring to a generation).

Although spontaneous behavior (*ziran*) is directed by the *Dao,* not by the agent's intentions, it also presupposes the particular nature of a thing, its *de,* which can be translated as "power," or as "(natural) virtue."[14] The nature of a particular thing *is* its power, according to the Daoist outlook. Daoist metaphysics considers "things" to be configurations of energy, in flux like the *Dao* that encompasses them. A thing's reality implies its dynamic contribution to the larger environment. The person in the condition of *wuwei,* not imposing a definite form onto his or her behavior, spontaneously manifests his or her character. This behavior, in turn, is an unimpeded response to the larger environment in its current tendencies. One is virtuous when one behaves "naturally," *in virtue of* what one is in the context of the larger current configuration of the *Dao.* Roger Ames clarifies the relationship between *wuwei* and *de* when he describes *wuwei* as "a negation of that kind of engagement that makes something false to itself."[15]

Obviously, Zhuangzi's characterization of virtue differs from many that have been central in Western thought. Notably, it contrasts with Aristotle's account. *Wuwei,* non-action or doing nothing, does not coincide with the Aristotelean emphasis on the activity of being virtuous. This difference may not be as extreme as it initially appears, however, for Aristotle would agree with Zhauangzi that one does not have to force oneself to act virtuously if one is genuinely virtuous.[16]

13. Chuang Tzu, "The Secret of Caring for Life (Section 3)," in *The Complete Works of Chuang Tzu,* 50–51. I take it that the "perception" that has come to a stop here is ordinary sensory perception, which has been replaced by spiritual intuition.

14. *De* is natural virtue in the sense of developing spontaneously from one's native endowment, as opposed to being artificially imposed upon it. This does not imply, however, that one does not need to cultivate *de,* but this cultivation, in the Daoist view, involves eliminating artificial aspirations and returning to a more natural state. For further discussion of *de,* particularly as used by the Daoists, see P. J. Ivanhoe, "The Concept of *de* ('Virtue') in the *Laozi,*" in *Religious and Philosophical Aspects of the Laozi,* ed. Mark Csikszentmihalyi and P. J. Ivanhoe (Albany: State University of New York Press, 1998), 239–257. Ivanhoe emphasizes that both Daoist and Confucian thinkers emphasize the positive impact virtue has on others and on the community as a whole, an emphasis that he sees as lacking in contemporary Western ethical discussions.

15. Roger T. Ames, introduction to *Wandering at Ease in the Zhuangzi,* 7.

16. Aristotle actually objects to generic negative formulations of the virtues, but for a reason that Zhuangzi might endorse: they are too blanket.

More obviously in contrast with Aristotelian virtue, *wuwei* is not the outcome of practical reason. Not only is it not directed by reason, it is not even directed by consciousness. Zhuangzi's virtuous characters are often craftsmen who claim they have perfected their skill by stilling their minds to the point that they "forget" everything they know about it. For example,

> Arisan Ch'ui could draw as true as a compass or a T square because his fingers changed along with things and he didn't let his mind get in the way . . . You forget your feet when the shoes are comfortable. Understanding forgets right and wrong when the mind is comfortable. . . . You begin with what is comfortable and never experience what is uncomfortable when you know the comfort of forgetting what is comfortable.[17]

Another of Zhuangzi's characters, the Barrier Keeper Yin, compares the perfect man (Zhuangzi's ideal of virtue) to someone who is too drunk to know he has anything to worry about.

> "When a drunken man falls from a carriage, though the carriage may be going very fast, he won't be killed. He has bones and joints the same as other men, and yet he is not injured as they would be, because his spirit is whole. He didn't know he was riding, and he doesn't know he has fallen out. Life and death, alarm and terror do not enter his breast, and so he can bang against things without fear of injury. If he can keep himself whole like this by means of wine, how much more can he keep himself whole by means of Heaven! The sage hides himself in Heaven— hence there is nothing that can do him harm."[18]

"Heaven" here has the connotation of the natural order of things. Elsewhere, Zhuangzi appropriates Confucius, the emblematic teacher, as a character. Defining the statement, "His powers are whole," Zhuangzi's Confucius says,

---

[I]t is by reason of pleasures and pains that men become bad, by pursuing and avoiding these—either the pleasures and pains they ought not or when they ought not or as they ought not, or by going wrong in one of the other similar ways that may be distinguished. Hence men even define the virtues as certain states of impassivity and rest; not well, however, because they speak absolutely, and do not say 'as one ought' and 'as one ought not' and 'when one ought or ought not,' and the other things that may be added.

Aristotle, *Nicomachean Ethics*, trans. W. D. Ross, *The Basic Works of Aristotle,* ed. Richard McKeon (New York: Random House, 1941), 1104b, l. 20–28.

17. Zhuangzi, "Mastering Life (Section 19)," in *The Complete Works of Chuang Tzu,* 206–207. In pinyin, "Ch'ui" would be "Chui."

18. Ibid., 198–199.

"Life, death, preservation, loss, failure, success, poverty, riches, worthiness, unworthiness, slander, fame, hunger, thirst, cold, heat—these are the alternations of the world, the workings of fate. Day and night they change place before us. . . . [T]hey should not be enough to destroy your harmony. If you can harmonize and delight in them, master them and never be at a loss for joy, if you can do this day and night without break and make it be spring with everything, mingling with all and creating the moment within your own mind—this is what I call being whole in power."[19]

Virtue is its own reward, according to Zhuangzi.

Zhuangzi's largely negative approach to virtue contrasts with some of the prominent concerns within contemporary virtue ethics. First, he rejects the idea that virtue can be linked with a clear distinction between right and wrong actions. In this respect he counters both virtue ethicists (such as Rosalind Hursthouse and Michael Slote) who contend that virtue can be used as a basis for delineating right action and with critics of virtue ethics (such as J. B. Schneewind) who consider it a failing that virtue ethics is not determinately action-guiding.[20] He is closer to contemporary particularists such as Jonathan Dancy, who rejects the goal of formulating moral principles to determine what to do in every particular instance. Zhuangzi's views might also remind the contemporary philosopher of contentions by Dancy and John McDowell that moral insight is a matter of perception, not universal principle.[21] But Zhaungzi goes further than either of these thinkers. He would question their emphasis on moral judgment and on salient facts, aspects, or concerns, for these notions require the kind of conceptualization and distinction making that he considers undesirable.

Zhuangzi not only rejects the idea that we can generate a clear distinction between right and wrong through a proper understanding of virtue; he considers the very attempt to do so an indication that one has failed to understand it. In the first place, he denies that there *is* a firm distinction that can be conceptually clarified. Zhuangzi's view is expressed by his character Wang Ni: "The way I see it, the rules of benevolence and righteousness and the paths of right and

19. Zhuangzi, "The Sign of Virtue Complete (Section 5)," in *The Complete Works of Chuang Tzu*, 73–74.

20. See, for example, Rosalind Hursthouse, "Virtue Theory and Abortion," *Philosophy and Public Affairs* 20 (1991): 223–246; Michael Slote, *From Morality to Virtue* (New York: Oxford University Press, 1992); and J. B. Schneewind, "The Misfortunes of Virtue," *Ethics* 101 (1990): 42–63.

21. See Jonathan Dancy, "Ethical Particularism," *Mind* 1011/368 (1983): 530–547, and John McDowell, "Virtue and Reason," *The Monist* 62 (1979): 331–350. Opposition to universal moral rules or precepts also has earlier precedents in the West, in the views of such figures as Aristo of Chios and Nietzsche, for example.

wrong are all hopelessly snarled and jumbled."[22] The *Dao* in general cannot be captured in definite rules and formulas; accordingly, neither can the virtue of any entity within the *Dao*.

Zhuangzi's negative characterization of virtue depends on rejecting the activity of distinction making on which an account of right and wrong depends.[23] The person who is characterized by *wuwei* behaves appropriately, responding to the situation that he or she apprehends through undistorted perception. Rules that formulate which actions are right and which wrong interfere with such perception, for they urge one to judge what one perceives in accordance with preconceived ideas. Contrary to the Confucian tradition's characterizations, Zhuangzi presents Confucius as warning against any such definite rules. Zhuangzi's Confucius praises a man he considers a sage and comments, "A man like this doesn't know what his ears or eyes should approve—he lets his mind play in the harmony of virtue."[24] This sage is virtuous, in other words, because he does not confine his mind with categories but spontaneously responds to the world, which he perceives without interference.

Zhuangzi's Lord of the North River similarly contends, "It is impossible to establish any constant rule."[25] "Do not strive to unify your actions, or you will

22. Chuang Tzu, "Discussion on Making All Things Equal (Section 2)," in *The Complete Works of Chuang Tzu*, 46.

23. Perhaps Zhuangzi's rejection of principles of right and wrong as determinants of action accounts for the impression many Westerners have that Daoist virtue is concerned with something other than morality. A. C. Graham, for example, considers the Daoist program to be fundamentally epistemological rather than moral.

[I]f like Chuang-tzu we sweep away all moral and prudential standards, certainly "Respond with awareness" will remain in force. Nothing is involved after all but preferring intelligence to stupidity, reality to illusion; of the traditional Western values, Truth, Good, and Beauty, only the first is assumed. (A. C. Graham, "Taoist Spontaneity, 'Is,' and 'Ought,'" in *Experimental Essays on Chuang-Tzu*, ed. Victor H. Mair, Asian Studies at Hawaii Series [Honolulu: University of Hawaii Press, 1983], 12.)

Roger Ames, by contrast, describes *wuwei* as primarily aesthetic rather than moral.

Wuwei describes a productively creative relatedness. *Wuwei* activity "characterizes"—that is, produces the character or ethos of—an aesthetically contrived composition. There is no ideal, no closed perfectedness. Ongoing creative achievement itself provides novel possibilities for a richer creativity. *Wuwei* activity is thus fundamentally qualitative: an aesthetic category and only derivatively, an ethical one. (Roger T. Ames, introduction to *Wandering at Ease in the Zhuangzi*, 8.)

Many have also read Zhuangzi as a moral relativist. For an account of the debates on this point, see P. J. Ivanhoe, "Was Zhuangzi a Relativist?" in *Essays on Skepticism, Relativism, and Ethics in the Zhuangzi*, ed. Paul Kjellberg and P. J. Ivanhoe (Albany: State University of New York Press, 1996), 196–214. Ivanhoe takes the view that Zhuangzi was not a moral relativist. He also claims that the Zhuangzi offers "considerable resources . . . for those seeking to develop a pluralistic ethic of human flourishing" (211), a view which I certainly endorse.

24. Chuang Tzu, "The Sign of Virtue Complete (Section 5)," 69.

25. Chuang Tzu, "Autumn Floods (Section 17)," in *The Complete Works of Chuang Tzu*, 180.

be at sixes and sevens with the Way!"[26] "What should you do and what should you not do? Everything will change of itself, that is certain!"[27] Efforts to conform to definite standards require that one understand one's situation in terms of pre-established categories. Such understanding may be conceptually consistent, but it will not maintain its connection with the Dao.

One should be cautious even in characterizing certain actions as virtuous, and one should certainly not do so categorically. Ruo (Jo) of the North Sea observes, "From the point of view of the Way, what is noble or what is mean? These are merely what are called endless changes."[28] Zhuangzi reports on a conversation he had with his friend and mentor, the eminent logician Huizi. Huizi, true to his penchant for clear distinctions, wants to know why Zhuangzi describes a sage as having no feelings. Zhuangzi explains, "When I talk about having no feelings, I mean that a man doesn't allow likes or dislikes to get in and do him harm. He just lets things be the way they are and doesn't try to help life along."[29] Elsewhere Zhuangzi has Confucius contend, "Discard goodness and goodness will come of itself."[30] The goodness to be discarded is the conception of goodness. Like all set conceptions, this "goodness" attracts attention and deflects one's openness to new perceptions. If one gets rid of such pre-conceived notions, one's perceptions will enable one to be really virtuous.

Zhuangzi's virtue is that of the virtuoso: it is concerned with consummate performance.[31] Formulated rules interfere with such performance, particularly if one keeps them prominently in mind. We might compare scripted virtue to scripted interpersonal conversations. Imagine a person who wants to ask the boss for a raise and rehearses a set speech for this purpose. Upon actually seeing the boss, even if the time and place were appropriate for such a request, this person would create a bad impression if his or her words seemed too rehearsed. So much the worse if the person disregarded indications that the time and place were not appropriate. The person who attempts pre-formulated virtue or "good action" regardless of the circumstances is a bit like the person so committed to his request speech that he forges ahead with it even after hearing that the boss has just been informed of a family emergency. Though asking for a raise may have been a good idea when the person first considered it, it is not at this mo-

26. Ibid., 181.
27. Ibid., 182.
28. Ibid., 181.
29. Chuang Tzu, "The Sign of Virtue Complete (Section 5)," 75–76.
30. Chuang Tzu, "External Things (Section 26)," in *The Complete Works of Chuang Tzu*, 299.
31. See Peter Hershock's account of Ch'an Buddhism's emphasis on virtuosic performance in Peter D. Hershock, *Liberating Intimacy: Enlightenment and Social Virtuosity in Ch'an Buddhism* (Albany: State University of New York Press, 1996).

ment, and it is a particularly poor idea to force the issue with a script that can make no adjustment to circumstances.

Zhuangzi even objects to garden-variety names for virtues insofar as these terms are used to designate standard guideposts to regulate behavior. He presents a conversation between Yi Erzi (Yi Erh-tzu) and Xu You (Hsü Yu), a famous recluse. The recluse asks Yi Erzi what the emperor has been offering by way of assistance.

> Yi Erh-tzu said, "Yao told me, 'You must learn to practice benevolence and righteousness and to speak clearly about right and wrong!'"
> "Then why come to see *me?*" said Hsü Yu., "Yao has already tattooed you with benevolence and righteousness and cut off your nose with right and wrong. Now how do you expect to go wandering in any far-away, carefree, and as-you-like-it paths?"[32]

Tattooing and cutting off one's nose were common punishments in ancient China. The recluse is claiming that what Yi Erzi describes as the emperor's assistance has effectively been punishment, in that it violates the integrity of one's body. Zhuangzi's reclusive character is claiming that set standards of virtue and of right and wrong, even those offered by a benevolent ruler, do violence to one's original nature, which is attuned and responsive to the *Dao*. Carefree or "free and easy" wandering is a recurrent metaphor in Zhuangzi for the lifestyle of the person characterized by *wuwei*, for such a person is carried by the currents of the *Dao* in directions that are not predictable.[33] Formulaic virtues are, in effect, their own punishment. They are false virtues that interfere with the truly joyous and efficacious life.

Besides contradicting the idea of using virtue to generate a sharp distinction between right and wrong, Zhuangzi's understanding of virtue contrasts with a second prominent concern in current discussions of virtue. Contemporary philosophers often describe virtuous behavior as being praiseworthy and vicious behavior as being blameworthy. The tendency to correlate virtue and vice with praise and blame is long-standing in the Western tradition. Aristotle uses the argument that the virtues and vices cannot be passions because we are praised and

---

32. Chuang Tzu, "The Great and Venerable Teacher (Section 6)," in *The Complete Works of Chuang Tzu*, 89.

33. The first section of the Zhuangzi is entitled, in Watson's translation, "Free and Easy Wandering" (Watson). Victor H. Mair translates the title as "Carefree Wandering" in *Wandering on the Way: Early Taoist Tales and Parables of Chuang Tzu*, trans. Victor H. Mair (Honolulu: University of Hawaii Press, 1994). A. C. Graham translates it as "Going Rambling without a Destination," in *Chuang-Tzu, The Inner Chapters*, trans. and ed. A. C. Graham (Indianapolis: Hackett, 1989).

blamed for virtues and vices, but not for the passions.[34] Hume contends that to recognize virtue is to feel a particular type of satisfaction in contemplating a character, and that this feeling "constitutes our praise or admiration."[35]

By contrast, Zhuangzi opposes characterization of virtue in terms of praise and blame, or of being admirable. According to Zhuangzi, such terms emphasize a point of view within the external world, while virtue requires attunement with the present configuration of energies flowing into one's own situation. Praise and blame are irrelevant to virtue, and they are even harmful, in that they encourage the potential agent to act deliberately in such ways that prompt encomiums. Zhuangzi's predilection for handicapped protagonists reflects his rejection of standards of praise and blame, for in his time a person lacking a hand or a foot was typically suspected of having been mutilated by the civil authorities as punishment for some crime. Zhuangzi insinuates that those marked by blame may well be sages. Blame only hinders us from seeing this.

Third, Zhuangzi's account of virtue contrasts with Western efforts (such as those of Slote and Michael Stocker[36]) to ascribe virtue to particular acts on the basis of their motives. Zhuangzi's *wuwei,* to the extent that it is compatible with a notion of behavior, involves motive-less behavior, at least if we limit our sense of "motives" to the intentions of the conscious person. Zhuangzi's account does not require intention as a key to the behavior of a virtuous person. Perception itself, when combined with *wuwei,* results in spontaneous action. In this respect, Zhuangzi resembles Plato's Socrates in considering knowledge to be virtue (although we must keep in mind that Zhuangzi's sense of knowledge is neither conceptual nor rational). An advantage to Zhuangzi's account of virtue, perhaps, is that *akrasia* defined as acting against what one perceives as appropriate is ruled out.[37] If a person exemplifies *wuwei,* the distinction between perception and motivation is collapsed.

Besides these ways in which Zhuangzi rejects approaches that are currently prominent, he takes interesting stances on a number of other issues within contemporary virtue ethics, concerning, for example, (1) the unity of the virtues and (2) whether the virtues are eudaemonistic. Zhuangzi does propose a conception of virtue that is unified, in that the fully virtuous person acts completely in accordance with the *Dao,* which includes the tendencies of his or her own nature

34. *Nicomachean Ethics,* 1105b, l. 30.
35. David Hume, *A Treatise of Human Nature,* ed. L. A. Selby-Bigge (Oxford: Clarendon, 1975), bk. 3, sec. 2, 471.
36. See, for example, Michael Stocker, "The Schizophrenia of Modern Ethical Theories," *Journal of Philosophy* 73 (1976): 453–466.
37. Those who think that *akrasia* obviously does occur in real life might consider this a disadvantage. But Zhuangzi agrees with Plato that apparent *akrasia* is actually an indication that one lacks genuine knowledge (although their conceptions of knowledge differ).

at any given moment. However, specific virtues drop out of consideration when this ideal is achieved (and Zhuangzi questions the desirability of cataloguing virtues in any case). There is no room for *wuwei* to conflict with other competing virtues in one's behavior. The person characterized by *wuwei* allows the flow of present energies to act through him as it will. Thus the precondition for internal conflicts of virtues—incompatible objectives or inconsistency of manner—is lacking.

The Daoist image of the Uncarved Block (representing the original nature to which the virtuous person has returned) reflects the lack of multiple aspects that might contradict one another. Zhuangzi's premise is that one's original nature is internally harmonious and in equilibrium with the environment. One experiences conflict as a result of either embracing goals that rigidify one's responses or of imposing concepts on one's context that are alien to it.[38] The achievement of *wuwei* restores equilibrium between the person and the environment, for it involves attuning oneself with the prevailing tendencies of the *Dao*. Zhuangzi's Confucius summarizes, "Virtue is the establishment of perfect harmony. Though virtue takes no form, things cannot break away from it."[39]

To the question of whether the virtues are eudaemonistic, Zhuangzi would say yes and no. Living well or flourishing are front and center, but one's inherent nature is what thrives. This achievement is particularistic, both in the sense that one's nature is specific to oneself and that its manifestation is spontaneous only insofar as it is attuned with the larger dynamic of the environment at a given moment. Zhuangzi's virtue is not eudaemonistic in the sense of objective fulfillment, understood as a common standard for *the* good life. In this sense, Zhuangzi is not an Aristotelian.

These contrasts may make Zhuangzi's ethics seem rather distant from the concerns to of those who are currently theorizing about virtue ethics. *Wuwei* and the conception of the good life that it presupposes may also sound alien to Western virtue ethicists for another reason. When I first presented this paper, one auditor dismissed *wuwei* as offering support for such practices as footbinding. This strikes me as an extremely unfair accusation, since it seems to judge a culture's ideal of virtue on the basis of whether or not all actual practices in the culture are virtuous. Sadly, there is a gap between ethical aspiration and actual behavior in every culture. The fact that no ethical ideal is perfectly instantiated by the culture that developed it does not offer a prima facie case that its ethical ideals are no good.

38. See Hall and Ames, *Thinking from the Han*, 48. Hall and Ames observe that Chinese thought generally does not consider the self to be internally conflicted.
39. Chuang Tzu, "The Sign of Virtue complete (Section 5)," 74.

This criticism also fails to acknowledge that Daoism was not the only source of ethical standards in China. Confucianism and Buddhism also offered ethical guidance within the Chinese tradition, sometimes guidance that conflicted with Daoist ethical thought. One would need to examine Chinese ethics more generally and to isolate the Daoist strand to establish the extent of its influence on cultural practice. Even if one could judge the soundness of ethical ideals on the basis of whether people lived up to them, the practice of footbinding would not reflect on Daoist ethics as such. In the first place, footbinding only became a common practice in China many centuries after Zhuangzi's text was written.[40] Second, footbinding directly clashes with Daoist ethical aspirations. Zhuangzi and the *Dao De Jing* both encourage one to follow nature and to avoid artificial practices that distort it. They challenge any fashionable practice that damages one's health, no matter how widely accepted or authoritatively prescribed.

Perhaps the concern voiced in the objection, however, is not footbinding or any other *particular* practice. It may instead be that Daoism encourages passivity, and that it does not have the resources to object to any practice whatever, since it proposes as virtue a stance of going with the flow. If so, the criticism still misses the mark. This objection does not do justice to the prescriptive character of Daoist texts, including the *Zhuangzi*. Zhuangzi is not a moral relativist. He endorses behavior that accords with nature—one's own nature and that of one's environment—and he strenuously opposes behavior that does not. How one ascertains what is natural is another question; but Zhuangzi clearly makes non-relativistic moral prescriptions.

What might mislead one into thinking that Zhuangzi has no basis for criticizing any behavior is that he is a moral particularist. He objects to generalizing from cases to fixed rules, and this may sound like openness to any course of behavior whatsoever. We should keep in mind, however, that Zhuangzi's ethical ideals presuppose the value of flourishing in attunement with nature. This value, coupled with perception of one's immediate situation, yields clear insight into appropriate behavior. It does not imply that it does not matter what one does.

Zhuangzi himself expresses strong views about good and bad ways of behaving. His insistence on flexibility reflects his views about what mental stances and habits will interfere with clear perception of one's real situation. He stresses that language, which involves the use of stable markers to represent things that are changing, inherently distorts reality by representing the dynamic as static and by classifying idiosyncratic particulars through general terms. Accordingly, we must recognize these limitations of the language that we use even while using it. Although Zhuangzi, like all language users, makes statements that sound like sta-

---

40. My thanks to Eric Hutton for drawing this to my attention.

ble generalizations, he stresses that any such generalities fall short of the mark with regard to one's actual situation.

Only by cultivating one's sensitivity to the nuances of changing circumstances can one overcome the distorting crudeness of linguistic categories. Hence, Zhuangzi's ethics are focused on the means by which one can develop this sensitivity. His promotion of flexibility is directed at cultivating sensitivity and undermining habits. Zhuangzi does not favor the kind of flexibility that enables one to rationalize anything—indeed, Zhuangzi is convinced that the tendency to rationalize is one of the habits that one should overcome through developing one's responsiveness.

To those who consider precise moral formulas the only safeguard against rationalizing, Zhuangzi counters that such formulas are often the tools of rationalizing. Moreover, they are not ethically practical. Precision in formulating principles of right and wrong will not close the gap between unvarying abstract formulations and the subtly shifting dynamics of actual life, for which varying responses are appropriate. Although Zhuangzi describes types of behavior (particularly types that by definition further or counter one's health and responsiveness), he always does so with the caveat that principles regarding action-types have only the status of rules of thumb.[41]

Western thinkers may still find the idea of simply allowing nature to work through oneself to be alarmingly passive and an evasion of responsibility. If so, they are probably operating with a more autonomous conception of the self than Zhuangzi's. The person who plays music with the feeling that something larger than the individual is operating is paradigmatic of someone flowing with the *Dao*. One's identity is not separate from the flow of reality, but instead it finds its effectiveness through this flow. The conception of "putting things in God's hands" is a common Western notion that resembles the idea of attuning oneself to the *Dao* (except that God is usually considered to be transcendent, while the *Dao* is immanent within our world). Is the religious person who takes this attitude toward his or her experience adopting a stance of passivity to the point of being unable to resist any perceived evil? Such a religiously interpreted Western outlook would not seem to have any advantages over Zhuangzi's ethics regarding the potential to counter harmful developments in one's world.

In fact, one's ability to counter such developments is enhanced by attuning one's energies to those of the larger world. One responds more appropriately and effectively the more one's energies are coordinated with the energies of the environment. To make a banal comparison, one drives well when one is atten-

41. Seneca makes a similar point in a letter. See Lucius Anneus Seneca. *Letter from a Stoic: Epistulae Morales ad Lucilium,* trans. George Long (New York: Viking, 1969), 22.7–8. He proposes that virtue is situation-specific. From a Stoic point of view, he insists, determination is good in cases in which it is worth the effort and does not require any base behavior, but not in other circumstances.

tive to those other beings and machines that are moving nearby. To drive without a penumbral awareness of everything moving around one is both dangerous and exhausting. Indeed, one may eventually be altogether prevented from moving forward by such inattention, for it can lead to a collision. Far from being passive, the driver who is attuned and responsive to the flow of other traffic is much more effective as a driver than one who is not.

On the other hand, the configuration of energies within one's immediate situation may dictate that a particular course of behavior cannot be efficacious at the moment. This may lead one to conclude, for example, that a given strategy for resistance to something should not be pursued just then. To return to the example of the driver, the driver who is stuck in traffic is not a more efficient driver if he or she remains bent on going forward at that moment. This driver is not adjusting to the current situation, which calls for waiting until the drivers in front depress their accelerators.

Those who contend that Zhuangzi's approach is incompatible with intervening in one's situation should also note that Zhuangzi's text does, in fact, depict characters making interventions to improve circumstances. For example, Zhangzi himself accepts the request of a prince of Chao to attempt to reason with his father, the king, who is so fond of swordsmanship that he has let every other aspect of his kingdom fall into decline. In order to be more persuasive, Zhuangzi abandons the attire of a scholar and puts on a swordsman's costume before confronting the king. Zhuangzi is prepared to fight with the swordsmen the king has gathered, but he persuades the king that to prefer such bouts among swordsmen is to choose a lesser kind of swordsmanship over a greater. The result is that the king abandons his addiction to such spectacles.[42] In another passage, Zhuangzi's Confucius stops his student Yan Hui from going to remonstrate with a king who is not ruling with sufficient concern for his people. Confucius tells Yan Hui that he has not yet cultivated himself sufficiently. The remainder of the section involves Confucius instructing Yan Hui on how he should go about self-cultivation, presumably as a preliminary to such political intervention as Yan Hui has in mind.[43] The point is not that one should not try to be politically effective, but that Daoist cultivation is the most powerful means for doing so.[44]

Zhuangzi does, then, have resources for criticizing certain behavior on the basis of the overarching value of healthy participation within the flow of the

42. See Chuang Tzu, "Discoursing on Swords (Section 30)," in *The Complete Works of Chuang Tzu*, 339–343.

43. See Chuang Tzu, "In the World of Men (Section 4)," in *The Complete Works of Chuang Tzu*, 54–58.

44. Along these lines one would do well to consider the martial arts of Japan, which are influenced by Zen Buddhism, derived from a sect of Chinese Buddhism that is itself influenced by Daoism. Zen

Dao. Rather than delineating precise proscriptions, however, he takes the more positive approach to ethics of emphasizing the development of skills that enable one to respond appropriately to one's situation, regardless of how unexpected it is. Clearing one's mind of preconceptions is more important for this purpose than is elaborating a system of well-formulated and mutually consistent statements (themselves preconceptions) about good and bad actions.

I have been considering Zhuangzi's ethical outlook in comparison with contemporary debates within virtue ethics. But is Zhuangzi really a virtue ethicist by current standards? For those who are convinced of the centrality of some of the emphases in contemporary discussion to understanding virtue (e.g. praiseworthiness, practical reason, or the guidance of action), Zhuangzi may seem to be dismissible. However, Zhuangzi's alternative to current formulations of virtue ethics challenges some of our typical presuppositions, raising questions that might refocus our discussion. Is virtue necessarily a matter of imposing rational form on our action? Might it not be a matter of making space for undistorted responsiveness? How does moral virtue relate to what might be seen as the epistemological virtue of perceiving clearly? And how practical is our practical reason? Does action that is "guided" by well formulated theoretical ideas necessarily excel that which is more intuitive? Are we perhaps better guided by anecdote and metaphor than by definitions that delineate the necessary and sufficient conditions for particular virtues?[45] Might the virtues of the free spirit be superior to the virtues of the practical reasoner?

By proposing that the virtue that leads to flourishing is a matter of efficacious performance and simply allowing one's nature to blossom, Zhuangzi suggests that virtue is neither rationalistic nor constraining, nor achieved by being conscientious. Instead, it amounts to a health of one's entire being, an equilibrium with the environment that makes one capable of wandering at ease and of doing nothing at all.[46]

Buddhism, like Daoism, seeks to return the practitioner to a state that is without preconceptions, and the martial arts related to Zen prescribe this as the appropriate stance for the warrior. The rationale is that without preconceptions one will not hesitate in acting responsively to one's opponent. Moreover, one will not attempt to carry out an action according to a plan. Instead, one will directly confront the opponent in accordance with his or her movements. One can then use the opponent's movements, positioning, and even weight to one's own advantage. Effectiveness in these arts is achieved by avoiding scripted strategies and by exploiting the resources of one's immediate situation. For further discussion of this topic, see Graham Parkes, "Ways of Japanese Thinking," in *From Africa to Zen: An Invitation to World Philosophy,* ed. Robert C. Solomon and Kathleen M. Higgins (Lanham, Maryland: Rowman and Littlefield, 1993), 25–53.

45. See Ames, introduction, 8.

46. As a final note, I wish to thank Eric Hutton for his thoughtful and helpful advice on this paper.

CHAPTER 7

Virtue Ethics and Human Development: A Pragmatic Approach

JENNIFER WELCHMAN

1. The Problem

A striking feature of contemporary virtue theory is the near universal tendency to treat moral agents as if they sprang into being as full adults: adults, moreover, who if they sometimes face death (for how else could they display their courage?) never display the incremental decline that comes with the increasingly long lives people today can expect. The virtues most discussed in the literature are traits associated with the middle period of our lives, the period when we possess the means and the opportunity to be just, merciful, or charitable towards others, prudent or temperate with our resources, and honest, vainglorious, or modest about our accomplishments. By contrast, dispositions closely associated with periods of dependency, such as gratitude, loyalty, and trust, however serviceable they may be to ourselves or others, are either ignored outright or grudgingly allowed an inferior status.

This narrow focus on a single period in our lives is understandable in the principle-based ethical theories that are among the continuing legacies of Kantian and high Modern thought. If one presumes that morality is a matter of reasoning from and about moral principles, then naturally the only sorts of agents who matter will be those agents fully competent to perform as autonomous moral reasoners.[1] Principle-based theories have been criticized for the narrowness of their conception of moral personhood, not infrequently by proponents

---

1. Children, psychologically impaired adults, and the declining elderly are interesting, if at all, as "marginal" cases who may present theoretically interesting challenges to moral agents but who are not themselves moral agents.

of character-based approaches. But to judge by the literature, these criticisms have not often been taken to heart. Most virtue theorists give no more serious attention to the development of morally important character traits throughout a lifetime than do their principle-based counterparts.[2] The virtue ethics literature focuses almost exclusively on our early to middle adulthood. The malleability that underpins moral development, so far from being a subject of interested attention, is not infrequently deplored as a sign of weakness or degeneration in a moral agent. Thus virtue theorists usually turn out to be talking about essentially the same group of agents that principle-based theorists do: individual, independent, autonomous adult moral reasoners.

Contemporary virtue theorists are, of course, not alone in this. The classical models on which so many draw treat human development as the realization of an essential human nature. Though Plato, Aristotle, and Cicero themselves give considerable attention to the process by which this self-realization is accomplished, the essentialism of these theorists limits the period of moral agency during which virtues and vices can be possessed almost as severely as do principle-based accounts. For prior to one's mature realization of one's potential character, one either has no character at all or a character not truly one's own. Thus any virtues or functional excellences associated with this early developmental period are either not virtues at all or not truly one's own virtues.[3] And once one has realized one's potential for character and self-development as fully as one is able, further progress is impossible. Henceforth, to change is to regress or degenerate as a person. Again any functional excellences associated specifically with this later stage of life can not properly be called virtues at all or not truly one's own. For anyone approaching middle life, these accounts paint a disturbing picture of one's moral future, even granting the comfortable assumption of these less youth oriented societies that no one can really be called mature before she is fifty.

Contemporary philosophers put the realization of character much earlier and so also the beginning of the rot. Although most reject essentialism, few it seems are confident about the possibility of significant development of character past our early adulthood. Joel Kupperman writes that "people typically have what we would unhesitatingly call characters only when they are past the years of *early* childhood."[4] Gregory Trianosky discusses the case of a "nobly motivated *young*

---

2. There are some notable exceptions to this generalization, but even they will agree that they *are* exceptions.

3. The first are not truly virtues because their value is purely instrumental to the development of adult character (e.g., docility in children); the latter though possibly virtuous, are not truly one's own because one ceases to possess them on reaching maturity (e.g. the "innocence" which does not survive childhood.)

4. Joel Kupperman, *Character*, (New York: Oxford University Press, 1991), 15–16 (emphasis mine).

adult . . . now set in the ways of his childhood," putting the formation of character only slightly later.[5] Similarly, Jonathan Jacobs holds that "there is a difference between having characteristics and having a settled character. The young
person [i.e., a child or an adolescent][6] has characteristics that *may* become fixed,
but there is still plasticity of character that can be shaped by voluntary action"
(20), which suggests that our characters are pretty well settled by our early
twenties.

As I look back over the two decades that have passed since I was in my early
twenties, I find it utterly incredible that however my life may have changed, my
character has not. My closet refutes it. There on the floor are the sensible shoes
I was once convinced I would never wear—in not one but three colors. Twenty
years ago I had no hobbies, unless you were to count reading. Now I drive an-
tique trams—my blue motorman's uniform is just there on the left. Reading
isn't something I have much time for now. Twenty years ago there were no
exercise clothes in my closet, because I threw them away when I escaped manda-
tory school sports. But today I have microfibre t-shirts, leggings, and race-
walking shoes, because knee trouble has recently forced me to give up running.
My closet used to be crammed with the collapsible backpacks, duffle-bags, and
totes that were required for the sort of strenuous travel I favored. Now that I
travel with children, I have enormous suitcases that have to be stored in the base-
ment. Besides, hotel porters are more willing to help with suitcases than they
are with duffle-bags and totes. I could go on, but why bother? I am sure your
own closets tell similar tales. The important question is what we should make
of them.

One might say, "nothing." Your tastes in footwear have changed, so what?
Raising children may change your luggage and your vacation choices, but surely
it does not change your character. Nor do hobbies or exercise. Such incidental
changes are no indication of a change in one's character. But that conclusion
may be premature.

As to the first point, it is not my aesthetic appreciation of shoes that has
changed, it is the value I assign to them. I still think my sensible shoes are un-
attractive. Attractiveness is no longer as important a quality in shoes for me as
it once was. I used to spend my time at school, in libraries, hanging out, going
to clubs. Now, during the day, I stand for hours in lecture halls and after work I
chase toddlers down supermarket aisles or stand at the sidelines of muddy soc-

5. Gregory Trianosky, "Natural Affection and Responsibility for Character: A Critique of Kantian
Views of the Virtues," in *Identity, Character, and Morality*, ed. Owen Flanagan and Amélie Oksenberg Rorty
(Cambridge: MIT Press, 1990), 93–110 (emphasis mine).

6. Jonathan Jacobs, *Choosing Character: Responsibility for Virtue and Vice* (Ithaca: Cornell University
Press, 2001).

cer fields. As to the second, parenting has changed a great deal more than my luggage—for parenting behavior is not easily switched off and on. I find I look at my students with a motherly eye I certainly did not have even ten years ago. And I worry more about them than I used to. Third, I do not read as much now because increasingly I prefer to spend my leisure time in group activities. I started running when a group of neighbors did. I drive trams in part because I enjoy working with the volunteer organization that restores them.

In his latest book, Jacobs claims that "when a person changes for the better in significant ways it can be very difficult to ascertain whether the positive change occurs because conditions are now favorable to bringing out the good that was in him or because he is making dramatically new acknowledgments and re-composing his character."[7] From a pragmatic point of view, the idea that we can possess dispositions to act that are not expressed in our actions (except in extreme and unusual circumstances) is hard to credit. I find it equally hard to credit the idea that a sustained change in a person's behavior is not good evidence of a change in his or her character. If a person's patterns of activity change substantially over time, then the dispositions from which one acts must also have changed. So though my temperament has not altered and I retain many of the same tastes and interests I had in the past, the consortium of predominant dispositions that determine my choices and actions—i.e., my *character*—has changed. The changes have been far from radical. Constancy of temperament and of my social environment assures that. But though incremental, the changes are cumulatively significant. Some of the changes were involuntary, others the effects of deliberate tinkering on my part. And judging by my mother's closet, the process is not over yet.

2. A Deweyan Perspective

This conception of the relation of character and action is one I have taken over from John Dewey. As a pragmatist, Dewey viewed ideas and theories, descriptive and evaluative, as socially constructed instruments for managing human experience. His constructivism was not limited to his understanding of our beliefs, scientific and moral. He also viewed human *character* as largely constructed rather than given. We are biological creatures born with physiological and temperamental traits that are the basic stuff of our development as persons. Development of a functional and well-integrated character out of the multiple and competing drives that constitute our raw human nature is an achievement,

7. *Choosing Character,* 64.

not a given. If you and I are free, autonomous persons who can claim virtues of character, it is not because we were born so but because interaction with others has taught us to reflect upon and to take some control over ourselves and our actions.[8]

Initially most of the credit goes to our social group, whose inculcation of habits of thought, reflection, approval, and disapproval gave us the tools to recognize and reflect upon, and inhibit or reinforce our first-order dispositions and temperamental promptings in accordance with more or less coherent schemes of value. The credit, thereafter, is increasingly our own, as we reflect upon and revise the membership and rank-ordering of the consortium of higher order action guiding dispositions that for Dewey constitute our characters. But the credit never becomes entirely our own. Early socialization leaves enduring legacies for good or ill. And characters are never transparent to their possessors. A Deweyan conception of character does not entail that radial character reform would be easy or frequent. But it does involve commitment to the position that, as he puts it, "conduct and character are strictly correlative."[9] Character traits with no externally observable influence on conduct are traits whose existence we have no business positing. By the same reasoning, since individuals' patterns of conduct vary over time, we have no business positing that character once formed remains constant. These changes are indicators of life-long, if gradual, character change.

Of course, Dewey is not the only possible source for such a view of character. There are other, more or less pragmatic, conceptions around. But what is unique and particularly valuable about Dewey's own theory is the way he integrates his notion of the continuous evolution of character into his conception of human flourishing and of the role of the virtues within it. Unfortunately, his approach has been under-appreciated by moral philosophers, because it is most fully developed in his philosophy of education, especially texts such as *Democracy and Education* and *Education and Experience,* and not in his better known contributions to moral philosophy, such as *Human Nature and Conduct* or *Ethics.*[10]

---

8. The reflection required need not involve a particularly high degree of abstraction, conceptual analysis, or articulation of one's ideas. Simple "pattern-matching" comparisons between my own behavior and the behavior of those I admire can be sufficient to show me whether I am or am not characteristically acting admirably or poorly and to show how I may reform my character. Adolescents are clearly capable of this sort of self-reflection and evaluation. So are many pre-adolescent children.

9. As a rule, he says, we may think of our characters and our conduct as "morally the same thing, taken first as effect and then as [the] casual and productive factor." John Dewey, *Ethics* (1932), vol. 7 of *Later Works* (Carbondale: Southern Illinois University Press), 172–173. But although every act says *something* about us, it's clearly not going to be the case that all acts will be directly traceable to nor revealing of the dispositions most central to our characters.

10. In fact, the latter are quite deliberately discouraging. Like most philosophers in the first half of the twentieth century, Dewey associated virtue theory with classical and Christian perfectionist theories. When he discussed the virtues at all, it was usually only to critique perfectionist accounts of value and human nature.

The reasons for this were twofold. First, Dewey feared that virtue language was so inextricably linked with classical or theological perfectionist theories as to be unsalvageable by post-Darwinian naturalistic philosophies. Second, despite his resistance to twentieth-century philosophy's linguistic turn, his own moral philosophy became preoccupied with many of the same issues of the language, logic, and ontology of morals that everywhere were pushing questions of character to the periphery of philosophical debate.

The situation was different in educational circles. Progressive era educational reformers had seized upon Rousseau's notions of education as a basis for reforming public schools. Traditional schools, they argued, distorted child development, because they interfered with the natural unfolding of the child's latent potential. Though a critic of traditional education himself, Dewey could not let what he considered to be a misappropriation of Rousseau go unopposed. In his responses, he began to work out the basis for a pragmatic conception of character and the virtues.

In *Democracy and Education* and *Education and Experience*,[11] Dewey argues for recognition of continual growth as a sine-qua-non of a "good" or meaningful life. "Our net condition is that life is development and that development, growing, is life. Translated into its educational equivalents, that means (1) that the educational process has no end beyond itself, it is its own end; and that (2) the educational process is one of continual reorganizing, reconstructing, and transforming."[12] However we define human flourishing, Dewey reasons, we must recognize that human beings change profoundly over time as do the physical and social environments in which they operate. Thus there is no particular condition or state of affairs that will constitute flourishing for any person throughout their lives. Flourishing and its requirements inevitably change over time. If we are to flourish, we must continually be able to adapt our dispositions to our perpetually shifting circumstances. As early as 1897, Dewey was pointing out to educators that "it is impossible to foretell definitely just what civilization will be twenty years from now. Hence it is impossible to prepare the child for any precise set of conditions."[13] Nor can one tell what anyone's abilities, interests, opportunities, or resources will be twenty years hence. Peter Pan could step out of time and live in an endless present. We cannot. Our dispositions, resources, and abilities are not static. The question is whether we are content simply to change as circumstances dictate or whether we prefer to grow.

Dewey defines growth as the development of new interests and abilities that

11. John Dewey, *Democracy and Education: An Introduction to the Philosophy of Education* (1916; New York: The Free Press, 1944); *Experience and Education* (New York: Macmillan, 1938).

12. *Democracy and Education*, 50.

13. "My Pedagogical Creed," in *Early Works of John Dewey, 1882–1898*, ed. Jo Ann Boydston (1895–1898; Carbondale: Southern Illinois University Press, 1972), 5:84–95.

can take the place of or transform failing interests or abilities over time. Growth differs from mere change in that it is a directed transformation, development, or reconstruction of abilities, interests, and activities. As such, growth is desirable as a means of promoting flourishing for oneself and others. But it is more—it is desirable for its own sake. Thus growth, he argues, is the key to flourishing.

Although the claim that growth is desirable is hardly new, Dewey argues, it has in the past almost invariably be misinterpreted. In educational theory,

> Our tendency [is] to take immaturity as mere lack, and growth as something which fills up the gap between the immature and the mature . . . We treat it simply as privation because we are measuring it by adulthood as a fixed standard.[14]

That is, growth is treated as a process of a development that ends on arrival at a state called "maturity." Once maturity is reached, growth is over—we can only regress or decay. Dewey agrees that when we cease to grow, our character and welfare do begin to decline. What he rejects is the idea that we reach a point beyond which further growth is unnecessary or undesirable. Thus, he writes:

> Normal child and normal adult alike, in other words, are engaged in growth. The difference between them is not the difference between growth and no growth but between the modes of growth appropriate to different conditions. . . . we may say the child should be growing in manhood. With respect to sympathetic curiosity, unbiased responsiveness, and openness of mind, we may say that the adult should be growing in childlikeness. One statement is as true as the other.[15]

Normal adults can continue to grow in this sense, that is, to develop, reconstruct, and transform their interests and abilities and thus the contents of their closets. But the natural and spontaneous pre-dispositions that support growth in children seem to wither away unless they are deliberately cultivated in later life. Dewey identifies these capacities as the child's natural *dependence* and *plasticity*. He notes that "it sounds absurd to hear *dependence* spoken of as something positive, still more absurd as a power."[16] And it sounds equally absurd to speak of *plasticity* as a "power."[17] But Dewey insists that the child's psychological *dependence* is not mere helplessness. It is a set of powers to elicit and maintain assistance in growing by encouraging and rewarding social interaction.[18] Similarly the *plasticity* on

---

14. Ibid., 42.
15. Ibid., 50.
16. Ibid., 42.
17. Ibid., 44.
18. Adults are often said to "fall in love" with their children, as if the children were purely passive

which growth depends is not simply malleability. It involves powers to respond constructively to internal and external changes. *Dependence* and *plasticity* are thus complexes of capacities, interests and dispositions to act, more or less spontaneous in children, that must nevertheless be cultivated to foster ongoing personal growth.

3: The Implications:

Dewey does not analyze these powers or abilities much further. But we can begin to do so for ourselves by asking which dispositions or interests, especially pronounced in children, seem to make the greatest contribution to their growth as persons. We must remember that these will not necessarily be traits that make children appear "good" in their elder's eyes, i.e., docility, obedience, or quietness.[19] Actively growing and changing beings are often unpredictable and so more difficult to manage than we might like. But from the child's point of view, the characteristics making them difficult to raise may turn out to be the most desirable. If, moreover, these traits, so desirable for their contribution to the child's growth, are also desirable in themselves, then these will be plausible candidates for recognition as virtues of plasticity and dependence.

Of course, the virtues of our minority would not be virtues proper according to classical theories of the virtue. For example, Aristotle remarks, "The child is imperfect, and therefore obviously his virtue is not relative to himself alone, but to the perfect man and to his teacher."[20] To be specific, their worth is relative to their tendency to help us achieve the virtues of our majority, i.e., courage, benevolence, temperance, justice, et cetera. To have any further need of the traits that help us develop, the virtues would indicate arrested development. As Aristotle says of the feeling of shame, "we think it right for young people to be prone to shame since they live by feeling and hence often go astray, but are restrained by shame . . . No one, by contrast, would praise an older person for readiness to feel disgrace, since we think it wrong for him to do any action that causes a feeling of disgrace."[21] Because the virtues of minor children are virtues spe-

---

beneficiaries of the process. In fact, children devote enormous energy to cultivating their parents' and other adult's attention and support with smiles, giggles, hugs, demands to "look at me," "play with me," "let me help," and so forth. By these means, children transform their own growth into a social project whose success rewards their care-givers as well as themselves.

19. Nor, for obvious reasons, will these be traits that adults are prone to find charming in children, such as innocence or *naïveté*.

20. See Aristotle, *Politics*, in *The Basic Works of Aristotle*, ed. Richard McKeon, trans. Benjamin Jowett (New York: Random House, 1941), [1260a] 1145.

21. See Aristotle, *Nicomachean Ethics*, trans. Terence Irwin (Indianapolis: Hackett Publishing, 1985), [1128b].

cific to *minority*—he views them as precursors to virtues rather than virtues themselves.

Indeed if they were not outgrown, the virtues of minority might even undermine the virtues of majority, precisely *because* the former promote growth and change. If a virtue proper is the stable realization of a mature human disposition, then traits fostering continual change threaten our virtues. Dispositions and interests that keep us plastic and interdependent beyond childhood are weaknesses to be overcome, not strengths to be encouraged. Thus for Aristotle, it is virtuous to be benevolent, but not to inspire benevolence in others. It is virtuous to have cause for self-esteem, but not to have cause to esteem others. And it is virtuous to be trustworthy in the face of danger, but not to be trusting.[22]

Although his reasons would differ, David Hume would have been no less quick to reject the virtues of minority as virtues proper. Hume holds any disposition or ability to be a virtue if it is customarily either useful or immediately agreeable to its possessor or other people. But Hume's broad definition rests in part on his denial of the traditional distinction between natural abilities as involuntary attributes and dispositions as acquired traits: "it being," he claims, "almost impossible for the mind to change its character in any considerable article."[23] If character is unchangeable, then the minor virtues cannot customarily be useful or agreeable for promoting life-long character development. Any esteem or approbation associated with such traits must have some other source. For Hume, then, as for Aristotle, the denial of value or importance to the traits that make us plastic or interdependent appears to arise solely from presuppositions about the nature and extent of character development—presuppositions which we have little reason to share.

A pantheon of what I shall call our *minor virtues* will thus differ significantly from more traditional pantheons, classical or modern. But which dispositions will it include? It would be impossible in the space available to present and defend any set of dispositions as complete or definitive. For the moment, I will just suggest seven likely candidates: curiosity, playfulness, confidence, sympathy, trust, gratitude, and loyalty. All arise more or less spontaneously in children, though most must be cultivated to become significant ingredients in their characters.

---

22. Aristotle not only denies that childish traits can be virtues, he denies that children possess virtues at all—a denial common from *Nicomachean Ethics* on through such recent texts as Christine McKinnon's *Character, Virtue Theories, and the Vices* (Peterborough: Broadview, 1999). His objection goes directly to the plasticity of children's characters. Children are incapable of the voluntary cultivation of virtues necessary to make them true virtues, Aristotle thinks, in part because they are so plastic and changeable. None of their choices are sufficiently "firm and unchangeable" to count. McKinnon agrees, describing children as possessing "personalities" rather than moral characters (62).

23. David Hume, *A Treatise of Human Nature*, ed. L. A. Selby-Bigge and P.H. Nidditch, 2nd ed. (Oxford: Oxford University Press, 1978), 608.

Each may be said to foster growth in at least one of the two ways Dewey mentions, i.e., in keeping us plastic and/or interdependent in desirable ways. And each is arguably valuable in itself to its possessor as well as instrumentally. Indeed, each is arguably of greater value to its possessor than are any one of the traditional virtues of majority.

Major virtues such as courage, prudence, and benevolence are not, upon reflection, dispositions we want highly developed in children. Courage in the face of threats to life and limb is not desirable in children and not only because children, especially younger children, lack the phronesis required to make wise choices about what risks to accept and for which sorts of projects. It is also because the sorts of projects that warrant serious risks are adults' projects and not the business of children to care for.[24] Confidence in the future serves children better than courage in facing the challenges of education and growth. Prudence is a virtue in adults, but like courage it is not particularly desirable in children. Prudence in a child suggests an inappropriate close-mindedness to the new and untried.[25] Curiosity and playfulness foster development better than prudent husbandry of existing skills or enjoyments.

Even benevolence seems out of place in young children, and again, not simply because children lack the capacity to make wise decisions about others' wants and needs. Benevolence is a disposition to devote one's resources or one's efforts to others. But children lack resources they can devote to others. And all their efforts are required for well-rounded growth. Wise parents take care to exhibit benevolence in ways children can comprehend. But they focus on cultivating children's natural but impulsive sympathetic responsiveness to others into the more stable and reliable sympathy that is a sine qua non of a truly benevolent character.

We approve and encourage children's trust in others, especially adults. Trust is essential for cooperation, which a child needs to grow physically and psychologically.[26] But we also encourage trust (and the sense of security that goes with it) as desirable in itself. Mistrustfulness, we think, can poison a child's experience of interaction with others. We try to inculcate the virtues of beneficiaries—gratitude and loyalty—by which children can reward and positively reinforce their benefactors.[27] We do this not simply for their respective instru-

24. It is not because children make bad soldiers that we deplore the use of child soldiers. Children make excellent soldiers. We deplore it because we understand that soldiering, however noble the cause, unmakes children, morally and spiritually.

25. For a discussion of the dependence of such virtues to the agent's age and state of development, see Michael Slote, *Goods and Virtues* (Oxford: Oxford University Press, 1983).

26. On trust, including trust in children, see Annette Baier's "Trusting People," in *Moral Prejudices: Essays on Ethics* (Cambridge: Harvard University Press, 1995).

27. Neither loyalty nor gratitude figures importantly in traditional pantheons of the virtues. For reviews of recent discussions of the claims of either to be virtues, see respectively Jennifer Welchman, "The

mental values, but also because they are agreeable in themselves. Beneficiaries can suffer from feelings of inferiority in relation to their benefactors, if they feel unable to make a return (as Aristotle's disdain for gratitude and loyalty attest). To be genuinely grateful or genuinely loyal is to have a happy appreciation of others' beneficial influence over one's life and character that acknowledges and honors beneficence, thus supporting rather than detracting from self-esteem.

What curiosity, playfulness, sympathy, confidence, trust, gratitude, and loyalty do for children, they also do for adults. Curiosity and sympathy for others fosters the redeployment and transformation of goals, projects, and purposes that prevent physical aging and decline from entailing the decline of meaningful activities. Trust in others and confidence in the future help us to face discouragement in learning new skills. Gratitude and loyalty make us fit companions of the colleagues and family who support our endeavors.

Some may nevertheless feel a mistake is being made, that although loyalty or gratitude, curiosity, or trust may make one better in performing specific social roles, they do not make one better as a person. Loyalty, it may be argued, makes one a better colleague, but is a better colleague necessarily a better person? Curious people are more likely to prove entertaining and informative dinner guests, but surely one could be a bore and be none the worse for it as a person? Sympathy is both useful and agreeable in doctors, lawyers, and other professionals whose services one may employ, but it is no guarantee that they are in other respects admirable people. Confidence is always an attractive quality but are there not diffident, self-deprecating people who have excellent characters despite their lack of confidence?

What seems to underlie all such questions is a common but often unstated presumption that to function well socially is somehow peripheral to one's functioning as a person. Human sociality is treated as if it were just another instrumentality we have developed to help us overcome material obstacles to our species' survival; another artifact like stone tools, irrigation, or electric lights. But sociality is not an human artifact, it is our nature. We are incapable of leading flourishing lives that are not focused around active social relationships. Social interaction is as necessary to our flourishing as food or shelter. Thus it is no surprise to learn from sociologists that two-thirds of the conversations of people in every walk of life, including university professors, are devoted to social gossip. We are unendingly fascinated with the minutiae of social interaction. Depression and anxiety are predictable results of the failure or create and maintain good working social relationships.[28]

Virtues of Stewardship," *Environmental Ethics* 21 (1999): 411–423; and Christopher Heath Wellman, "Gratitude as a Virtue," *Pacific Philosophical Quarterly* 80 (1999): 284–300.

28. Even cloistered, celibate, inhabitants of religious orders are in relationships with one another and

We are all familiar these days with the expression, "use it or lose it." We know we stand to lose physical fitness and well-being if we do not use our bodies as nature designed them to be used. We did not evolve in environments that favored sedentary lifestyles combined with high calorie diets. To ignore this is to risk health problems that can seriously reduce the quality of one's later life. Increasingly, it seems that "use it or lose it" also applies to our mental flourishing. If we fail to develop substantial mental skills and abilities in early life or fail to cultivate and maintain these skills afterwards, we are at greater risk of developing serious cognitive impairments later in life, impairments that threat our quality of life.[29]

Happily for us, this means philosophers are not predisposed to developing dementia—whatever non-philosophers may suppose—given the high-levels of early education most of us have had. And since philosophers usually engage in what occupational psychologists consider "cognitively demanding jobs," we are at less risk still. Studies of people with cognitively demanding occupations suggest they retain greater intellectual flexibility into later life than others in less demanding situations. But it is extremely important to understand what makes our work "cognitively demanding," for it may not be the features that most readily come to mind.

To quote one researcher: "the more diverse the stimuli, the greater the number of decisions required, the greater the number of considerations to be taken into account in making these decisions, and the more ill defined and apparently contradictory the contingencies" together with the degree of "self-direction" involved, the more demanding the work environment.[30] Cognitively demanding jobs are not necessarily jobs that require higher education. Supervision of other people by contrast, whether the work is skilled or unskilled, may rate as highly cognitively demanding. Jobs requiring a high-degree of self-direction in

order their lives around what they take to be the most important relationship of all, that between human beings and their creator.

29. Low levels of education constitute a risk factor for dementia in later life. Cognitive functioning in later life seems to be conditional in large part on the reserve of cognitive abilities and skills one had developed in one's earlier years. See Karin Anstey and Helen Christensen, "Education, Activity, Health, Blood Pressure and Apolipoprotein E as Predictors of Cognitive Change in Old Age: a Review," *Gerontology* 2000 (46): 163–177. And see B. Schmand, J. H. Smit, M. I. Geerlings, and J. Lindeboom, "The Effects of Intelligence and Education on the Development of Dementia. A Test of the Brain Reserve Hypothesis," *Psychological Medicine* 1997 (27): 1337–1344; and Y. Stern, G. E. Alexander, I. Prohovnik, L Stricks, B. Link, M. C. Lennon, and R. Mayeux, "Relationship between Lifetime Occupation and Parietal Flow: Implications for a Reserve Against Alzheimer's Disease Pathology," *Neurology* 1995 (45): 55–60.

30. See Carmi Schooler, Mesfin Samuel Mulatu, and Gary Oates, "The Continuing Effects of Substantially Complex Work on the Intellectual Functioning of Older Workers," *Psychology and Aging*, 1999 (14): 483–506; and see K. Warner Schaie, "Intellectual Development in Adulthood," in *The Handbook of the Psychology of Aging*, ed. James E. Birren and K. Warner Schaie, 3rd ed. (San Diego: Academic Press, 1990), 291–309, esp. 300.

workers are liable to be more cognitively demanding than those that are less so. Thus even housekeeping can turn out to be a cognitively demanding occupation that maintains intellectual flexibility in those engaged in it.[31] Upon reflection, what makes professorial activity cognitively demanding may have less to do with our research and writing than with the time we spend engaged in teaching, evaluating, and advising our students and serving on committees with our colleagues. It seems likely that these aspects of professorial work, the ones calling upon interpersonal skills and dispositions such as sympathy, confidence, trust, and loyalty, may count as much, if not more, towards making the occupation cognitively demanding, and so beneficial to one's long-term flourishing, as the more outwardly "intellectual" ones.

Cognitively demanding occupations, paid or unpaid, seem to be ones in which people who have cultivated the minor virtues are apt to fare better. Indeed people who have cultivated the minor virtues are more apt to seek them out in the first place. Curiosity allows a work-place fraught with uncertainties to be rewarding. Playfulness makes it possible to view the necessary departures from previous learned strategies as entertaining. Sympathetic interest in others makes coping with the unpredictability of co-workers, employees, or clients enjoyable. Gratitude and loyalty to others makes it possible to reward those from whom help must be sought with the result that accepting help is not felt to be as weakness or powerlessness. And so forth. While we need not go so far as to predict that people who are disloyal colleagues, incurious bores, unsympathetic professionals or simply diffident, are necessarily the worse as persons, it is not unreasonable to fear that they may become the worse, over time, if they do not reflect upon and try to cultivate the minor virtues.

4. Conclusion

I am *not* arguing that the major virtues are not also virtues because they do not promote plasticity and interdependence as the minor virtues do. Virtues like courage, prudence, benevolence, and justice are valuable for the reasons usually given. But I think the argument does suggest that the major virtues may have been *over*-valued. At the very least their status as non-dependent, intersubjectively valuable virtues should be questioned. First, their value appears to be restricted to the relatively short period of our lives when we are mature and fully

31. See C. Schooler, M. L. Kohn, K. A. Miller, and J. Miller. "Housework as Work," in *Work and Personality: an Inquiry into the Impact of Social Stratification,* ed. M. L. Kohn and C. Schooler (Norwood: Ablex, 1983), 242–260.

independent beings, suggesting they are highly context-dependent. By contrast, the minor virtues seem desirable as primary constituents of personal character through the whole of our lives. Second, the major virtues may be *dependent* in another sense, i.e. directly dependent on the prior cultivation of the minor virtues. It is difficult to see how a person without sympathy for others could succeed in recognizing when benevolence or mercy are appropriate. It is equally difficult to see how a person mistrustful of others would display charity or generosity towards them. Even critics of loyalty's claim to be a virtue have recognized its necessity for the development of virtues such as justice, equity, and impartiality.[32] Prudence in the absence of curiosity about the untried could become a fearful conservatism. Thus of the two groups of virtues, it seems that the minor virtues might be the more central to human flourishing.

Though more central, however, they are not sufficient in themselves. Growth and development ultimately present problems for which the minor virtues alone are not enough to cope successfully. This seems too obvious to require much elaboration. The independence of adulthood inevitably makes temperance important. The investment of unrecoverable time and energy into long-term projects makes prudence desirable. Opportunities to exercise power over others invite disaster, personal and social, if justice is lacking. But if the minor virtues are not sufficient for human flourishing, they seem collectively necessary to it.

In summary, then, Dewey's incorporation of development into his account of human flourishing has interesting and important implications for traditional accounts of the virtues. From this perspective, any account will be seriously incomplete if it does not include growth-promoting dispositions as crucial virtues of character. Dispositions, especially associated with children, such as sympathy, curiosity, playfulness, confidence, trust, gratitude, and loyalty, turn out to be virtues central to human growth and flourishing. If, as I have surmised, they prove equally important through out the course of a life-span, then, on a pragmatic approach, the minor virtues turn out to be better candidates for recognition as primary or cardinal virtues than the traditional virtues of majority. Thus in appropriating and reconstructing traditional virtue theories for our own use, we should take a cue from the character of children.

---

32. See Andrew Oldenquist, "Loyalties," *Journal of Philosophy* 79 (1982): 173–193.

PART 4

VIRTUE ETHICS
AND ITS ENVIRONS

CHAPTER 8

Hume on Virtue, Utility, and Morality

ROGER CRISP

In the recent revival of so-called "virtue ethics," among past philosophers it is Aristotle who, rightly enough, has provided the greatest source of inspiration. David Hume, however, offers much penetrating insight into the virtues and almost certainly deserves greater attention in this regard than he has received. One reason, perhaps, for the relative neglect of Hume is that he is often construed as a utilitarian, and the prevailing view is that virtue ethics is opposed to utilitarianism.[1] The two positions, of course, can be, and often are, defined so that this is indeed the case. But it is always important to enquire of any particular ethical theory exactly which question it is seeking to answer. If we do that in the case of Hume, I shall argue, we find that his position combines *both* a form of

---

1. A good deal of debate has taken place over whether Hume is a utilitarian. For the view that in some sense he is, see J. Laird, *Hume's Philosophy of Human Nature* (London: Methuen & Co., 1932), 236; A. C. MacIntyre, "Hume on Is and Ought," *Philosophical Review* 68 (1959): 451–68, at 457–8; R. D. Broiles, *The Moral Philosophy of David Hume* (The Hague: Martinus Nijhoff, 1964), 25, 94; J. Plamenatz, *The English Utilitarians* (Oxford: Blackwell, 1967), 22, 28; R. J. Glossop, "The Nature of Hume's Ethics," *Philosophy and Phenomenological Research* 27 (1967): 527–36, at 535–6; J. Rawls, *A Theory of Justice* (Oxford: Oxford University Press, 1972), at 22 n. 9; J. Harrison, *Hume's Theory of Justice* (Oxford: Clarendon Press, 1981), 33, 88; F. Rosen, introduction to J. Bentham, *An Introduction to the Principles of Morals and Legislation,* ed. J. H. Burns and H. L. A. Hart (Oxford: Clarendon Press, 1996), lxiii; J. H. Sobel, "Hume's Utilitarian Theory of Right Action," *Philosophical Quarterly* 47 (1997): 55–72, at 58. Utilitarian interpretations are denied by B. Wand, "Hume's Non-utilitarianism," *Ethics* 72 (1962): 193–6; A. Botwinick, "A Case for Hume's Nonutilitarianism," *Journal of the History of Philosophy* 15 (1977): 423–35; N. Capaldi, *Hume's Place in Moral Philosophy* (New York: Peter Lang, 1989); D. Long, "'Utility' and the 'Utility Principle': Hume, Smith, Bentham," *Utilitas* 2 (1990): 12–39, at 12–13, 23, 26; A. Baier, *A Progress of Sentiments* (Cambridge, Mass.: Harvard University Press, 1991), 250; G. Sayre-McCord, "Hume and the Bauhaus Theory of Ethics," *Midwest Studies in Philosophy: Moral Concepts,* vol. 20, ed. P. A. French, T. E. Uehling (Jr.), H. K. Wettstein (Notre Dame: University of Notre Dame Press, 1996): 280–98, at 280.

common-sense morality which could plausibly be described as a kind of virtue ethics *and* a form of utilitarianism: Hume is *not,* in the usual sense, a utilitarian of any kind (and here I include so-called "indirect" or "two-level" utilitarianism) in that his answer to the question, "What should I do?" makes no special theoretical reference to utility; but utilitarianism *does* enter his theory in answer to the question, "Which virtues, character, or motives should I have?" and also at a deeper level in his explanation and justification of the very phenomenon of morality itself. Indeed, his answer to the question about character rests on this deeper level and is grounded on an account of the nature of morality which may have the implication that it is impossible coherently to state non-utilitarian views of character. Both these views seem to me intrinsically interesting and worthy of further thought. So one moral of this paper is that it is likely to be helpful for any moral philosopher not only to be clear about exactly which question or questions her ethical theory is intended to answer, but also to consider what implications her view of the origin and nature of morality might have for her first-order normative theory, that is, for her views about how we should live, what character we should have, how we should act, and so on.

1. Hume the Moral Anthropologist?

Before proceeding with any examination of Hume's first-order ethical position, I must first deal with the objection that he has no such position, and that he is best seen merely as a philosophical anthropologist out to discover the nature of morality.[2]

There is no doubt that much of Hume's ethics is descriptive. His broad brush portrait of morality, as well as the detailed sketches of individual virtues and character traits, must rank as among the most significant since Aristotle. Further, Hume himself seems to characterize his project as entirely descriptive. He introduces the *Treatise* with the claim: "The sole end of logic is to explain the principles and operations of our reasoning faculty, and the nature of our ideas: morals and criticism regard our tastes and sentiments."[3] And he closes it by drawing an analogy between himself and an anatomist, saying:

2. For this common view, see J. L. Mackie, *Hume's Moral Theory* (London: Routledge & Kegan Paul, 1980), 5–6, 152; S. Darwall, "Hume and the Invention of Utilitarianism," in *Hume and Hume's Connexions,* ed. M. A. Stewart (Edinburgh: Edinburgh University Press, 1994), 61. See also the many references in R. Shaver, "Hume's Moral Theory?" *History of Philosophy Quarterly* 12 (1995): 317–31, at 317; Shaver's paper provides further arguments against a purely descriptive interpretation of Hume.

3. *A Treatise of Human Nature,* ed. L. A. Selby-Bigge, rev. P. H. Nidditch, 2nd ed. (Oxford: Clarendon Press, 1978) (henceforth "T"), introduction, xv. Future references to T will locate passages according to book, part, section, and page, respectively. I shall use both the *Treatise* and the *Enquiry concerning the Prin-*

The anatomist ought never to emulate the painter: nor in his accurate dissections and portraitures of the smaller parts of the human body, pretend to give his figures any graceful and engaging attitude or expression. . . . An anatomist, however, is admirably fitted to give advice to a painter. . . . [T]he most abstract speculations concerning human nature, however cold and unentertaining, become subservient to *practical morality*.[4]

We must not lose sight of the fact that a central aim of Hume in his ethical writings is to *explain* morality: to offer an "anatomical" account of its origin, its nature, and its content. But even here he is suggesting that just as the painter can learn from the anatomist, so the moral agent can learn from abstract philosophy. And in his later writings Hume came to state more clearly that the very distinction between abstract speculation and practical morality was not as sharp as these passages from the *Treatise* might suggest, and that the moral philosopher might have a directly normative contribution to make to practical ethics.[5] In an essay published before the *Enquiry*, Hume is indeed wary of seeing it as part of the role of philosophy to offer advice on the ends to be sought in life. But, he says, "to satisfy you, I shall deliver my opinion upon the matter, and shall only desire you to esteem it of as little consequence as I do myself. By that means you will neither think it worthy of your ridicule nor your anger."[6] Hume goes on to argue that "the happiest disposition of mind is the *virtuous*" and notes that one role of philosophy is that "[it] insensibly refines the temper, and it points out to us those dispositions which we should endeavour to attain, by a consistent bent of mind, and by repeated *habit*."[7] This, presumably, is what he sees himself as doing in the *Enquiry* when he describes the several qualities of Cleanthes, noting: "A philosopher might select this character as a model of perfect virtue."[8]

In the *Enquiry* itself we find strong implications of normative positions. In the

---

ciples of Morals in interpreting Hume, since, though the latter places greater stress on utility, the fundamentals of the position I shall attribute to Hume are in both works.

4. T 3.3.6.620–1. Cf. *An Enquiry concerning Human Understanding*, ed. L. A. Selby-Bigge, rev. P. H. Nidditch, 3rd ed. (Oxford: Oxford University Press, 1975), 10. For an interesting reading of the quoted passage, which sees it as drawing the engaging/accurate distinction rather than the prescriptive/descriptive distinction, see Shaver, "Hume's Moral Theory," 319.

5. See G. Sayre-McCord, "On Why Hume's 'General Point of View' Isn't Ideal—and Shouldn't Be," *Social Philosophy and Policy* 11 (1994): 202–28, at 203–4. It is likely that Hume was, to some extent, stung by Hutcheson's complaint that the *Treatise* lacked "a certain Warmth in the Cause of Virtue"; see Mackie, *Hume's Moral Theory*, 24.

6. "The Sceptic," in *Essays: Moral, Political, and Literary*, ed. E. F. Miller (Indianapolis: Liberty Fund, Inc., 1985), 161–2.

7. Ibid., 168, 171.

8. D. Hume, *An Enquiry concerning the Principles of Morals*, ed. T. L. Beauchamp (Oxford: Clarendon Press, 1998) (henceforth "E"), sect. 9, para. 2. (Future references to E will be to section and paragraph, respectively.) See Shaver, "Hume's Moral Theory?" 320.

first section, for example, Hume suggests that no one can avoid making moral judgments: "Let a man's insensibility be ever so great, he must often be touched with the images of RIGHT and WRONG."[9] It is pretty easy, he claims, to enumerate "estimable or blameable" human qualities, and then:

> The only object of reasoning is to discover the circumstances on both sides, which are common to these qualities; to observe that particular in which the estimable qualities agree on the one hand, and the blameable on the other; and thence to reach the foundation of ethics, and find those universal principles, from which all censure or approbation is ultimately derived.[10]

We can deduce, then, that Hume to some degree accepted the morality he describes, and that he would have seen his own praise and blame for the qualities he describes as resting on the principles he outlines. The philosophical anthropologist arrives, one might suggest, at some of his conclusions through introspection of his own commitments. If this is right, then the morality Hume describes is likely to be, in large part, his own practical morality.

It is true that in the *Enquiry* Hume continues to see the aim of his project as "being more the speculative, than the practical part of morals."[11] But note the comparative nature of his remark here, and the fact that he makes it after admitting that he has "forgotten" this fact, and has provided various considerations in favor of the view that the social virtues are "estimable." He continues:

> [N]o qualities are more entitled to the general good-will and approbation of mankind, than beneficence and humanity, friendship and gratitude, natural affection and public spirit, or whatever proceeds from a tender sympathy with others, and a generous concern for our kind and species.[12]

The end of the *Enquiry,* moreover, is a clear admission by Hume that he saw the respective analytic and protreptic aims of abstract speculation and of practical morality as both within his purview:

> Having explained the moral *approbation* attending merit or virtue, there remains nothing, but briefly to consider our interested *obligation* to it, and to enquire, whether every man, who has any regard to his own happiness and welfare, will not find his account in the practice of every moral duty. If this can be clearly ascer-

9. E 1.2; cf. 5.39.
10. E 1.10.
11. E 2.5.
12. Ibid.

tained from the foregoing theory, we shall have the satisfaction to reflect, that we have advanced principles, which not only, it is hoped, will stand the test of reasoning and enquiry, but may contribute to the amendment of men's lives, and their improvement in morality and social virtue.[13]

Hume goes on to suggest that his philosophical account of morality has represented virtue "in all her genuine and most engaging charms," thus recognizing that a description can itself attract people to its object.[14] And, of course, the conclusion of the *Enquiry* is a paean to virtue, closing with an anticipation of Mill's suggestion that virtue is a higher pleasure, itself taken from Plato's *Republic:* "These natural pleasures, indeed, are really without price; both because they are below all price in their attainment, and above it in their enjoyment."[15]

Nor is Hume's view in the *Enquiry* a change of mind as opposed to one of emphasis, despite what the "anatomical analogy" may in isolation suggest. If we look back in the *Treatise*, we shall find the same recognition that descriptions can engage or attract:

> Were it proper in such a subject to bribe the readers assent, or employ any thing but solid argument, we are here abundantly supplied with topics to engage the affections. All lovers of virtue (and such we all are in speculation, however we may degenerate in practice) must certainly be pleas'd to see moral distinctions deriv'd from so noble a source, which gives us a just notion both of the *generosity* and *capacity* of our nature.[16]

In recent years, it has become common to attribute to Hume a form of practical skepticism, based on his view of motivation, which would also threaten my interpretative project. Christine Korsgaard, for example, suggests that "Hume's view is that there is no such thing as practical reason at all," and Garrett Cullity and Berys Gaut ascribe to Hume the position that "there are no normative practical reasons."[17]

Anything approaching a full discussion of this issue is beyond the scope of this paper, but it does seem to me that the case for such a strong form of skepticism is far from proven. Consider, for example, the fact that Hume is "con-

---

13. E 9.14.
14. E 9.15.
15. E 9.25. See Plato, *Republic,* 580d3–88a11; J. S. Mill, *Utilitarianism,* ed. R. Crisp (Oxford: Oxford University Press, 1998), ch. 2, para. 6, lines 7–10.
16. T 3.3.6.619.
17. See C. Korsgaard, "The Normativity of Instrumental Reason," in *Ethics and Practical Reason,* ed. G. Cullity and B. Gaut (Oxford: Clarendon Press, 1997), 222; G. Cullity and B. Gaut, introduction to Cullity and Gaut, *Ethics and Practical Reason,* 7.

tented with saying, that reason requires" certain conduct.[18] Of course, he believes that what we think of as the reason that *opposes* passion is in fact itself a
"determination" of a passion, a calm one.[19] But this is a view about what practical reason is: his skepticism is about not practical reason as such, but a particular conception of it. And it is important to remember also that this
determination is itself "founded on some distant view or reflexion," and that it
"correct[s]" the (violent) passions.[20] It has, that is, a cognitive grounding,[21] and
Hume provides us with the resources for claiming, if not reasonableness, then
"correctness" for certain calm passions. More on this below.

Hume is contented to speak also of normative reasons. He asks, for example,
if I have borrowed some money, "*What reason or motive have I restore [it]?*".[22] Also,
it is worth recalling that Hume thought his view that virtue and vice lie "in the
senses" had no implications for the "reality" of these qualities, or for moral practice or first-order ethical theory.[23] Even if the most plausible interpretation of
Hume is as some kind of skeptic about practical reason, he inoculates normative ethics against any potentially paralyzing implications of metaethics.

So, though Hume is not sanguine about the effectiveness of philosophy as a
normative enterprise, we can conclude that not only did he attribute this role
to it, but he was prepared to allow his own philosophy to play that role. I am,
therefore, entitled to ask my question of Hume.

2. Ethics of Action, Ethics of Motive

First order ethics usually focuses on actions. The act-utilitarian will claim that
the right action is that which maximizes utility, the Kantian that which is performed on the basis of the Categorical Imperative, and so on. Hume is certainly
prepared to make judgements about actions. It is clear, for example, that he

---

18. T 3.3.1.583.

19. Ibid.

20. Ibid. See also T 3.3.1.585. These calm passions can also be "corroborated by reflection" (T
2.3.8.437). For a plausible explanation of how these claims can be fitted into Hume's subjectivist framework, see R. Cohon, "The Common Point of View in Hume's Ethics," *Philosophy and Phenomenological
Research* 57 (1997): 827–50, at 835–9.

21. Cf. R. Kydd, *Reason and Conduct in Hume's Treatise* (London: Oxford University Press, 1946), 137;
B. Stroud, *Hume* (London: Routledge & Kegan Paul, 1977), 192; D. F. Norton, *David Hume: Common-
Sense Moralist, Sceptical Metaphysician* (Princeton: Princeton University Press, 1982), 120, 129.

22. T 3.2.1.479. It is true that Hume does not, in this passage or elsewhere, distinguish as clearly as
one might like between motivating and normative reasons. But the context here suggests that he is im-
plying that he himself would be motivated to return the loan by his concern for justice, and that his being motivated would itself consist partly in his taking justice to be a "sufficient [normative] reason for"
him to make the return.

23. "The Sceptic," 166 n. 3. Cf. T. 3.1.1.469.

thinks I have a duty to repay a debt.[24] This obligation is, in part at least, one of justice. In order to understand Hume's view of the rightness of actions, then, let me consider his account of the virtue of justice.[25]

Hume suggests that human beings are driven to a great extent by self-interest, and by love of those close to them. Unregulated, these passions would be destructive of society, and harmful to all, so the institution of justice develops to solve this problem. It is not itself consciously instituted, but develops as a convention in the way that two men rowing a boat fall into a certain rhythm without agreeing beforehand. So justice is artificial, a device to deal with two important features of the human situation: our limited generosity and the scarcity of goods. Were we not partial, or were the goods with which justice is concerned not scarce, the institution of justice would be unnecessary.

As yet, the moral sentiments have not entered the story.[26] They do so through the operation of a remarkable human faculty: sympathy. Once the institution of justice is in place—protecting our property, for example—I shall feel an unpleasant sensation if I see you about to break some principle of justice protecting some of my property. But because of my capacity to sympathize, I shall feel the same "uneasiness" if I see you about to threaten someone else, or even hear of some breach of justice long ago, to someone not known to me. This uneasiness is a moral sentiment, and a natural one, and it is impartial in the sense that it does not vary in proportion to the intensity of my concern for the threatened individual. The institution of justice has to work, so it cannot repeat the biases towards self and near and dear which it is its function to counteract. It has to work as a system of communication between all people, so it rests on "the general survey,"[27] an impartial point of view from which each person should, as it were, see and feel things the same way. This natural sentiment is also "augmented by a new artifice, and . . . the public instructions of politicians, and the private education of parents, contribute to the giving us a sense of honour and duty."[28] "*Thus self-interest is the original motive to the* establishment *of justice: but a* sympathy *with public interest is the source of the* moral approbation *which attends that virtue.*"[29]

24. T 3.2.1.479.
25. See T 3.2.2; E 3.
26. Hume believes they arise after the laws of justice have been established on the basis of self-interest: T. 3.2.6.533. Note that it is not only sympathy that explains the moral sentiments. Reason also plays a central role: "Men are superior to beasts principally by the superiority of their reason" (T 3.3.3.610), and it is on account of their inferior "knowledge and understanding" that animals "have little or no sense of virtue or vice . . . and are incapable of" participating in institutions such as those of "right and property" (T 2.1.12.326). Cf. K. Tranöy, "Hume on Morals, Animals and Men," *Journal of Philosophy* 56 (1959): 94–103, at 100.
27. T 3.2.2.499. I discuss this notion further in section 4 below.
28. T 3.2.6.533–4.
29. T 3.2.3.499–500. Cf. T 3.2.6.529.

Hume's account of the virtue of justice seems, on the face of it, to be thoroughly utilitarian:

> [J]ustice is a moral virtue, merely because it has that tendency to the good of mankind; and, indeed, is nothing but an artificial invention to that purpose. The same may be said of allegiance, of the laws of nations, of modesty, and of good-manners. All these are mere human contrivances for the interest of society.[30]

A similar story may be told regarding the "natural" virtues, such as benevolence.[31] If you are my sister, a mere natural desire to help you is not sufficient to ground my sentiment as a moral one. Moral sentiments are based on impartiality, so that I shall view my helping you, and some stranger's helping another stranger, as morally equivalent, and worthy of the same praise or admiration. And, just as the institution of justice emerges to provide various social benefits, so do the natural virtues:

> The necessity of justice to the support of society is the SOLE foundation of that virtue; and since no moral excellence is more highly esteemed, we may conclude, that this circumstance of usefulness has, in general, the strongest energy, and most entire command over our sentiments. It must, therefore, be the source of a considerable part of the merit ascribed to humanity, benevolence, friendship, public spirit, and other social virtues of that stamp.[32]

According to act-utilitarianism, the right action is that which maximizes utility, or expected utility. Given Hume's grounding of a virtue-centered, common-sense morality on its utility, it may be tempting to offer a "two-level" act-utilitarian interpretation of Hume, according to which the right action is that which maximizes utility, and the best way to decide how to act is to follow the norms of common-sense morality.[33]

---

30. T 3.3.1.577. Cf. T 3.2.6.618. Geoffrey Sayre-McCord has objected to a utilitarian interpretation of Hume's conception of justice that Hume is concerned with not the good of all, but the good of each: "Hume and the Bauhaus Theory of Ethics," 280, 289–90. Hume, however, is quite prepared, as we see in this passage, to speak of the good of society as a whole, and because he believed justice to be in the interest of all (T 3.2.2.497), he had no reason to draw any distinction between the good of all and the good of each such as might be necessary for one considering whether the overall good might justify the sacrifice of the good of an individual.

31. The natural virtues, according to Hume (T 3.3.1.579), do not require artificial institutions, being based on sentiments which human beings will feel naturally and without acculturation. Further, every exercise of a natural virtue will do good, while in the case of the artificial virtues it is only the *system* as a whole that has utilitarian value.

32. E 3.48. What Hume means by the claim that "usefulness" is a source merely of a part of the merit ascribed to the social virtues here will be discussed in the following section.

33. For the most well-known modern version of such a view, see R. M. Hare, *Moral Thinking: Its Methods, Levels, and Point* (Oxford: Clarendon Press, 1981), ch. 2.

Hume is not an act-utilitarian. This can be seen clearly in those cases of artificial virtue in which we are required to act in accordance with the virtue, and
not to override it in order to bring about a greater good. A two-level act-utilitarian interpreter of Hume may well argue that we should be loath to override
the rules of common-sense morality because of the difficulty of predicting consequences reliably. And she may point, for example, to Hume's allowing that, in
the several cases that come before a judge, "'tis impossible to separate the good
from the ill."[34] But Hume in fact thinks that we should praise an action emerg-
ing from a virtuous trait of character even when we *know* that that action is un-
productive of utility. "When a man of merit, of a beneficent disposition, restores
a great fortune to a miser, or a seditious bigot, he has acted justly and laudably,
but the public is a real sufferer."[35]

Nor, it is clear, is Hume any kind of rule-utilitarian, who appeals to the consequences of the following of moral rules in some imagined situation, such as
that in which the majority accepts those rules.[36] Justice is a good because it is
actually in the public interest, not because it would be so in some imaginary
circumstances.

At the level of the rightness of actions, then, Hume is best understood as not
any kind of utilitarian at all, but as a virtue-centered, common-sense moralist,
who will praise and blame actions in accordance with his best understanding of
a common-sense morality upon which there is general agreement.

But—and this is further to justify my use of "virtue-centered" to describe
Hume's version of common-sense morality—Hume's focus in ethics is not *primarily* upon actions at all.

> 'Tis evident, that when we praise any actions, we regard only the motives that pro-
> duced them, and consider the actions as signs or indications of certain principles
> in the mind and temper. The external performance has no merit. We must look
> within to find the moral quality. This we cannot do directly; and therefore fix our

---

34. T 3.2.2.497.

35. T 3.2.2.497. It may be objected that Hume is assuming that the praise itself will be justified by
act-utilitarianism, but there is no evidence that Hume took an instrumental attitude towards praise. By
"laudable" here we must, then, take him to mean something close to morally right. Hume does allow
that in conflicts within commonsense morality, we should appeal to considerations of utility; see E 2.17,
a passage discussed in my text below in connection with the notion of utility-maximization. And if justice *as a practice* can be seen to be "pernicious," then it should be abandoned: "Of Passive Obedience,"
Essays: Moral, Political, and Literary, 489; see E 3.32. But the essential point is that Hume nowhere offers
an act-utilitarian criterion of right action, and is prepared to praise individual acts in accordance with
common-sense morality. Incidentally, I take it that in this passage beneficence is mentioned as an "ordinary" virtue that might constitute a possible counterweight to justice, but one in fact insufficient to tip
the scales.

36. See R. Brandt, *A Theory of the Good and the Right* (Oxford: Clarendon Press, 1979), ch. 15; B.
Hooker, *Ideal Code, Real World* (Oxford: Clarendon Press, 2000).

attention on actions, as on external signs. But these actions are still considered as signs; and the ultimate object of our praise and approbation is the motive, that produc'd them.[37]

It is tempting to assume that Hume is making a somewhat proto-Kantian point, that what we are concerned about in ethics is not the action as an "external event," but the agent's intentions. For these, it may be suggested, are what we are and may be held responsible for.

This, however, is certainly not Hume's view. He sees no clear or significant distinction between mere natural abilities and moral virtues and refuses to distinguish between them on the ground of whether their possessor holds them voluntarily or not.[38] First, many moral virtues, such as fortitude, are involuntary. Second, virtue and vice *could* be entirely involuntary, since the notion of vice emerges from the pain or pleasure we feel from the "general consideration of any quality or character," and qualities can produce pleasure and pain even when they are involuntary. Third, there is anyway no such thing as free will.

This is not to say that Hume fails to recognize the significance of intention.[39] If you cause me some injury, and I blame you for it, I shall withdraw my criticism if I find that the injury was accidental. But this is not to say that if it were not accidental I should be blaming you because you have performed, voluntarily, a wicked action for which you are morally responsible:

'Tis not enough, that the action arise from the person, and have him for its immediate cause and author. This relation alone is too feeble and inconstant to be a foundation for these passions. It reaches not the sensible and thinking part, and neither proceeds from any thing *durable* in him, nor leaves any thing behind it; but passes in a moment, and is as if it had never been. On the other hand, an intention shews certain qualities, which remaining after the action is perform'd, connect it with the person, and facilitate the transition of ideas from one to the other.[40]

It is, then, the durability or the steadiness of moral qualities that leads to their being the primary concern of ethical judgements. As we have seen, Hume is prepared to make common-sense moral judgments about actions. But he in-

---

37. T 3.2.1.477. For objections based on this passage to a utilitarian interpretation of Hume, see Wand, "Hume's Non-utilitarianism," 193; Mackie, *Hume's Moral Theory,* 152; Sayre-McCord, "Hume and the Bauhaus Theory of Ethics," 287; see also Darwall, "Hume and the Invention of Utilitarianism," 59–60. Sobel ("Hume's Utilitarian Theory of Right Action," 56) ascribes to Hume a utilitarian theory of right action based on his utilitarian view of motives. But this seems to me to miss the force of Hume's redirecting our reflective consideration from actions to motives.

38. T 3.3.4.608–9.

39. T 2.2.3.348–50.

40. T 2.2.3.349. Cf. T 3.3.1.575.

terprets those judgments as themselves referring to certain moral qualities—
virtues—in the agent. We may, then, ask not "which actions should one perform?" but "which qualities should one possess?" Hume's answer is utilitarian:
qualities are morally justified to the extent that they promote utility.

In this respect, Hume's view may be seen as similar to what Robert Adams
has called "motive-utilitarianism."[41] As Adams characterizes it, this view is that
"the morally perfect person . . . would have the most useful desires, and have
them in exactly the most useful strengths; he or she would have the most useful among the patterns of motivation that are . . . possible for human beings."[42]
The best set of motives for me, then, is not those that would, *in my special circumstances,* maximize utility, but those which are most useful in general for human beings to have. Compare Hume:

> [T]he tendencies of actions and characters, not their real accidental consequences,
> are alone regarded in our moral determinations or general judgments. . . . Why is
> this peach-tree said to be better than that other; but because it produces more or
> better fruit? And would not the same praise be given it, though snails or vermin
> had destroyed the peaches, before they came to full maturity?[43]

Now it is important to note that Adams himself distinguishes motives from,
for example, traits of character.[44] Hume speaks of motives, qualities of character, virtues, and so on, without drawing clear distinctions between them. But if
we take "motive" in its broad Humean sense, Hume's view appears to be a form
of motive-utilitarianism. But, as I shall suggest in section 4, Hume's motive-utilitarianism, though it is indeed a first-order view in the ethics of character (as
opposed to the ethics of action, in which, as I have shown, Hume is best understood as a virtue-centered, common-sense moralist), emerges from a utilitarian understanding of the very phenomenon of morality itself. His first-order
utilitarianism, that is to say, rests on what one might call "utilitarian metaethics."
But before discussing this, I must first deal with two common objections to any
kind of utilitarian interpretation of Hume.

41. R. M. Adams, "Motive Utilitarianism," *Journal of Philosophy* 73 (1976): 467–81. Cf. D. D. Raphael,
"Hume and Adam Smith on Justice and Utility," *Proceedings of the Aristotelian Society* 73 (1972–3): 87–103,
at 102; J. Harrison, *Hume's Theory of Justice,* 33, 88.

42. "Motive Utilitarianism," 470. The language of maximization and exactness here is alien to Hume,
as I shall show in the following section. But the essence of the position—that motives are to be judged
in accordance with the principle of utility alone—is entirely Humean.

43. E 5.41, n. 24.

44. "Motive Utilitarianism," 467. It is worth noting also that I do not wish to attribute to Hume the
view that there is a *single* set of motives for *every* human to have, as opposed to the view that the list of
virtues and vices at any time and place to some extent depends on the circumstances then prevalent. But
it may be that Adams would allow his motive-utilitarian also to adopt this latter view.

3. *Maximandum* and Maximization: Two Objections

According to the first objection, if Hume were a utilitarian, he would have to claim that the virtues are based on utility alone. In fact, he says that, in the case of the social virtues, "the public utility of these virtues is the *chief* circumstance, whence they derive their merit."[45]

Hume does indeed state that in addition to conduciveness to public utility there are three further classes of quality that serve as the foundation for our esteem of the virtues: (1) qualities useful to ourselves, such as discretion, industry, or frugality;[46] (2) qualities immediately agreeable to ourselves, such as cheerfulness, greatness of mind, and courage;[47] (3) qualities immediately agreeable to others, such as good manners, wit, or decency.[48] But in fact he is merely distinguishing between what may be seen as different sources of utility.

A quality, such as discretion, recommended for its usefulness to oneself is still being recommended on the basis of its promotion of happiness. My own good is part of the social good.[49] It might be objected that these qualities could be being recommended purely on the basis of self-interest. But, in fact, though Hume may allow such recommendation, he also stresses that these virtues are esteemed for the sake of utility, and from the same impartial moral point of view as those virtues conducive to the good of society as a whole.[50]

But what about the "agreeableness" of classes (2) and (3)? Is this not something independent of utility? Not really.[51] Hume is merely distinguishing between qualities which produce pleasure indirectly, and those which do so directly, as soon as they are confronted.[52] If I am discreet, that will be to my long-term advantage. My discretion here can be seen purely instrumentally, but it comes to be admired as a virtue because of its usefulness in the long term in the production of pleasure. In the case of qualities such as cheerfulness, how-

---

45. E 5.4 (italics added); cf. E 3.48 quoted in the text above. For the objection, see e.g. Mackie, *Hume's Moral Theory*, 151–2.; Sayre-McCord, "Hume and the Bauhaus Theory of Ethics," 280; N. Capaldi, *Hume's Place in Moral Philosophy*, 304; Baier, *A Progress of Sentiments*, 205, 250; Beauchamp, "Editor's Introduction" to Hume's *Enquiry*, 40. Long argues that Hume's notion of utility is primarily aesthetic, and not to be understood in terms of expedience: "'Utility' and the 'Utility Principle,'" 26. But in fact exactly the opposite is the case: Hume's aesthetics is itself utilitarian; see T 3.3.1.576–7.

46. E 6.

47. E 7.

48. E 8. The categories are not mutually exclusive. Courage, for example, as well as being agreeable, is of clear utility "both to the public and to the person possessed of it" (E 7.11).

49. See Glossop, "The Nature of Hume's Ethics," 535.

50. E 6.2–3.

51. *Pace* Baier, *A Progress of Sentiments*, 204–5.

52. See N. Kemp Smith, *The Philosophy of David Hume* (London: Macmillan, 1941), 164; Wand, "Hume's Non-utilitarianism," 193; Glossop, "The Nature of Hume's Ethics," 535.

ever, the pleasure "which they communicate to the person possessed of them" is "immediate."[53]

> No views of utility or of future beneficial consequences enter into this sentiment of approbation; yet it is of a kind similar to that other sentiment, which arises from views of a public or private utility.[54]

The same contrast between immediate and non-immediate pleasure, of course, also underlies the category of "qualities immediately agreeable to others." As Hume puts it in the *Treatise*, "The very essence of virtue . . . is to produce pleasure, and that of vice to give pain."[55] The four categories of the virtues merely distinguish between who feels the pleasure and pain as a result of the quality in question and whether it is felt immediately or not.

A second common objection to any utilitarian interpretation of Hume concerns the notion of maximization. According to a utilitarian theory, the rightness or moral goodness of whatever is the focus of that theory depends on its producing the greatest balance of happiness over unhappiness.[56] Hume, however, never speaks of "maximization," and the technical apparatus of aggregation, calculation, cost/benefit analysis, and so on, is entirely absent from his writings.[57]

This objection is, as far as it goes, largely correct. Hume does suggest that even common-sense morality demands "just calculation, and a steady preference of the greater happiness."[58] But the apparent difference between Hume's position and that of modern, technical utilitarians is indeed striking.

We should not, however, expect a technical version of utilitarianism in Hume. His project begins with everyday morality as it is, seeking justification for those rules we have as opposed to having no rules at all.[59] Once he has demonstrated the huge amount of good produced by institutions such as justice, a question may arise about whether these are the *best* institutions, or the best forms of such institutions, that we might have. Here, however, Hume believes there is an undeniable degree of vagueness in calculating utilities.

---

53. E.29.

54. Ibid.

55. T 2.1.7.296. This seems the clearest evidence that Hume does not hold what Sayre-McCord calls a "Bauhaus" theory, which avoids "any commitment to there being a single overarching standard for evaluating all solutions to problems" ("Hume and the Bauhaus Theory of Ethics," 287). Also see T 3.3.1.580.

56. See Mill's reference to the *Greatest* Happiness Principle, at *Utilitarianism*, ch. 2, para. 2, line 2.

57. For the objection, see Botwinick, "Case for Hume's Nonutilitarianism," 429, 431, 435; Mackie, *Hume's Moral Theory*, 152; Sayre-McCord, "Hume and the Bauhaus Theory of Ethics," 280; Beauchamp, introduction, 40. Note that Hume is prepared to speak of prudence as aiming at one's "greatest possible good" (T 2.3.3.418).

58. E 9.15.

59. See Beauchamp, introduction, 40.

That there be a separation or distinction of possessions, and this separation be
steady and constant; this is absolutely required by the interests of society, and hence
the origin of justice and property. What possessions are assigned to particular persons; this is, generally speaking, pretty indifferent; and is often determined by very
frivolous views and considerations.[60]

Hume believes that attempts to calculate the different utilities of individual
components of some moral institution will generally be a waste of time. "To reduce life to exact rule and method, is commonly a painful, oft a fruitless occupation."[61] So, since individual moral agents are not being charged with maximizing
utility, and since there is little hope of improving the moral institutions we have,
any talk of "maximization" would be otiose. This is not, of course, to say that
Hume is entirely conservative. When the overall harms of some element of common-sense morality, or some version of it, are salient, he recommends its aban-
donment, as in the case of the "monkish" virtues—celibacy, self-denial, humility,
solitude, and so on.[62] But, here again, talk of maximization would be pointless.

The lack of any notion of maximization in Hume is, then, entirely explica-
ble. Nor is the spirit of maximization absent, though doubtless Hume would
have found the technical calculations of Bentham and his followers somewhat
barbarous. When disagreements arise about what common-sense morality requires, Hume recommends reference to the principle of utility:

[W]herever disputes arise, either in philosophy or common life, concerning the
bounds of duty, the question cannot, by any means, be decided with greater certainty, than by ascertaining, on any side, the true interests of mankind.[63]

There seems no reason to think that Hume would deny that one should
choose the best option from the point of view of overall utility. But he would
stress that exactly what that option is may well be undecidable. "[Q]ualities are
approv'd of, in proportion to the advantage, which results from them."[64] Or, as
he might have put it, "*roughly* in proportion."

60. E App. 3.10, n. 65. See also the text of E 3.10 itself. Note that Hume believes that such rules of
justice are adopted as "*best* serve the . . . end of public utility" (E App. 3.6, italics added).
61. "The Sceptic," 180. See J. Griffin, *Value Judgement* (Oxford: Clarendon Press, 1996), 105. See also
Mackie, *Hume's Moral Theory*, 152: "Hume repeatedly deprecates any enquiry about what would be the
best way of distributing property or the best form of government or the best choice of rulers; though it
is true that his argument in each case is that the public interest would actually be harmed by attempts to
promote it in such detailed ways, because of the disputes and conflicts and insecurity that would result."
62. E 9.3.
63. E 2.17. See n. 35 above for an explanation of why this passage should not be taken to commit
Hume to utilitarianism in the ethics of action.
64. T 3.3.4.612.

But if Hume is so vague about the calculation of utility, should we continue to call him a utilitarian? We should, since other central figures in the utilitarian tradition have been equally pessimistic about maximization, saying little or nothing about it and concentrating their attentions on elements of common-sense morality which they saw as clearly pernicious rather than on delicate balancing between principles or virtues whose presence was more beneficial than their absence.[65] Any weighty commitment to a theoretical or practical role for maximization is best not seen as an essential element of utilitarianism.

A central component, however, of any utilitarian view must be impartiality from the moral point of view between amounts of utility. This notion is central not only to Hume's motive-utilitarianism, but also to his understanding of the nature of morality itself, which itself grounds his motive-utilitarianism and explains his unreadiness to propose anything like act-utilitarianism. This topic will be the subject of the next section.

4. Utilitarian Impartiality and the General Point of View

We have seen that Hume is a kind of motive-utilitarian. When asked how people ought to act, Hume will answer as a virtue-centered, common-sense moralist (albeit one whose common-sense morality is itself shaped by utilitarian considerations). But when asked about the motives or qualities of character that people ought to have, he will claim that they should possess those qualities that, in general, are productive of overall utility. But there is a very important difference between his form of the theory and that offered by contemporary moral theorists such as Adams. Ordinarily, motive-utilitarianism is a view *within* morality. That is, the motive-utilitarian will see herself as in disagreement with, say, a deontologist, about what makes a motive right, good, or justified. But Hume's motive-utilitarianism is a view not merely within morality, but *about* morality itself. As Hume sees it, the very institution of morality is to be understood in motive-utilitarian terms. In other words, Hume is answering not just the question, "Morally speaking, which motives ought I to have?" as if there were already some kind of agreement on what morality consists in, but he is attempting primarily to deal with a quite different question of "What is morality?" And here is one of the points where he might hope that his description, based as it is on social utility, might prove an "engaging" one.

Hume, as we have seen, accepts that human beings are concerned primarily for themselves and those close to them. He explains this in terms of the effects

65. Consider, for example, Mill.

of "contiguity" on the vivacity of our impressions and hence on our will: "When I am a few miles from home, whatever relates to it touches me more nearly than when I am two hundred leagues distant."[66] We care most for ourselves, then for our friends and relatives, and finally for strangers, and this partiality affects our ideas of vice and virtue. We find ourselves blaming someone who pays all his attentions to his family and similarly someone who pays them no attention and prefers the interests of strangers:

> From all of which it follows, that our natural uncultivated ideas of morality, instead of providing a remedy for the partiality of our affections, do rather conform themselves to that partiality, and give it an additional force and influence.[67]

Further, Hume notes, this partiality in our sympathies might seem to pose a problem for the view that morality, which is impartial and does not so fluctuate, rests on our sympathies.[68] His explanation of the development of morality and of the moral point of view turns out also to be a series of arguments in favour of morality. The first argument—which I shall call the *conflict-resolution argument*—is implicit in the quotation just above: the practice of cultivated, or impartial, morality provides a "remedy" for the problems of partiality, a remedy which we have seen is of benefit to all.

Relatedly, the adoption of a "common point of view" makes possible the expression of our natural and impartial sentiments of "humanity."[69] According to the *communication-enabling argument,* then, impartial morality not only provides a motivational counter to our partial affections, but enables us to express our impartial sentiments of sympathy. And this, of course, makes possible the whole enterprise of evaluation—with all its potential for informing and guiding.[70] We learn by experience what to expect from a person described as "cruel," for example, just as we learn from experience what a piece of gold will buy us in the market.[71] If we were merely to express our sentiments from our own partial and constantly changing points of view, there could be no "intercourse of sentiments."

Hume's third argument in favour of the impartial common point of view is the *veridical argument.* The common point of view is the *correct* point of view, and

---

66. T 1.3.8.100.
67. T 3.2.2.489. This passage makes it clear that it is uncultivated morality that Hume has in mind at T 3.2.2.483 when he says that "we always consider the *natural* and *usual* force of the passions, when we determine concerning vice and virtue."
68. T 3.3.1.581.
69. E 9.8.
70. T 3.3.1.583, 3.3.3.602–3; E 5.42.
71. T 3.2.2.490.

represents things as they are, "real and intrinsic value" as opposed to appearance. Consider an aesthetic analogy.[72] If I find pleasure in a beautiful face, and the owner of it moves away from me, it will from a distance appear like any other face. But I shall not judge the face in the light of that appearance, preferring to correct it in the light of my knowledge that, were I to approach it, I should feel the same pleasure at its beauty as I did previously. Similarly, we correct appearances of size via an understanding of perspective.[73] The same goes for morality. Moral sympathy consists in an impartial concern for the happiness of all sentient creatures.[74] From the common point of view, we judge the value of a character trait by its actual effects on the person who possesses it and on others: " 'Tis only when a character is considered in general, without reference to our particular interest, that it causes such a feeling or sentiment, as denominates it morally good or evil."[75]

When we adopt the moral point of view, we must be entirely impartial between ourselves, those close to us, and strangers.[76] If we were not, the moral point of view would not be one which all could adopt in common. One must "forget" his own interests, and "depart from his private and particular situation."[77] But what kind of impartiality does Hume have in mind? For there are other conceptions of impartiality than the utilitarian view, according to which equal moral weight attaches to equal amounts of utility. Indeed, it may be urged that Hume nowhere explicitly says that "forgetting" one's own interests is equivalent to utilitarian impartiality, with its lack of what Rawls calls "the distinction between persons."[78]

It is indeed true that Hume nowhere explicitly advocates utilitarian impartiality. But one can judge his conception of the impartiality implicit in the common point of view by what is delivered from that point of view. And since what emerges from that point of view, in the ethics of character, is motive–utilitarian, we should conclude that the common point of view is itself utilitarian. If it were

---

72. T 3.3.1.581–2.
73. E 5.41.
74. See T 3.3.1.588.
75. T 3.1.2.472; cf. T.3.3.1.577. Also see: "tho' sympathy be much fainter than our concern for ourselves, and a sympathy with persons remote from us much fainter than that with persons near and contiguous; yet we neglect all these differences in our calm judgments concerning the characters of men" (T 3.3.3.603; cf. E 5.42).
76. Cf. J. Laird, *Hume's Philosophy of Human Nature*, 220; D. G. MacNabb, *David Hume: His Theory of Knowledge and Morality* (London: Collins, 1951), 195; J. B. Stewart, *The Moral and Political Thought of David Hume* (New York: Columbia University Press, 1963), 94. On the similarity between Hume's view and Adam Smith's Impartial Spectator model, see Glossop, "Nature of Hume's Ethics," 530; J. Harrison, *Hume's Moral Epistemology* (Oxford: Clarendon Press, 1976), 114; Mackie, *Hume's Moral Theory*, 67.
77. T 3.3.1.591; E 9.6. Cf. T 1.4.2.198, 3.3.1.588; E 9.5.
78. Rawls, *Theory of Justice*, 27.

not, it would produce a different first order morality. Imagine that the common point of view required partiality towards, say, one's family and friends. Then, when describing the basis of virtues such as justice and benevolence, Hume would mention the special weight to be attached to the interests of those individuals. But he does not. Rather, the virtues are such because of their tendency to the good of "mankind," or "society," as a whole.

Why did Hume not consider a less stringent conception of impartiality, one which would perhaps even allow some of the natural bias towards persons that is exemplified in all human beings? The answer lies primarily, I suggest, in the nature of his arguments. As the quotation above suggests, Hume would have seen the inclusion of any kind of partiality within the common point of view as a diminution of its effectiveness. If the problem is partiality, then partiality cannot be part of the solution. When it comes to communication-enabling, it is important that we attach the same sense to evaluative terms. If "kind" means "kind-from-my-perspective," you can learn nothing useful from my attributions of kindness, since you do not occupy the same perspective, and may know nothing of my situation. Finally, for the perspectival analogy to go through for the veridical argument, there must be only one answer to the question of how valuable something is, just as there is only one answer to the question how large some object is.

One further reason for Hume's adopting a utilitarian conception of impartiality may have been an analogy between the temporal impartiality of prudence and the "spatial" impartiality of morality.[79] Prudence—"what in an improper sense we call *reason*"—requires me to be entirely impartial between different times in my life, and it is an easy step to the notion that morality consists in complete impartiality between people.[80]

These reasons explain rather than justify Hume's conception of impartiality. It is not clear why a conception that allowed for partiality—on the agent-neutral or universalizable assumption that everyone's reasons for partiality are the same— would not do the jobs Hume requires of the common point of view.[81] Consider a conception of impartiality, for example, which allowed, first, that each person has reason to give himself and those close to him *some* priority, and, second, that *some* priority be given to the worst off. This conception would presumably give rise to a first order ethics of character that, though it included the virtues of friendship and justice, would nevertheless serve as well to provide a moral motivation to counter excessive partiality. Further, given that each per-

79. T 3.2.7.536. I owe this point to Elizabeth Ashford.
80. See Rawls, *Theory of Justice*, 26–7.
81. See Cohon, "The Common Point of View in Hume's Ethics."

son would view the moral world in the same way, communication would not be prevented. Again, there seems no reason to deny that this conception of impartiality might not be said to be veridical. It is, after all, a single conception, and one with independent attractions. Finally, the problems arising from the separateness of persons with the direct extension of prudential principles into morality are, of course, well known.

It is true that Hume's impartial, motive–utilitarian conception of morality may permit partiality in practice. Indeed, as we have seen, Hume claims that pure impartiality in practice would be beyond human capacity and that encouraging it would lead not to an increase in the overall good so much as the drying up of more partial but nevertheless productive moral concern:

> [W]hile every man consults the good of his own community, we are sensible, that the general interest of mankind is better promoted, than by any loose indeterminate views to the good of a species, whence no beneficial action could ever result, for want of a duly limited object, on which they could exert themselves.[82]

But this, of course, will not be enough to satisfy those who deny that morality itself is to be understood in terms of strict utilitarian impartiality. Indeed, they may use Hume's plausible claims about the limitations of the human will against his own conception of morality. Given those limitations, is it not more likely that the common point of view itself would have incorporated some of that partiality human beings find it so difficult to expunge from their everyday lives?

5. Conclusion: Moral Questions, and the Nature of Ethics

We have seen that Hume's views on virtue, utility, impartiality, and the nature of morality are surprisingly complex. At the level of right action, Hume is best understood as a virtue-centered, common-sense moralist who will recommend those actions that are in line with his own conception of common-sense morality. But he sees praise or blame of actions as directed ultimately at qualities of their agents—virtues—and these qualities are themselves justified, from the

---

82. E 5.38 note 22. Cf. E 5.42 note 25. Note also the passages concerning the sources of justice in self-interest and those concerning different sources of utility discussed above. At T 3.3.3.602–3, Hume suggests that, though we are quite aware of the partiality of human beings towards their friends and family, we approve of such partiality from an impartial perspective of sympathy which takes all into account. In general, Hume is a lot more pessimistic about the possibility of first order impartiality than, say, William Godwin, Mill, Peter Singer, or Shelly Kagan.

moral point of view, by their promoting overall utility. Finally, the moral point of view itself is to be characterized in impartial utilitarian terms. The institution of morality itself emerges only because of its utility value: "Common interest and utility beget infallibly a standard of right and wrong."[83] It might be argued, then, that Hume has removed the ground from beneath the feet of non-utilitarian or deontological positions in the ethics of character. Since the phenomenon of *morality itself* is utilitarian, a non-utilitarian moral position on which character or virtues we should have turns out to be, for him, a conceptual impossibility. Even if his non-utilitarian opponents remain unpersuaded, it is, I suggest, incumbent on them to reflect, as Hume did so carefully, upon the origin and nature of morality and the implications of that reflection for first-order ethics.[84]

83. E 4.20. Cf. E 9.8, cited above; Mill, *A System of Logic Ratiocinative and Inductive*, in *Collected Works*, ed. J. Robson (Toronto: Toronto University Press, 1961–91), 8:849–50. I discuss the tendency in the utilitarian tradition to "instrumentalize" morality in "Teachers in an Age of Transition: Peter Singer and J. S. Mill," in *Singer and his Critics*, ed. D. Jamieson (Oxford: Blackwell, 1999), 95–7. "Utilitarian metaethics"—the view that the actual institution of morality is founded on utility—is commonly found in the empiricist tradition. Locke, for example, offers a theistic version: "For God, having, by an inseparable connection, joined *virtue* and public happiness together; and made the practice thereof, necessary to the preservation of society, and visibly *beneficial* to all, with whom the virtuous man has to do; it is no wonder, that every one should, not only allow, but recommend, and magnify those rules to others, from whose observance of them, he is sure to reap advantage to himself." *An Essay Concerning Human Understanding*, bk. 1, ch. 3, sect. 6, abr. and ed. J. Yolton (London: Dent, 1977).

84. For comments on and discussion of earlier drafts, I am grateful to the Thames Valley Ethics Group; the Centre for Politics, Law and Society, UCL; the Philosophy Dept., University of Rome La Sapienza; delegates at the Hume Studies in Britain II conference, Edinburgh, September 2002; Elizabeth Ashford, Julia Driver, Stephen Gardiner, and David Wiggins. An earlier version of parts of this paper appeared in Italian as "Hume è un utilitarista?' *Iride* 36 (2002): 251–61.

CHAPTER 9

Nietzschean Virtue Ethics

CHRISTINE SWANTON

1. Introduction

In *Gorgias* (S.506) Plato claims that "all good things whatever are good when virtue is present in them."[1] Provided virtue is understood in the Greek sense of *arete,* or excellence, the claim marks the fact that goodness in things is to be understood through the idea of excellence, as opposed to quantities or amounts of, say, pleasantness or power. This is the key not only to understanding virtue ethics, in general, but to understanding Nietzschean virtue ethics, in particular.

Nietzsche's rejection of Hedonism (the idea that only pleasure is intrinsically good) is well known; what is less clearly appreciated is that despite certain ambiguities and exaggerations, for Nietzsche goodness (or value) is not to be understood through the idea of will to power (as such) either. It is rather to be understood through the idea of will to power exercised well or excellently, or (as I shall put it) undistorted will to power. Given that a virtue is a disposition of excellent or good responsiveness to items in its domain (such as threatening or dangerous situations, pleasure, friends or potential friends), a Nietzschean virtue ethics based on the idea of will to power will require that an agent not be motivated by will to power as such, but by undistorted will to power.

In providing an account of undistorted will to power, I seek to remove the major obstacle to a Nietzschean virtue ethics, namely, the specter of immoralism. It is interesting that in *Natural Goodness* Philippa Foot cites Nietzsche as a potential ally with respect to morality's structure (though not its content), "for

---

1. Cited in Michael Slote, *Morals From Motives* (Oxford: Oxford University Press 2000), 155.

what Nietzsche is denying of the supposed virtue of charity is exactly the connection with *human good that was earlier said to give a character trait that status.*"[2] I
shall appeal to aspects of Nietzsche's thought not emphasized by Foot, to question her view of him as an immoralist. However my primary aim is not to defend Nietzsche himself from that charge, but to develop a Nietzschean virtue
ethics.

The claim of immoralism stems from two connected sources: (1) an overly
narrow understanding of will to power, and (2) a failure to appreciate the aretaic (or excellence related) aspects of Nietzsche's notion of will to power. To re-
but the immoralism charge, but more importantly to develop a Nietzschean
virtue ethics, we need briefly to give an account of will to power. That will be
done in the next section. Sections 3 and 4 discuss two forms of undistorted will
to power: will to power as healthy will to power and will to power as excellent
forms of life affirmation. Section 5 attempts to integrate apparent tensions between those two forms by developing a Nietzschean virtue ethics in which the
notion of a virtue is relativized to excellence or goodness in "becoming," as opposed to an end-state of perfection.

2. Will to Power

Will to power as a genus must be distinguished from various of its species. As
a genus, it is a highly general idea, applicable to all life forms. "A living thing desires above all to *vent* its strength—life as such is will to power . . ."[3] As applied
to humans, the need to "vent one's strength" (or expand) is connected essentially with their nature as active, growing, developing beings, rather than mere
receptacles of pleasure or welfare.

On the face of it, this broad notion of will to power is almost devoid of content, and as such seems an unpromising base for a virtue ethics. Maudmarie
Clark claims, for example, "that the psychological doctrine of the will to power
. . . does not deserve serious consideration as an empirical hypothesis."[4] Her reason for this claim is that it does not explain anything, for will to power is "at
work everywhere."[5] The will to power hypothesis can survive this objection, in
her view, only if it ceases to be monistic. "Will to power" would have to be defined so that at least some *possible* motives are not instances of it.[6] I shall pro-

---

2. (Oxford: Clarendon Press, 2001), 107.
3. *Beyond Good and Evil,* trans. R. J. Hollingdale (London: Penguin Books, 1973), 44.
4. "Nietzsche's Doctrines of the Will to Power," in *Nietzsche,* ed. John Richardson and Brian Leiter
(Oxford: Oxford University Press 2001), 139–149, at 140.
5. Ibid., 141.
6. Ibid.

pose an account of the ethical dimensions of will to power that can survive the objection. The account has several aspects. The first is structural. Will to power is understood through the multifarious ways it can be distorted. J.L. Austin's attack on the notion of real did not eliminate the notion, or restrict the broad range of phenomena to which it could be applied. Rather we had to divest ourselves of certain essentialist understandings. We had to focus on the various disparate ways things are not real if we were to secure a substantive contentful understanding. Again, Austin argued, it is unfreedom or lack of freedom, and not freedom, that "wears the trousers." As far as will to power is concerned, the situation is more complex. We give content to "will to power" not by considering the various ways it can be absent, but by considering the various ways it can be distorted.

This brings us to the second aspect of the account: a relation between the idea of distorted will to power and its ethical dimensions. Distorted will to power underlies vice, whereas virtue is marked by an absence of such distortion. Pity as a vice can thereby be distinguished from virtuous altruism, which Nietzsche frequently calls "overflowing"; laziness as a vice can be distinguished from virtuous "letting things be"; resignation or "willessness" distinguished from sublimation, and (virtuous) solitariness; courage from self destructive recklessness; and anxiety ridden fear from proper prudence.

Thirdly, and finally, will to power can have explanatory power only if the disparate forms of distorted will to power can be seen to be related in a theoretically interesting way. That requires that the notion be fleshed out within a psychological framework that gives substantive content to the various virtues and vices. Such a framework, I suggest, may be provided by the development of Nietzsche's psychology along the lines of Alfred Adler's views and those of later theorists and practitioners. Maudmarie Clark's criticism of will to power, I conclude, has bite only if will to power is seen as a simple positive motive without complex normative dimensions.

The confusion of will to power as a genus with species of will to power (or power) as e.g. augmenting influence and power over, as well as the neglect of the aretaic, have led to immoralist interpretations of Nietzsche. For example, in Stephen D. Hales's consequentialist interpretation of Nietzsche,[7] the distinction between will to power generally, and unhealthy, distorted will to power is not drawn. On Hales's interpretation of Nietzsche, the value to be promoted is power as such, whether or not it expresses or promotes distorted forms. "It appears that his consequentialism ultimately aims at the maximisation of power."[8] By contrast, on my view, Nietzsche distinguishes between "life-affirming" and

---

7. "Was Nietzsche a Consequentialist?" *International Studies in Philosophy* 27 (1995): 25–34.
8. 32.

"life-denying" will to power, a distinction giving some content to the idea of distorted versus undistorted will to power. This idea is present in psychology, where, for example, Erich Fromm contrasts "malignant" and "benign" forms of aggression.[9]

I have suggested that the idea of will to power, properly understood, can provide a basis for a rich psychologically informed conception of virtue. However, if such an understanding is to be garnered from Nietzsche, some kind of unity in his theory is not easy to find. There seem to be two starting points for an account of undistorted will to power: will to power that is not unhealthy, and will to power that is not life denying. Note, however, that these notions are best understood, not as prescribing a monistic blueprint for a virtuous life, but as permitting multiple options constrained by (non-absolute and sometimes conflicting) requirements to avoid various forms of distortion.

3. Undistorted Will to Power: Life-Affirmation

It is time now to give an account of undistorted will to power, for that account makes for normativity—in short, for an ethics. However, wresting such an account from Nietzsche is difficult. For Nietzsche's (or a Nietzschean) notion of undistorted will to power has at its heart two central ideas: life affirmation and health. Unfortunately (from the point of view of presenting a unified theory) these two ideas do not appear to pull in the same direction. Of most concern is that what may count as life affirming may be said on depth psychological criteria apparently favored by Nietzsche to be sick. In short we have two potential criteria for undistorted will to power—will to power that is life affirming or not life denying, and will to power that is healthy or not sick.

Let us now investigate the moral theoretic underpinnings of a morality that is based on life affirmation. The life affirmative aspects of Nietzsche's thought bear the hallmarks of a value-centered morality. The values in question are the "life affirming" ones of, for example, creativity, self-assertion, spontaneity, overflowing, lightness of spirit, play. Life affirming value theory may or may not be virtue ethical. It is virtue ethical only if the life affirming values of creativity, spontaneity, play, etc. are to be understood as aretaic; that is, as having excellence or virtue built into them. Non-aretaic value centered moralities rely on the provision of a set of "base-level" values (such as spontaneity, creativity, and play) specified independently of virtue. Such moralities then define virtues as dispositions to respond to these values appropriately—e.g. to promote them, honor

---

9. *The Anatomy of Human Destructiveness* (London: Penguin Books, 1977).

them, or (as on Thomas Hurka's view) to love them.[10] "Virtue" is thus understood derivatively in terms of certain sorts of responsiveness to, or dispositions to, act favorably towards those values.

A virtue ethics requires by contrast aretaic interpretations of the relevant values—creativity must be creativity that is free from all vice (or more weakly, some relevant vices); play cannot be, for example, mocking, or (in competitive sport) must be competitive without violating standards of fair play. Is an aretaic reading of the life affirming values a plausible reading of Nietzsche? I think so. A unifying aretaic value central in Nietzsche's thought is the absence of something described as "the greatest ugliness"—mediocrity. The absence of mediocrity is inherently an aretaic idea; indeed, it connotes the satisfaction (to a sufficient degree) of standards of excellence. The substantive task, of course, is to provide theories about what constitutes mediocrity in, for example, music, the visual arts, politics, relationships, philosophy, and other areas of human endeavor and culture. The specification of spontaneity, play, self-assertion, as *aretaic* values cannot be given without having to hand theories of excellence in those endeavors.

If the absence of mediocrity provides the aretaic value which unifies the various "life affirming" values, may it not provide too, the central value which underpins the second understanding of undistorted will to power—that is, the healthy will to power or will to power that is free of sickness? If so, then the two understandings of undistorted will to power can be combined into a single Nietzschean virtue ethics. Unhealthy and life denying will to power could then be seen as both expressing and promoting mediocrity, for Nietzsche. Much of Nietzsche's thought does indeed support this idea. Pity, a manifestation of "sick" will to power (for reasons to be explained), is also harmful to life affirming values, by undermining the achievements of "man's lucky hits" (i.e. those free of sickness), and by not accepting "meaningful suffering," so needed for the finest creativity and the avoidance of mediocrity.

However, there are two problems with this unificatory move. First, not all "sickness" and life denial seems connected with mediocrity. There is no doubt that Nietzsche regarded the self-laceration of Christian saints (such as St. Teresa of Avila) as unhealthy and life denying, but it would be hard to describe such saints as mediocre. Rather, their actions and motivations are unhealthy and life denying because of their connection with a sense of individual worthlessness.

It may be replied that I have just cited self-assertiveness as a life affirming value, and as such, as one of the values unified by the aretaic value of absence of mediocrity. Indeed this is so. But the kind of lack of self-assertiveness which is particularly associated in Nietzsche's thought with mediocrity, is the pas-

---

10. See *Virtue, Vice, and Value* (Oxford: Oxford University Press, 2001).

sivity of herd-like behavior condemned by Nietzsche in passages such as the following:

> For this is how things stand: the withering and levelling of European man consti-
> tutes *our* greatest danger, because it is a wearying sight . . . Today we see nothing
> with any desire to become greater, we sense that everything is going increasingly
> downhill, thinning out, getting more good natured, cleverer, more comfortable,
> more mediocre, more indifferent, more Chinese, more Christian—man, there is
> no doubt, is 'improving' all the time . . .[11]

Although in Nietzsche's view one could describe St. Teresa of Avila as suffering from a highly problematic sense of worthlessness, one could not describe
her as herd-like or mediocre.

Here is the second problem with the unificatory move. In Nietzsche's view,
it seems, the halting of the slide to mediocrity can be achieved by certain expressions of what, in views recoverable from Nietzsche, could be regarded as
sick. Consider the apparently grandiose artist or philosopher living the ethics of
creativity. Of such a person, Nietzsche claims: "he is not far from the sinful wish:
pereat mundus, fiat philosophia, fiat philosophus, fiam!"[12] ["Let the world perish, but
let there be philosophy, the philosopher, me!"] Such a philosopher "does *not*
deny existence, he rather affirms *his* existence and *only* his existence."[13] Even
the sickness of bad conscience is lauded by Nietzsche, if it has a creative vigor:
if it becomes "*active* bad conscience" and "[brings] to light much that is new and
disturbing in the way of beauty and affirmation . . ."[14]

So let us think of life-affirmation and health as two somewhat independent
aspects of undistorted will to power and move on now to health.

4. Undistorted Will to Power: Health

Anticipating psychoanalytic theory, Nietzsche not only largely understands
health through the idea of sickness, but also shares that view's general pessimism.
"For man is more sick, more uncertain, more mutable, less defined, than any
other animal . . . he is *the* sick animal." And, "He is . . . the most endangered,
the most chronically and deeply sick of all sick animals . . ."[15] The sickness that

---

11. *On the Genealogy of Morals,* First Essay, 12, trans. Douglas Smith (Oxford: Oxford University Press, 1996), 28.
12. Ibid., Essay 3, 7; 87.
13. Ibid.
14. Ibid., Essay 2, 18; 68.
15. Ibid., Essay 3, 13; 100.

is at the forefront of Nietzsche's attention is resentment: a manifestation of what Alfred Adler was later to call the inferiority complex. In this complex, according to Adler, there is a gap between the despised self and the ego-ideal that at an unconscious level are in conflict. In the inferiority complex, the conflict results in various sorts of neurotic resolution with neurotic "symptoms." The symptom of resentment, at least in its supposed Christian form, is the topic of Nietzsche's best known discussion, but he is remarkably insightful on two other species of inferiority complex: what Karen Horney was later to call the expansionist solution or the desire for mastery (grandiosity and cruelty) and the solution of resignation.[16] The intellectualist version of the latter is the frequent target of Nietzsche's scorn. He excoriates philosophers who retreat to the world of abstraction and pure reason. I shall concentrate on the Christian version of a resentment-filled inferiority complex (called by Karen Horney the self-effacing solution of love) that is particularly important for a Nietzschean distinction between virtue and closely allied vices, as we shall presently see.

What, according to Nietzsche, is resentment? As Bernard Reginster puts it, Nietzsche's person of resentment is inhibited by a feeling of incurable impotence, while retaining "pride" or "arrogance" and a desire at some level to lead a life of nobility and strength.[17] Furthermore, the conflict between the sense of weakness and expansionist strivings is not resolved: either by a stoical elimination of desire or by a full (self loving) acceptance of one's objectively-based weakness.

The conflict between a desire to lead a life of strength, nobility, or achievement and a sense of being impotent and worthless creates a need for resolution. As a manifestation of this conflict, resentment consists in a certain sort of distorted resolution of this conflict, one that valorizes the welfare of the weak, and thereby the altruistic virtues, while at the same time failing to overcome a sense of impotence. This results in externalized self-hate. Hence the manner in which the altruistic virtues are expressed is one of repressed hostility and revenge, as is highlighted in Nietzsche's discussion of pity in *Daybreak*.

> An accident that happens to another offends us: it would make us aware of our impotence, and perhaps of our cowardice, if we did not go to assist him. Or it brings with it in itself a diminution of our honour in the eyes of others or in our own eyes. Or an accident and suffering incurred by another constitutes a signpost to some danger to us; and it can have a painful effect upon us simply as a token of human vulnerability and fragility in general. We repel this kind of pain and offence and requite it through an act of pity; it may contain a subtle self-defense or even

16. Karen Horney, *Neurosis and Human Growth: The Struggle Toward Self-Realization* (New York: Norton, 1970).

17. "*Ressentiment*, Evaluation and Integrity," *International Studies in Philosophy* 27(1995): 117–124, 118.

a piece of revenge. That at bottom we are thinking very strongly of ourselves can be divined from the decision we arrive at in every case in which we *can* avoid the sight of the person suffering, perishing or complaining: we decide *not* to do so if we can present ourselves as the more powerful and as a helper, if we are certain of applause, if we want to feel how fortunate we are in contrast, or hope that the sight will relieve our boredom.[18]

In Nietzsche, non-virtuous altruism—pity—is characterized by self-referential comparisons masking externalized hostility. By contrast, genuine virtuous altruism is an overflowing expression of self-love, where the distorted will to power of pity is absent. This is clear in the following passage. "In the foreground stands the feeling of plenitude, of power which seeks to overflow, the happiness of high tension, the consciousness of wealth which would like to give away and bestow."[19] This sentiment, even the language, is echoed by Erich Fromm.

> For the productive character, giving has an entirely different meaning. Giving is the highest expression of potency. In the very act of giving, I experience my strength, my wealth, my power. This experience of heightened vitality and potency fills me with joy. I experience myself as overflowing, spending, alive, hence, as joyous.[20]

The overflowing and, indeed, passional nature of many of Nietzsche's virtues is a phenomenon approvingly discussed by Robert Solomon.[21] But there is a problem with Nietzsche's valorizing such virtues on the grounds that they are life affirming. Grandiosity and grandiose self-destructiveness are, in Horney's view, one of the faces of the neurotic "expansionist" solution. This is what Horney calls a "streamlined" neurotic solution to the problem of dynamic conflict between the "superior" self (the "ego-ideal"—to use Adler's term) and the despised self, in the inferiority complex. In this version of streamlined solution, the inferior self is ruthlessly suppressed, in contrast to the self-effacing solution in which the superior self—the ego-ideal—is suppressed. I am not suggesting that all "overflowing" is sick as opposed to expressing a genuine "plenteousness": a Nietzschean term favored also by Fromm and C. S. Lewis to describe genuine agapeic love. But certainly some kinds of overflowing favored by Nietzsche seem, on the face of it, to be suspect. Consider the following from *Thus Spoke*

---

18. Nietzsche, *Daybreak*, sec. 133, trans. R. J. Hollingdale (Cambridge: Cambridge University Press), 84.
19. *Beyond Good and Evil*, sec. 260, trans. Walter Kaufmann (New York: Vintage Books 1996), 205.
20. Erich Fromm, *The Art of Loving* (1957; London: Unwin Paperbacks, 1975), 26.
21. See his "Nietzsche's Virtues: a Personal Inquiry," in *Nietzsche's Postmoralism: Essays on Nietzsche's Prelude to Philosophy's Future*, ed. Richard Schacht (Cambridge: Cambridge University Press, 2001), 123–48.

Zarathustra: "I love him whose soul squanders itself, who wants no thanks and returns none: for he always gives away and does not want to preserve himself. I love him whose soul is overfull, so that he forgets himself, and all things are in him: thus all things spell his going under."[22]

5. Nietzschean Virtue Ethics: Content and Structure.

In this section, I shall claim that the apparent tensions revealed in the previous two sections between ideals of health and life affirmation can be resolved by the development of a Nietzschean virtue ethics based on Nietzsche's ideas of "self overcoming," or "becoming who you are": an ethics that does not presuppose the idea of an individual end state of perfection. In brief, in this resolution, we are not to see health and life affirmation as end states of perfection. There are two broad possibilities for resolution. First, one could imagine that those who are to become "who they are" are a select few, for this is the means to realize the perfectionist-consequentialist goal of cultural excellence. This does not entail that *individuals* have, or should have, a definite goal in mind when they improve themselves in "self-overcoming." Second, one could reject consequentialism while maintaining the aretaic value of avoiding mediocrity. "Becoming who you are" is an injunction for all to follow, by exemplifying worthwhile achievement in one's own life and not destroying or undermining the achievements of others.

I shall adopt the second of these strategies. The central idea is that the tensions can be resolved if we conceive of Nietzschean virtue as essentially tied to self improvement (self-overcoming) which does not presuppose an end-state of individual perfection, in contrast to Aristotelian conceptions of virtue as end-states of perfection. If both health and life affirmation are seen as end states of perfection, and virtue as exemplifying both these ideals, then a virtue ethics based on them would appear to have an incoherent conception of virtue, since, it seems, they are conflicting ideals of perfection. By contrast, if norms of health and life affirmation are to be embedded in a virtue ethics of self-improvement, the tensions between these norms can be resolved. I shall claim that one can do this by recognizing that their function as norms is constrained by norms of development, such as "do not be virtuous beyond your strength."

Both the consequentialist and non-consequentialist strategies for overcoming the tensions between health and life affirmation as ideals presuppose that we

22. *Thus Spoke Zarathustra*, in *The Portable Nietzsche*, ed. and trans. W. Kaufmann (New York: Penguin Books, 1976), 127–128.

can speak of excellence in a process of betterment—in a process of what Nietzsche calls "overcoming." For we can attempt to improve ourselves in ways that fall short of satisfying norms of development by, for example, running before we can walk (emulating the supremely virtuous), seeing an analyst when we should not be, or not seeing an analyst when we should, being overly reflective or insufficiently reflective, and so on. However, how this idea features in the consequentialist strategy is quite different from the way it figures in non-consequentialist views.

Before developing the non-consequentialist alternative, let us take a quick look at the consequentialist strategy, for this has been a dominant interpretation of Nietzsche. Many commentators have understood Nietzsche as a particularly nasty exemplar of perfectionistic consequentialism. Perfectionism, whether consequentialist or non-consequentialist, is the view that goodness or value is to be understood as "the realization of human excellence in the various forms of culture."[23] Perfectionism in this sense is virtue-theoretic, if these excellences include, in a central way, the virtues (however they are conceived in that theory). However, a virtue-theoretic form of perfectionism may be consequentialist, in which case it would not be virtue *ethical* on normal understandings. In fact, John Rawls ascribes to Nietzsche what Conant calls "excellence-consequentialism," which means "(1) that the perfectionist is concerned with optimizing the conditions which promote the achievement of excellence in the arts and sciences, and (2) that the goodness of an action is to be assessed in accordance with the degree to which it maximises such forms of excellence."[24]

There is some textual evidence that Nietzsche supports this view. An example of such evidence occurs in *Beyond Good and Evil:*

> The essential thing in a good and healthy aristocracy is, however, that it does *not* feel itself to be a function (of the monarchy or of the commonwealth) but as their *meaning* and supreme justification—that it therefore accepts with a good conscience the sacrifice of innumerable men who *for its sake* have to be suppressed and reduced to imperfect men, to slaves and instruments. Its fundamental faith must be that society should *not* exist for the sake of society but only as foundation and scaffolding upon which a select species of being is able to raise itself to its higher task and in general to a higher *existence:* like those sun-seeking climbing plants of Java— they are named *sipo matador*—which clasp an oak-tree with their tendrils so long and often that at last, high above it but supported by it, they can unfold their crowns in the open light and display their happiness.[25]

23. James Conant, "Nietzsche's Perfectionism: A Reading of *Schopenhauer as Educator*," in *Nietzsche's Postmoralism.*

24. See 187.

25. *Beyond Good and Evil,* sec. 258; 193.

Insofar as this passage suggests a perfectionist consequentialism, norms of self-improvement, whether relating to health or life affirmation, are subservient to the promotion of the goal of overall cultural excellence understood in the following way. The measure of cultural excellence is given by the overall achievement of the best or most talented members of society. Tensions between ideals of health and life affirmation are resolved by understanding them in an instrumental way. If "sick" grandiosity in a talented artist enhances the realization of cultural achievement such "sickness" is to be tolerated, even applauded. However, the consequentialist understanding does not sit well with a central theme in Nietzsche: the requirement on all of us to "become who you are"; to work at discovering and expressing the genius within you. Let us now elaborate the second, non-consequentialist strategy for overcoming the tensions revealed in the previous section.

The dynamic features of a non-consequentialist Nietzschean ethics are captured in the aphorism, "Become who you are" where the injunction is intended to apply to all, and virtues are understood as expressive of an individual's living this maxim in her own life as opposed to their being seen as traits whose status as virtues is wholly dependent on their systematically promoting the consequentialist-perfectionist goal. The aphorism, however, is on the face of it mysterious, suggesting that there is a final state (of perhaps perfection) which is your *true* self and which you have a duty to reach. However this reading seems un-Nietzschean: as Alexander Nehemas points out, for Nietzsche, "becoming does not aim at a final state."[26] A less problematic reading is suggested by the expanded version of the aphorism in "Schopenhauer as Educator": "The human being who does not wish to belong to the mass needs only to cease being comfortable with himself; let him follow his conscience, which calls to him: "Be yourself! All you are now doing, thinking, desiring is not you yourself."[27]

As Conant puts it, "All one need do is become uncomfortable with the discrepancy between oneself and one's self—between who we are at present, and the self that is somehow ours and yet presently at a distance from us."[28] This does not entail that there is an end-state of "arrival" where the self, or one of the selves, presently at a distance from us, is the terminus of our endeavors. Self-improvement should be the basis of our endeavors, but that does not mean that we should have definite productive goals such as being a great artist, which now drive all our actions. Nor is there an *end*-state of perfection that one can reach such that one can say on reaching it that "I have arrived." Rather, improvement is a continuous matter of overcoming obstacles, becoming stronger, while deal-

---

26. "How One Becomes What One Is," in *Nietzsche,* ed. Richardson and Leiter, 255–80; at 261.
27. Nietzsche, "Schopenhauer as Educator," in *Untimely Meditations,* Third Essay; cited in James Conant, 197.
28. Ibid.

ing with the world and achieving worthwhile goals. These goals may themselves change as one becomes stronger and faces new obstacles and circumstances. John Richardson puts the point well.[29] Having argued that "will to power," or power, is not itself an end but is constituted by improvement, growth, or development in "patterns of effort" in achieving the various internal ends of "drives," he claims that

> This makes the connection between power and a drive's internal end even less direct than we expected: not only does power not lie in this end's achievement, it doesn't even lie in progress toward it but in improving this progress. Moreover, the criteria for this "improvement" aren't set by the end—it's not just an improvement in the route's efficiency for achieving the end. Rather . . . it lies in an enrichment or elaboration of the drive's activity pattern.[30]

Although there need be no final state to which we should aspire, which constitutes a norm of perfection, there do need to be norms of self improvement, if the idea of becoming who you are is to make sense as an injunction for self improvement.

How are norms of life affirmation and health constrained by developmental norms of self-improvement? Given that improvement is something that occurs step by step, what norms govern the steps we take? In *Zarathustra*, Nietzsche claims: "Do not be virtuous beyond your strength!"[31] Clearly this is not a recipe for complacency or timidity: it has to be given a dynamic reading. The point of the injunction is to warn us against directly emulating the supremely virtuous. For such emulation is not appropriate to one in a state of "convalescence." According to this view, a conception of a virtue such as generosity may be understood not merely as a threshold notion (such that it is possible that one is both virtuous and capable of improvement) but also as a continuum, relativized to the strength of the agent. Hence (virtuous) generosity for the self-improver may not be overflowing bounteousness, for attempts at such bounteousness in the relatively weak may constitute self-destructive, resentment-filled, self-sacrifice that is ultimately harmful to others as well as oneself. A core virtue, or core component of virtue, such as self love, will not have the same features at different points along the self improvement path. Just as a truly self confident society will be able to dispense with punishment according to Nietzsche, so the strongest individuals will be able to say: "Of what concern are these parasites to me?"[32] In other words, turning the other cheek is a virtue of the strong. By contrast,

---

29. See his "Nietzsche's Power Ontology," in *Nietzsche*, 150–185.
30. See 158.
31. *Thus Spoke Zarathustra*, pt. 4:13, "On the Higher Man," 403.
32. *On the Genealogy of Morals*, Essay 2, 10; 54.

such behaviour in the weak is likely to be a sign of regressive self-abasement. Though self love in the strong can manifest itself in a form of forgetfulness, in the weak, forgetfulness may be a form of repression in which anger is driven inwards and surfaces in various distortions: secretive revenge, bitterness, manipulativeness, jealousy. Better for the weak to display assertiveness, even of a retaliatory kind, to lessen their tendencies to be wounded. Nietzsche puts the point this way in *Ecce Homo:* "[The sick person] does not know how to get loose of anything, to become finished with anything to repel anything—everything injures. Human being and thing obtrude too closely; experiences strike one too deeply, memory is a festering wound."[33]

Again, to use another example of Nietzsche's, solitude as a disposition is a virtue of the strong; otherwise, it is loneliness, the escape *of* the sick as opposed to escape *from* the sick.[34] "In solitude, whatever one has brought into it grows— also the inner beast. Therefore solitude is inadvisable for the many."[35] In other words, though (proper) self sufficiency is a virtue, the proper cultivation and nature of that virtue is not straight forward—it will have different manifestations according to one's level of strength. The cultivation of solitude and a desire for such is not advised for the weak.

We are now in a position to see how a dynamic, non-consequentialist, Nietzschean virtue ethics resolves the tensions revealed in section four. Rather than health and life-affirmation being seen as somewhat independent states of perfection, norms of health and life-affirmation interact in differing ways in different contexts of self-improvement or "self-overcoming." Progress is not understood simply in terms of realizing an already given end, for the end itself is recreated more or less continuously, and in a variety of ways for a variety of reasons. First, one's "pattern of activity" is enriched and modified as one reshapes one's ends in the light of circumstances and developing desires and interests. Second, improving one's strength or health is not a smooth progress, for in a sense one must be careful not to overreach one's (current) strength. However, this is not to say that Nietzsche regards this as a universal injunction as opposed to a general warning. At times he appears to admire such overreaching. It would be a mistake to regard Nietzsche's norms as absolute and non-conflicting. Finally, virtue itself is shaped by norms of self-improvement. Though virtue rather than an amount of power, say, is at least a necessary condition of goodness in human beings, goodness should not be understood in terms of realizing an end state of perfection.

The proposed understanding of a Nietzschean virtue ethics poses a problem. For is it not the case that building self-improvement into the very fabric of virtue is an oxymoron? Is not a virtue a stable trait of character? Answering this ques-

33. *Ecce Homo,* 1, 6.
34. *Thus Spoke Zarathustra,* pt. 3, "Upon the Mount of Olives," 287.
35. *Thus Spoke Zarathustra,* pt. 4, "On the Higher Education of Man," 404.

tion fully presupposes an account of character traits—their robustness and malleability. My own view, which cannot be defended here, is that virtues are more or less robust depending on where the threshold of virtue is set in different contexts. Secondly and more importantly, since practical wisdom is at least characteristically an aspect of virtue, virtue involves self-knowledge, including knowledge of where one is placed on the self-improvement path, and of how large or small are the steps one should take. Relative robustness had better not be confused with rigidity, incapacity to develop further, and imperviousness to changing contexts. However, this is not to deny that virtue, at high levels, is constituted by a solid core of incorruptible integrity, honesty, and so forth: a core of virtue not readily undermined by corrosive social forces and institutions.

Let me now summarize the main features of a Nietzschean virtue ethics. I began this paper with the claim that Nietzsche's ethics is aretaic in the sense that goodness in things is to be understood as having excellence built into them. Where excellence in things is characteristically understood as their either being handled virtuously (say, virtuously handled money, honors, play, friendship, pleasure), or their being themselves virtuous (virtuous human beings), such an ethics is a candidate for being a virtue ethics.

The content of Nietzschean virtue ethics is to be understood in terms of undistorted will to power, which has two aspects: life-affirmation and health. However, these are not to be understood as end-states of perfection, but as norms of self-improvement. The idea of undistorted will to power enables us to distinguish between virtues and closely allied vices, such as the forms of altruistic virtue and vice.

A Nietzschean virtue ethics can be seen as a non-consequentialist version of perfectionism in the sense defined above. However, Nietzschean virtue ethics is a non-standard form of perfectionism insofar as the road traveled seems more important than the destination. Self-improvement is a process, itself having norms of excellence, but (1) those norms do not presuppose that there is a single goal suitable for all, for we are all different in strength, talents, interests, and circumstances of life, (2) in a process of "self overcoming" we do not necessarily have in mind a long term destination, for the good life may involve much experimentation, and (3) virtue itself should not be understood as an end state of perfection. Rather, insofar as "self-overcoming" is at the core of virtue, it is a dynamic process-notion, relativized to the strength of individuals as well as to their roles and circumstances.[36]

36. I owe grateful thanks to Steve Gardiner for his helpful suggestions for improvement, and for organizing the conference in Christchurch, New Zealand, for which this paper was written. Thanks also to the participants, especially Robert Solomon.

CHAPTER 10

The Virtues, Perfectionist Goods, and Pessimism

GEORGE W. HARRIS

Philosophers often appeal to a variety of tests for determining if a moral theory is acceptable. Can the theory solve the problem of relativism? Can it answer the egoist by providing a rational foundation for intrinsic concern for others? Can it refute the moral skeptic by providing a basis for moral knowledge? Does it result in a reflective equilibrium of our considered moral judgments? Does it provide an account superior to its competitors of the good, the right, and the virtuous? These and many other tests are often appealed to with different degrees of emphasis by contemporary analytic philosophers in their quest for a moral theory that requires our allegiance. Seldom invoked by these philosophers is another test that was central to philosophical thinking in the nineteenth century: the test of confronting pessimism, the philosophical view that the bad hopelessly outweighs the good.[1] The naivety with which this test is bypassed and left unaddressed by otherwise very sophisticated analytic philosophers is staggering, because even if a theory passed all the other tests, it would still face the formidable task, especially in light of the tragedies of the 20th and early 21st centuries, of showing that our lives and our world are on balance worth preserving.

Some might object that the only test of a moral theory is whether it is true, and it is made no better as a moral theory for providing a response to the philosophical pessimist. How, the worry goes, does the truth of a moral theory turn on responding to the pessimist, since the response to the pessimist is a conse-

---

1. Arthur Schopenhauer, *Philosophical Writings,* edited by Wolfgang Schirmacher (New York: Continuum, 1998), 13–18, 27–41.

quence of the truth of the theory? Should it, then, be a constraint on a moral theory that it be consistent with our having reasons for living? Suppose the answer to the last question is no, because on the true moral theory we (all of humanity) have moral reasons for not living, for ending human existence, because the facts of the world and moral values conspire in a way that yield the result that it would be morally better that there were no people. If we can imagine the latter, then it is not a constraint on the truth of a moral theory that it be consistent with our having reasons for living.

Since I believe that it is possible for us to imagine that it would be morally better if there were no people, the objection has real force. So how can I argue that the task of responding to the pessimist is a burden on the moral theorist?

Part of the answer is that truth is not the only desirable feature of a moral theory. We do not begin our theorizing about morality with a mere cognitive interest in moral truth. We begin also with the hope that reflection on our values, both nonmoral and moral, will provide us with reasons for living and with reasons for living one way rather than another. It is the burden of either grounding or dashing this hope that makes it a task of the moral theorist to answer the pessimist. How, for example, can we have the obligation to construct our basic institutions on the basis of, say, Rawls' difference principle (or any other principle) if pessimism is true? All or certainly most of the analytic moral theories currently in vogue blithely assume that moral hope is not mere wish but a rational attitude to take toward life. How else do we explain why advocates of those theories never even address whether the alleged truth of their theories justifies their optimism? The fact remains that any moral theory that says that the task of regulating our ongoing daily lives is justified assumes a minimal level of optimism. For such theories, it is a part of the alleged truth of those theories that pessimism is false. For these theories, it is just as much a burden to respond to the pessimist as it is a burden to respond to the skeptic. Why? Because on these theories it is just as much a part of the truth of morality that morality is consistent with our having reasons for living as it is that genocide is wrong. Another part of the answer is that regardless of whether a moral theory is optimistic or pessimistic, it is still surely a test of its plausibility that it must give a plausible answer to the question that pessimism raises, just as it must give a plausible answer to the questions raised by skepticism and relativism.

Suppose, then, I test a moral theory by asking if, according to the theory, my life is worth living? Does the intrinsic value of my life, according to the theory, give me good reasons to continue it? Or to put the question in global terms: is our world worth preserving? Does the intrinsic value of our world give us good reasons not to destroy it? Optimism says yes, and pessimism says no. One way, therefore, of adjudicating the dispute between virtue ethics and its theoretical competitors is by judging their responses to pessimism. So I begin with the thought that if a theory can plausibly give us good reasons for loving our world and our lives it is better, everything else being equal, than a theory that gives us reasons for hating them. A second thought is that we have good reasons for loving rather than hating our world and our lives if we have good reasons for thinking that they contain more good than bad.[2]

In what follows, I will consider Thomas Hurka's recent case against virtue ethics and his account of perfectionist goods in the context of the problem of pessimism, focusing on the good of knowledge. I will argue that the agent–neutral feature of his account distorts the value of knowledge, conceals the evil of ignorance, and threatens victory for the pessimist. In the process, I will contrast a different account of the good of knowledge and the evil of ignorance and suggest that the structure of virtue ethics need not deny the recursive value of the virtues. What it must deny, however, is the agent-neutrality of Hurka's account in favor of an agent-centered approach. So structured, virtue ethics provides firmer grounds for optimism regarding the balance of perfectionist goods over perfectionist evils than Hurka's account, especially the good of knowledge and the evil of false belief and ignorance.

1. Hurka, Recursiveness, and Pessimism

Hurka's general case against virtue ethics is his recursive account of the virtues, according to which virtue is accommodated within an agent-neutral form of consequentialism.[3] Though most consequentialists afford virtue only

2. The comparative judgment involved in this sentence does not dictate a certain familiar maximizing strategy associated with consequentialism. It does not imply that the goal of practical reason or morality is to "promote" some good that makes for optimal states of affairs. Rather, the thought is a simple one: sometimes life is not worth living and sometimes it is. What is it about a life worth living that makes it so? is a question to which there are a variety of answers, all of which imply some conception of balancing good over bad. Philosophers may disagree about what kind of balancing is at the heart of such judgments, but they cannot dismiss the issue of pessimism by tainting it as a relic of a consequentialist mistake. Moreover, the same is true of whether our world is worth preserving. That things might get bad enough in the world, all things considered, to raise doubts about preserving it is not an incoherent thought generated either by consequentialism or any other form of moral theory. Indeed, it is coherent to the proverbial "man on the street" and on any plausible conception of good and bad, consequentialist or otherwise. Any attempt, then, to eliminate the problem of pessimism by conceptual analysis is bound to fail. For virtue ethic criticisms of consequentialism, see Philippa Foot, *Natural Goodness* (Oxford: Oxford University Press, 2001), 48–50 and Christine Swanton, "Virtue Ethics, Value-Centeredness, and Consequentialism," *Utilitas* (July 2001): 213–235. See also, Elizabeth Anderson, "Practical Reason and Incommensurable Goods," in *Incommensurability, Incomparability, and Practical Reason*, ed. Ruth Chang (Cambridge, Massachusetts: Harvard University Press, 1997), 90–109.

3. Thomas Hurka, *Virtue, Vice, and Value* (New York: Oxford University Press, 2001).

instrumental value, Hurka affords it intrinsic value by distinguishing between generic goods and goods of virtue. Generic goods are goods like pleasure, achievement, and knowledge, and the virtues are appropriate attitudes toward generic goods, which themselves have intrinsic value. If x is intrinsically good, loving x for itself is also intrinsically good and being indifferent to or hating x is intrinsically evil. Conversely, if x is intrinsically evil, then loving or being indifferent to x is intrinsically evil and hating x is intrinsically good. For example, the relief of suffering is an intrinsic hedonic good and compassion is the virtue of hating suffering which itself has intrinsic value. What we should aim at from the moral point of view is maximizing intrinsic value from the global perspective. This means that we should maximize the highest balance of intrinsic good over intrinsic evil, considering both generic goods and evils and virtues and vices. It is this maximizing strategy from the global perspective that makes Hurka's theory an agent-neutral form of consequentialism. It will be a virtue, then, to love our world if we believe truly that it is on balance good and a vice to love our world if we believe truly that it is on balance bad.

How does this lead to an argument against virtue ethics? The structure of the argument is revealed in Hurka's refutation of the so-called "virtue defense" of the theistic problem of evil.[4] According to the virtue defense of theism, the intrinsic evil of suffering that exists in the world is counter-balanced by the good of the virtue of compassion (and any other virtues) it generates. So theistic pessimism is averted by the appeal to the intrinsic value of virtue. That this is a bad defense is established according to Hurka by the recursive account and a plausible account of the value of virtue in relationship to the generic goods to which the virtues are attached. The most plausible view, according to Hurka, is that the intrinsic value of a virtue *per se* is less than the value of the generic good to which it is attached. Compassion, therefore, has intrinsic value but less than the generic good to which it is related. Consequently, the relief of suffering is more important *per se* than the compassion it generates. The person who loves compassion more than the elimination of suffering fails to love the good in the appropriate way. A good God, then, could not have justified the existence of suffering as we in fact know it for the sake of the compassion it generates in good people. The burden Hurka shifts to those who would value virtue in a way that it could, as a matter of fact, make our lives or our world love-worthy when other values do not is a formidable one. The onus is the challenge of making plausible the claim that the virtues are either equally or more important than the generic goods to which they are attached. And it is a hard burden to bear.

So should we be optimists or pessimists? Should we love our lives and our

4. Hurka, *Virtue, Vice, and Value*, 129–61.

world, or should we hate them? On Hurka's recursive account, we can add to the value of a love-worthy life or world by adding the virtue of loving them, but, barring some very implausible empirical assumptions, we cannot make them love-worthy by loving them if they are not already so.[5] Not only does this undermine the virtue defense of theism, but it also undermines any secular attempt to solve the problem of pessimism by appeal to the value of virtue. If a life or a world is not love-worthy without virtue, they will not likely be made love-worthy with it. This is one sense, then, in which a proper account of the virtues undermines virtue ethics. The implication is that the value of virtue is best made sense of on a theory in which aretaic concepts are subordinate to concepts of non-aretaic goods, something Hurka takes virtue ethics in all its forms to deny.

Now suppose you are suffering more than you are subjectively flourishing and that it is not rational to believe that this will change. Make the same assumptions regarding the world, that it contains more suffering than subjective flourishing and that it is rational to believe that this is not going to change. Add to this that with regard to all other generic goods except perfectionist goods, there is a net loss in goodness. Then on the recursive account, if we put perfectionist goods aside, neither your life nor your world is worth loving. To love it is a vice, and to hate it a virtue. But there remains the possibility that it is still a virtue to love your life and your world. It will be so only if there is some other kind of good that can be added to your life or to the world to make them better. Perfectionist goods, goods that consist not in their contribution to subjective flourishing but just in their being some highly developed state of human capacities, might do the work. Your life might be worth living, then, if there is some threshold level of perfectionist goods that if added to your life or to the world would counterbalance the evil of subjective suffering and other generic evils to make for a net balance of good over bad.

To keep things simple and focused, bracket considerations of all perfectionist goods except knowledge, a good widely prized by philosophers. Might the value of knowledge, a highly developed state of your human cognitive capacities, make your life worth loving where pleasure, love, and achievement fall short, assuming that they do not fall woefully short? The thought is not that there is no love in your life but that it just isn't enough compared to the hatred and indifference it contains. It is not that there is no pleasure, but just that your life is not on the whole pleasant, but painful. Similarly with achievement. It is

---

5. Suppose a few people suffer but many, many people feel compassion for the few. The numbers might convince us at some point that the compassion generated outweighs the suffering incurred. There are problems with such a suggestion independent of its implications regarding the empirical facts, but that nothing like this kind of empirical condition obtains is enough to foreclose any argument depending on it for plausibility.

not that you have achieved nothing, but that on balance there is more failure or lack of attempt than success. Might you nonetheless have a life worth living because there is enough knowledge to tip the scales into the positive column of good over bad and thereby make your life love-worthy? The same sorts of questions could be asked about a range of perfectionist goods, but I will limit the inquiry here to knowledge.

2. Hurka and the Features of Knowledge as a Perfectionist Good

According to Hurka, there are three fundamental features of knowledge as a perfectionist good: (1) knowledge is an agent-neutral good, (2) the value of knowledge is in its formal features, and (3) the negative counterpart to knowledge is false belief.

Consider the agent-neutral feature. A consequentialist theory of the sort advocated by Hurka calculates the value of a world in terms of knowledge parallel to the way in which a hedonistic utilitarian calculates the value of the world in terms of pleasure.[6] Individual utilities are first calculated and then summed somehow across persons to get a notion of social utility. If we take individual lives as the units of individual utilities where knowledge rather than pleasure is the gauge of utility, then a life is love-worthy, everything else being equal, if it contains a positive balance of knowledge over its generic opposite. A world will be love-worthy if when summed across persons there is more knowledge in that world than there is of its generic opposite. Knowledge is best distributed across persons when it is distributed in a way that maximizes the highest balance available of knowledge over its generic opposite. In the most general terms, this is what it is, on Hurka's view, to say that knowledge is an agent-neutral value.

Now consider the second feature of knowledge as a perfectionist good, namely, its formal nature. For knowledge to be a perfectionist good, it must be the development of something. For it to be a generic good, its value must not be merely instrumental. For Hurka, this means that knowledge is the development of a network of justified true beliefs. One network is better than another, more developed than another, if it contains a greater unity of justified true beliefs than the other, regardless of what those beliefs are about. The value, then, of knowledge as a generic good is purely formal. Usefulness of belief is not a generic but an instrumental value. Therefore, when we value knowledge for its own sake, we value it for its formal features: truthfulness, unity, and extent. The maximization of knowledge at the individual level is thus the widest

6. Hurka, *Virtue, Vice, and Value*, 109, 114, 198–200, 207–11.

possible network of justified true beliefs with as much unity among them as possible.[7]

This does not mean that all true beliefs stand on a par. Some have a unifying function that others do not. Knowing a principle of inference or a physical law is more important than knowing a particular, nongeneralizable fact, like how many hairs are on one's head. A belief-network organized in an explanatory hierarchy is more developed than an alternative network with an equal number of distinctly justified true beliefs. Still, the ultimate criterion for one network of beliefs being more developed than another is in terms of the extent of justified true beliefs it facilitates with maximal unity. Nothing of intrinsic importance turns on what one believes. This is what it is to say that Hurka's account of the value of knowledge is purely formal.

At the personal level, we can compare the formal value of knowledge networks by the extent of justified true beliefs they contain. Suppose A's and B's networks are equally unified, then A's epistemic life is better than B's if A's is more extensive than B's. If adding knowledge to a life makes it better, then surely adding more knowledge with equal or greater unity makes it better. The positive ratio between justified true belief and false belief can be broadened both by eliminating false beliefs and by adding new justified beliefs that either sustain or do no detract from the unity of one's knowledge. The crucial point is this: theoretically the solution to the problem of interpersonal comparisons of utility applied to knowledge, where knowledge rather than pleasure is the measure of utility, is some mathematical function of the ratio between unity and extent of justified true belief over whatever the generic opposite of knowledge is. All this follows from the formal account of the value of knowledge.

But like utilitarian versions of agent-neutral consequentialism, the solution to the problem of interpersonal comparisons is only one of several problems that have to be solved. What do we do with the individual utilities when we get them so that we arrive at an agent-neutral concept of the good that can be employed to rank worlds or states of affairs from best to worst or to judge whether they are on balance good or bad? Do we add the numbers, add and divide, or what?[8]

---

7. See Hurka, *Virtue, Vice, and Value*, 13. Speaking of both knowledge and achievement, he says, "Finally, for both goods the degree of value of an instance of them is determined by formal rather than substantive criteria. The best knowledge is not that of any particular subject matter but that whose content extends farthest across times and objects—think of scientific laws—and which has the most other knowledge subordinate to it in an explanatory hierarchy."

8. One of the most notorious problems is the problem of the repugnant conclusion. See Derek Parfit, *Reasons and Persons* (London: Clarendon Press, Oxford, 1984), 419–42. Applied to the issue of knowledge, which is the better epistemic world, one in which there are many very knowledgeable people with extensive justified true belief networks—or another world in which there are vastly higher numbers of people with very low levels of knowledge—people with very restricted knowledge networks—but whose cumulative knowledge is very extensive?

Whatever we do with the numbers reflects a notion of epistemic well-being, development, and perfection as those notions apply to a world.

To settle this issue, we must address both at the individual level and the global level what generic evil must be weighed against the generic good of knowledge. This question brings us to the third feature of Hurka's account. We are already assuming that the sums of other positive generic values are in and that they come up short. Without perfectionist goods, pessimism is in order. So the question is not about how knowledge stands in regard to nonperfectionist goods or to other perfectionist goods. Rather, it is about what the generic evil is relative to knowledge. What detracts from pleasure is pain and from love is hatred and indifference, but what about knowledge? If pain is the Hyde to the Jekyll of pleasure, what is the Hyde to the Jekyll of knowledge?

Hurka's answer is that it is false belief.[9] On this view, we can sum the perfectionist value of knowledge as the development of a network of true beliefs over false beliefs both at the individual and global levels. At the individual level, A's level of epistemic development is measured in terms of the balance of knowledge (with due consideration to unity) over false belief in A's network of beliefs, regardless of the content of A's beliefs. If network P yields a 3:1 ratio of knowledge to false belief and Q yields a 2:1 ratio of knowledge to false belief, then if A believes P and B believes Q, and all other values are equal, then A's life is better than B's. It follows from the above analysis of Hurka's account that if all other values are equal (if all other goods and evils result in a neutral or negative balance), if R is a network of beliefs in which the ratio of knowledge to false belief is negative, say, one-half, and A believes and can only believe R, then A's life is not love-worthy and therefore not worth living. There would be more evil in it than good. If A, then, has the virtue of hating evil, as she would on Hurka's recursive account of the virtues, she will hate her life.

At the global level, we might calculate the intrinsic epistemic worth of a world in terms of the ratio of knowledge to false belief for the average person in that world's population. There are problems with this view, just as there are problems with average utilitarianism, but they can be put aside for present purposes.[10] The point is that something like this (or some other mathematical formula, it does not matter here which) might be used to calculate the value of knowledge for populations of countries, or cities, or universities, or the total population of the world. In any of these social rather than individual calculations, if we are good

9. Hurka, Virtue, Vice, and Value, 15.

10. The problem for average utilitarianism is that it yields strongly counter-intuitive judgments of social utility. Which is the better world, one with a robust number of people who are extremely ecstatic or one including those people plus an equal number who are ever so slightly less ecstatic? The parallel with knowledge should be obvious.

consequentialists of the sort Hurka has in mind, we will be aiming (by hypothesis) at the highest ratio of knowledge to false belief attainable for the average person in the social group, regardless of the content of the beliefs involved and consistent with the worth of other values.[11] Moreover, if the ratio of the knowledge of the average person that we can produce is negative, then the world is intrinsically evil as far as the intrinsic value of knowledge is concerned. If the ratio of all other goods and evils is either equal or negative, then if we have the virtue of hating evil and loving the good, we will hate this world, and, barring other considerations, will be justified in global pessimism.

3. Two Views of the Good of Knowledge and the Evil of Ignorance

Whether this is acceptable turns in part on how the good of knowledge is to be understood. Hurka's view, insofar as it considers false belief as the only generic evil relative to knowledge, seems to be that the value of knowledge is to be understood as epistemic felicity. We have beliefs, and they can be either intrinsically good or intrinsically evil. They are intrinsically good when they are felicitous, and felicitous when matched with the world and we are justified in having them. They are intrinsically evil when they are infelicitous, and infelicitous when they are false.[12] According to this view, where there is no belief there is no cognitive evil, because there can be no infelicity of belief where there is no belief. The evil alternate to knowledge seems to be a kind of cognitive embarrassment, the embarrassment of having failed in belief where belief was attempted. The value of knowledge, then, is epistemic felicity because it makes belief true and justified, whereas false belief is epistemic infelicity because it deprives belief of what makes it good: truth and justification.

But what about ignorance? Hurka does not see ignorance as a generic evil. He employs a model for cognitive value that parallels the model for hedonic value. Pleasure is good; pain is evil; and hedonic zero is neutral. Similarly: justified true belief is good; false belief is evil; and ignorance is neutral. But surely, it is just false that only false belief is the privation of knowledge. At least on tradi-

---

11. I am not attributing something analogous to average utilitarianism to Hurka but simply employing that notion of maximization to illustrate a point. Just what maximization notion Hurka himself would employ is unclear. There is, however, a complication worth noting. The ratio might employ a 1:1 relationship between a unit of knowledge and a false belief, or it might weight units of false beliefs more heavily than units of knowledge. It will include the latter kind of weighting on a theory that says that it is better to avoid evil than to promote good, that evil is worse than good is good. Some might think that this is a general truth about value. I do not, and the formulation in the text is purposefully ambiguous on this point.

12. Hurka, *Virtue, Vice, and Value*, 15.

tional understandings of perfectionism, the kind of evil that is relative to a perfectionist value is not the kind of evil that is relative to a nonperfectionist value. For example, pleasure is not a perfectionist value, and one crucial way of showing this is that its evil alternate is not the privation of pleasure but a distinct negative value. Of course, one can be pained at pleasure denied, but the pain of migraine is not a form of low-level pleasure. Nonperfectionist values have distinct evil correlates. Perfectionist values, at least on the traditional view, do not. Perfectionist evil is the privation of good. And it is just false that only false belief is the privation of knowledge. What prevents us from knowing the cure for AIDS is in all probability more to be found in what we do not know than in what we falsely believe. Of course, this is practically important knowledge, but the same point applies for any area of knowledge. What prevents me from having a greater understanding of music is in what I do not know about music than in my false beliefs about music. The same is true for physics, math, philosophy, and a host of other bodies of belief or knowledge. Moreover, as Hurka himself notes, false belief can play a positive role in rational development (witness Aristotle's biology).[13] Ignorance cannot. It lurks as an evil devouring opportunity after opportunity for knowledge that is valuable in itself.

Moreover, there is a tension between the view that ignorance is value-neutral and that extent is a formal feature of the value of knowledge, as it clearly is on Hurka's view. If belief network A is as truthful and unified as network B but contains more justified true beliefs than B, then A is better than B in its formal features. And clearly what might make B inferior in this regard is the ignorance it reflects. Ignorance, then, would have to be a bad making quality of a belief network in terms of its lack of extent, one of the formal features of the value of knowledge.

There seems, then, to be a tension in Hurka's thought about the value of knowledge. Formally, extent is a measure of the value of knowledge, but only false belief is a formal evil. Insofar as he thinks of the value of knowledge in terms of its generic opposite, he thinks of the value of knowledge as epistemic felicity, something that can be added to belief to make it good rather than bad. Contrary to this view, the value of knowledge might be thought of not as epistemic felicity—something that makes beliefs good if one has them—but as cognitive access, a good that it is bad not to have. For any good that it is bad not to have, the privation of that good is an intrinsic evil. The question is whether knowledge and perfectionist goods in general are goods of this sort.[14] We will think that plea-

---

13. Thomas Hurka, *Perfectionism* (New York: Oxford University Press, 1993), 10.

14. Hurka has pointed out to me in correspondence that the theodicies of both Aquinas and Leibniz tried to exonerate God for the existence of some evil by holding the view that perfectionist goods were such that their privation was not a distinct intrinsic evil—the point being that a perfectionist good is not

sure is not such a good if we think that hedonic zero is value-neutral. This is what Hurka thinks regarding pleasure, and he thinks that ignorance, while a privation of knowledge, is nevertheless value-neutral. That there are goods that it is bad not to have is not something Hurka need deny in general and that should be clear upon reflection on the value of good character. For all beings at all capable of character, the lack of good character, itself a perfectionist good, is an intrinsic evil, if anything is. So what about knowledge? If what is good about knowledge is that it provides justifiable, cognitive access to truth, then knowledge is a good that it is a bad not to have and ignorance is an intrinsic evil. To be epistemically virtuous, on this view, is to love being cognitively connected to the world and to hate being either cognitively isolated from it or misconnected to it. To be epistemically vicious is to hate or be indifferent to being cognitively connected to the world through knowledge. If so, then both ignorance and false belief are privations of the good of knowledge, which is consistent with an account of the value of knowledge that includes extent as a formal feature.

The contrast with Hurka's view is this: the value of knowledge as epistemic felicity is such that truth and justification are added to belief to make belief good as opposed to bad, whereas, the value of knowledge as cognitive access is such that what is important about knowledge is the access to truth it constitutes. On the epistemic felicity view, the generic value of the knowledge of physics consists in making whatever beliefs about physics one has justified and true as opposed to false. On the cognitive access view, the generic value of the knowledge of physics is that one has access to the truths of physics. By contrast, the epistemic felicity view has it that where there is no belief nothing about the generic value of knowledge is lost. Thus, indifference to ignorance of physics is not a vice. But on the cognitive access view, it is. It is a vice not to love and long for the truths of physics or the truths of any other domain. Of course, other loves may restrict our sense of loss occasioned by our ignorance, but this does not mean that indifference to ignorance is not a vice.[15]

---

a good that it is bad not to have (or not to exist). But if this is false, then these theodicies fail insofar as they rely on such an assumption. Moreover, it is one thing to assert that the privation of a good is not a distinct positive evil and quite another to assert that it is not an intrinsic evil. Pain is a positive evil distinct from the absence of pleasure, but if the absence of feeling—pleasurable or painful—is value-neutral, then pleasure is not a good that it is bad not to have. On the other hand, if knowledge is a good that it is bad not to have, then ignorance is not value-neutral, despite the fact that its badness consists in being the privation of a good. Finally, if both pleasure and perfectionist goods are not such that they are goods that it is bad not to have and if pain is a positive evil, then it is hard to see how the creation of perfectionist goods could ever justify the creation of sentient beings. How could a good that it is not bad not to have (or not to exist) ever provide a reason for allowing a bad that is a positive evil?

15. The view that ignorance is intrinsically evil does not mean that, all things considered, it is best

4. The Vices, Ignorance, and the Pessimistic Conclusion

In fact, Hurka's own account of the vices provides additional support for the view that ignorance as well as false belief are intrinsic evils that oppose the value of knowledge. If the account is supported by its application to false belief as an intrinsic evil and it applies equally well to ignorance, then that is a reason for thinking of ignorance as an intrinsic evil. The relevant features of the general account are these. At a very general level, vices divide into (1) pure vices and vices of indifference, (2) base-level and higher level vices, and (3) vices that are attitudes toward goods in view and attitudes toward goods about which one has not bothered to become aware.[16]

Pure vices are vices that involve either hating the good or loving the bad. Vices of indifference involve being indifferent either to the good or to the bad. When applied to knowledge as a good and false belief as an evil, hating knowledge or loving false belief would be a pure vice. But what about loving ignorance? If I can love false belief and hate knowledge—if I can love for itself, for example, that some people have false beliefs or hate for itself that some people have knowledge—then why can't I love ignorance, love for itself that some people are ignorant? Why would the love of ignorance not be a case of hating knowledge? Moreover, the rarity of both of these vices only supports the point: ignorance, like false belief, is a generic evil.

Far more common are vices of indifference, some of which are base level vices and others of which are higher level vices involving goods in view. Hurka lists callousness, apathy, and sloth as different ways of being indifferent to some base level good or evil that one has in view.[17] Just as one can be calloused, apathetic, or slothful in regard to the suffering of others, one can be calloused, apathetic, or slothful about the false beliefs of others and one's own. This observation illustrates that the application of vice-concepts such as callousness, apathy, and sloth transfer without difficulty from attitudes toward suffering to attitudes toward false belief. But where is the difficulty in making a similar transfer from false belief to ignorance? Why cannot one be calloused, apathetic, or slothful about ignorance, one's own or others'? In fact, the vices of indifference toward ignorance are likely far more common than those toward false belief, as is the higher order vice of shamelessness about ignorance. Shamelessness, according to

---

that we know everything. The effort it might take to know how many people pass by my office in a day might prevent me from realizing a more valuable intrinsic good, say, a period of rest from pursuing knowledge or avoiding ignorance. Just as some knowledge is too trivial to pursue given other values, some ignorance is too trivial to avoid.

16. Hurka, *Virtue, Vice, and Value*, 92–105.

17. Ibid., 94–95.

Hurka, is a higher order vice that reflects an indifferent attitude toward a base level attitude: shamelessness is indifference toward one's callousness, apathy, or sloth.[18] And just as one can be shameless regarding one's indifference toward suffering and false belief, one can be shameless regarding one's indifference toward ignorance.

Finally, consider the base level vice of thoughtlessness toward goods one has not bothered to consider and the higher level vice of smugness toward one's thoughtlessness.[19] Some people are thoughtless about the suffering of others in the sense that their ignorance of such suffering is a result of their not caring enough to inform themselves of it. Some people have the same attitude toward false belief. They do not care enough about false belief to even reflect on whether they or others might be mistaken in some of their beliefs. The issue does not come up for them in a way that they can take the attitudes of callousness, apathy, and indifference toward it. Rather, they are simply thoughtless in regard to false belief. But does this not also describe a clearly distinct kind of vice, namely, thoughtlessness about ignorance, one's own or others'? Moreover, this is a very prevalent vice, often even on university campuses. And smugness toward such thoughtlessness regarding ignorance is anything but rare.

We have every reason, therefore, to think that if indifference to false belief is an evil, then indifference toward ignorance is as well. And if the recursive account is correct, we cannot think that indifference toward ignorance is a vice without thinking of ignorance as a generic evil.

It would seem, then, as virtuous lovers of knowledge as a formal perfectionist good, we would want to revise Hurka's third feature to include ignorance along with false belief as a generic evil. If we do, and we retain the other features—agent-neutrality and formality—we should aim at the greatest ratio of knowledge possible to both ignorance and false belief, everything else being equal.

But now note the consequences. The ratio of knowledge to the combination of false belief and ignorance is far more likely to justify our hating our lives and our world than before. Why? Because it is now far more likely that the epistemic balance is negative. If we are virtuous lovers of knowledge and haters of its privation, it is far more likely that we will see ourselves as justified in both individual and global pessimism.

In fact, matters are even worse. As a perfectionist good, knowledge is intrinsically valuable independent of its contribution to subjective well-being. What is important is that the truth be known. If the emphasis is on the formal di-

18. Ibid., 95.
19. Ibid., 95.

mensions of knowledge from an agent-neutral point of view, the results for global consequentialism seem clearly disastrous. What we either do not know or cannot know is infinitely more extensive than what we in fact know. It would seem, then, a moral certainty that if we are virtuous we will hate our lives for what we do not know in comparison with what we do know and we will hate our world for its poverty in knowledge and its wealth of ignorance. Epistemic pessimism is a virtual moral imperative, no matter how well things are going on other fronts: the disvalue of infinite ignorance will dwarf the positive value of all other finite goods combined.[20]

Something has gone wrong somewhere.

5. An Optimistic Option

Perhaps the ancient skeptics were right and the view that ignorance and the suspension of belief is bliss is correct after all. Then, again, perhaps there is just something deeply wrong with consequentialism and its agent-neutral values when it comes to assessing the intrinsic value of knowledge as a perfectionist good. We get a better take on the intrinsic value of knowledge as a perfection-ist good when we study its place in the life of a person who loves knowledge for itself and to what degree such love gives a person reasons from his or her own point of view for living one way rather than another or for living at all. We get a better understanding of the generic value of knowledge as a perfectionist good by understanding the character of people who love knowledge than we do by trying to arrive at an independent account of the value of knowledge in order to understand what it is to have the virtue of loving it. To do this, we must shift from the agent-neutral point of view to the agent-centered point of view and put the study of character front and center.

We might do well in this regard to take the advice of the ancient virtue ethi-cists and think more naturalistically. When we become dehydrated, a natural affective response of our bodies is thirst. When our brains are deficient in serotonin, a natural affective response is depression. When we are isolated from our loved ones and deprived of intimacy, a natural affective response is loneli-ness. What are natural affective responses to deficiency in knowledge? Boredom and curiosity are instructive candidates. Just as loneliness is a painful affective re-

---

20. Ignorance aside, however, it is not clear to me that my belief network now contains more knowl-edge than false belief or that there is now more knowledge than false belief in the world. The radical de-mographic expansion of the last fifty years has probably expanded the global network of false belief more than the global network of knowledge. And while I am reasonably confident that my own network of knowledge has expanded, I do not have a good grip on how many of my beliefs are justified, on how many false beliefs I have acquired, or on the balance between the two.

sponse of people who love others as ends but who are denied intimacy with them, boredom is one of the painful affective responses of those whose love of knowledge as an end is expressed as curiosity but who are confined to ignorance. And there is much instruction in this fact for how to measure the intrinsic value of knowledge to organisms like us.

The desire to know is embedded in a psychology driven to understand. That is what curiosity can be. Lack of cognitive attachment hurts for organisms like us. That is what boredom sometimes is. If we were not subject to boredom, we would not value knowledge as a generic value in the way that we do. Nor would we be subject to boredom in the way that we are if we did not value knowledge in the way that we do. To be sure, false belief can stave off boredom in a way that ignorance cannot, but that is because when we believe falsely we take ourselves to be believing truly. When we discover that our beliefs are false, the drive to inquiry is fueled by a desire for cognitive attachment. We find respite from the disappointment of false belief in the activity of seeking the truth and settling on it. Entertainment and sports have some capacity for driving off boredom, but what they cannot do is satisfy our curiosity about what is true. When we are denied either the process of inquiry or the results of its success, we hurt. That is one exemplification of boredom. In this sense, boredom is how ignorance sometimes feels.

Of course, nothing said here establishes the exact relationships between ignorance and knowledge on the one hand and boredom and curiosity on the other. The central point is that there are affective and conative dimensions of our psychology that provide clues to the kind of value the development of our human cognitive capacities has for us. Boredom is not always the result of ignorance, but sometimes it is. Imagine an environment about which there was nothing that would evoke human curiosity. Any reasonably intelligent human being would eventually become bored in such an environment, no matter what else that environment contained. Now imagine an environment that evoked a lot of curiosity but no competitiveness or playfulness. It, too, might become boring, but not for the same reasons as the first. Finally, imagine an environment that evoked a lot of curiosity but no means of satisfying it. For any reasonably intelligent human being, it, too, would eventually become boring. Boredom, then, is sometimes how underdeveloped human cognitive capacities feel.

Moreover, contrary to the formal account of the value of knowledge, the pursuit of some truths is intrinsically more important to us than the pursuit of others. Why else do we ask questions the answers to which might destroy us psychologically?[21]

There is also a threshold, and this is very revealing, perhaps my most central

---

21. This is not to deny that we also value the formal features of knowledge. I believe we do.

point. We do not seek to insure a positive ratio of knowledge over the combination of false belief and ignorance as a goal for epistemic survival. The threshold of ignorance that triggers the affective pain of boredom is not measured by such a ratio. Rather, we avoid reasons for epistemic pessimism when our knowledge is sufficient to establish a level of cognitive intimacy with the world that does not leave us suffering from the extreme boredom of cognitive alienation. It is not that we love knowledge because it relieves boredom, but boredom sets in as a gauge for a lack of a certain kind of intimacy with the world. In this regard, it is cognitive loneliness (which is an altogether different pain than cognitive embarrassment). But just as personal loneliness can be dispelled without a majority of one's personal relations being personally intimate, cognitive loneliness can be dispelled by considerably less than a net balance of knowledge over false belief and ignorance. This is just a fact about our psychology as lovers of knowledge. Seen in this way, the value of knowledge and the love of it need not represent the threat that we might hate ourselves and our world for our ignorance in the way that more objectivist and agent-neutral views do.[22]

Of course, it might be objected that by taking recourse to the agent-centered view, I distort the value of knowledge as a generic good by reducing it to an element in subjective well-being. Further, it might be claimed that extending the account to other perfectionist goods would fall prey to the same difficulty and fail to be true both to the plurality of values and to the true nature of those values.

Though this is a serious objection, it does not succeed. It fails to note the difference between what we value for itself and the causal account of why we value it. Consider love. We love our loved ones for themselves, not for the fact that intimacy with them dispels the loneliness that accompanies their absence. Organisms who are vulnerable to loneliness are organisms that value others intrinsically in a certain way. The capacity for loneliness reveals what intrinsic values are encoded in a psychology vulnerable to the devastating effects of loneliness. The loneliness explains that a good is missing, but it also explains what kind of good is missing, and what is missing is not a good of subjective well-being but a certain kind of relationship with another person, which for creatures like us adds to our subjective welfare. A similar lesson applies to knowledge and boredom. The capacity for boredom reveals what intrinsic values are encoded

---

22. In correspondence, Hurka has raised the problem that my view that ignorance is evil might involve me in the contradiction of saying that ignorance is both intrinsically evil and intrinsically good, intrinsically evil as the lack of knowledge and intrinsically good as the lack of false belief. Saying that ignorance is value-neutral would avoid the difficulty. But I see no logical difficulty in saying that both false belief and ignorance are intrinsically evil in being privations of cognitive intimacy with the world, a good that it is bad not to have.

in a psychology vulnerable to the devastating effects of boredom. The boredom explains that a good is missing and what kind of good it is. And it is decidedly not a good of subjective well-being but a certain kind of relationship to truth. That subjective well-being is intimately related to an organism's ability to live in a way that accommodates what the organism cares most deeply about is not a surprising fact, but it is a fact from which some rather bad conclusions have been drawn about the structure of practical reason.

The moral is this: if you want to know about the structure of knowledge as a perfectionist value, you must study the character of those who love knowledge. Strongly influenced by the intuitionists, Hurka thinks that the recursive account shows that moral theory begins with an account of generic goods which then explains the value of the virtues. Virtue theory, therefore, is mistaken and structurally flawed. However, we may accept an agent-centered account of the recursive theory, which says that the value of a virtue is less than the good to which it is related, but reject Hurka's understanding of virtue theory and its structure. Virtue theory need not take the rather narcissistic turn of Stoicism that says that the single or primary goal of action is virtue. Aristotle certainly rejected this view. What virtue theory explains better than any other kind of theory is why one way of life is better than another. Hurka thinks that one way of life is better than another because one way of life includes a better balance of generic goods (and virtues) than the other. But the virtue ethics tradition, as I understand it, says that we see one set of generic goods and virtues as better than another because of the kinds of people we are. To be sure, we see one way of life as better than another because it includes the things we think are better, but we see some things as better than others because of the kinds of persons we are. And it is in this sense that the study of the good and the right proceeds through the study of character.[23] What ultimately explains the pull of the good of knowledge is in the knower, which explains why the pull is the pull of love and emo-

23. It is one thing for a theory to say that virtue plays a certain kind of justificatory role in morality and practical reason and another for it to say that it plays a certain kind of explanatory role. Some thinkers (in *Virtue, Vice, and Value*, Hurka cites Elizabeth Anscombe, Philippa Foot, Rosalind Hursthouse, Julia Annas, and Michael Slote [219–255]) believe that virtue ethics must give the virtues a more fundamental justificatory role than deontological or consequentialist theories do in order to constitute a third structural option within types of moral theories. I believe, as Hurka does, that this is a mistake. However, this does not exhaust the structural field. What explains why the good is good and the right is right? Pure practical reason? Non-natural moral properties? The commands of God? Virtue ethics, as I see it, explains why a practical reasoner sees a way of life as good because it expresses the deepest values of his or her character. To the extent to which deontological and consequentialist theories give other explanations, they are false. Virtue ethics does not have to claim that knowledge is good because it contributes to human flourishing. It can merely say that what explains the fact that we value knowledge as an intrinsic good is that we are the kinds of creatures who care deeply about knowledge for itself and hence the value of knowledge plays a certain justificatory role in our practical deliberations.

tion rather than mere cognition. In this fundamental sense, virtue ethics secures an advantage over consequentialism and deontology. *Of course,* the value of a virtue is often (maybe even always) less than the good to which it is related, but what explains this is the simple fact that it is fundamental to our character to care about things other than our own virtue.[24] What is surprising about that?[25]

24. I leave open the possibility that sometimes the value of a particular virtue in a life might not be given a recursive account.

25. I would like to thank the participants of the *Virtue Ethics: Old and New Conference* sponsored by the University of Canterbury, New Zealand, in May 2002 for many helpful comments; for excellent written comments, Steve Gardiner; and for helpful correspondence, Thomas Hurka.

Notes on Contributors

JULIA ANNAS is Regents Professor of Philosophy at the University of Arizona. She has also taught at St Hugh's College Oxford and Columbia University. She was the founder editor of *Oxford Studies in Ancient Philosophy* and has published many books and articles on ancient philosophy, particularly on ancient epistemology and ethics. Her books include *The Morality of Happiness, Platonic Ethics Old and New* and *Voices of Ancient Philosophy*. She is presently working on virtue ethics and on ethics in late antiquity.

ROGER CRISP is Uehiro Fellow and Tutor in Philosophy at St Anne's College, Oxford. He is author of *Mill on Utilitarianism*, editor of *Utilitas*, and a member of the *Analysis* Committee.

STEPHEN M. GARDINER is an Assistant Professor of Philosophy at the University of Washington in Seattle. He was previously on the faculty at the University of Canterbury, Christchurch, New Zealand, and the University of Utah. His main research interests are in ethical theory, political philosophy, environmental ethics and Aristotle's ethics. He has previously published in journals such as *Oxford Studies in Ancient Philosophy, Philosophy and Public Affairs,* and *Ethics.*

GEORGE W. HARRIS is Chancellor Professor of Philosophy at the College of William and Mary, and author of *Dignity and Vulnerability: Strength and Quality of Character* and *Agent-centered Morality: An Aristotelian Alternative to Kantian Internalism.* He is currently completing a book manuscript, *Reason's Grief: An Essay on Tragedy and Value* (supported by a National Endowment of the Humanities Fellowship).

KATHLEEN MARIE HIGGINS is Professor of Philosophy at the University of Texas at Austin. She is the author of *Nietzsche's Zarathustra, The Music of Our Lives, Comic Relief,* and (with Robert C. Solomon) *A Short History of Philosophy, A Passion for Wisdom* and the editor of *From Africa to Zen.*

T. H. IRWIN is Susan Linn Sage Professor of Philosophy and Humane Letters at Cornell University. His many publications include: Plato's *Gorgias,* Aristotle's *First Principles,* Aristotle's *Nicomachean Ethics, Classical Thought, Classical Philosophy,* and *Plato's Ethics.*

DANIEL RUSSELL is an Assistant Professor of Philosophy at Wichita State University. He is the author of the forthcoming book *Plato on Pleasure and the Good Life.*

ROBERT C. SOLOMON is Quincy Lee Centennial Professor of Business and Philosophy and Distinguished Teaching Professor at the University Texas at Austin. He is the author of *The Passions, In the Spirit of Hegel, About Love, A Passion for Justice, Ethics and Excellence, Up the University, The Joy of Philosophy* and (with Kathleen M. Higgins) *A Short History of Philosophy,* and many other books.

CHRISTINE SWANTON is a professor of Philosophy at the University of Auckland New Zealand, and the author of *Virtue Ethics: A Pluralistic View.*

JENNIFER WELCHMAN is an Associate Professor of Philosophy at the University of Alberta, working in the history of ethics and virtue theory. She is author of *Dewey's Ethical Thought* and is currently editing an anthology, *The Practice of Virtue.*

Index

achievement, 196
acquired virtues, 60
actions: character and, 73, 144–45, 146n9; formal principle and, 66; knowledge and, 115–17; praise/blame of, 135–36, 177–78; self-respect and, 114; virtuous character vs., 130
act-utilitarianism, 164, 166–67, 167n35, 168n37, 173
Adams, Robert, 169, 173
adaptability, 138–40
Adler, Alfred, 181, 185
agapé: eros vs., 91, 93; Kant and, 89; as moral virtue, 81; Nietzschean overflowing and, 186–87; as personal, 88; as universal, 98
agent(s): calculation of utility and, 172; intentions of, 168; normative priority of, 35, 40; praise/blame of, 177–78
agent-centered point of view, 206–10
agent-neutrality, 195–98, 199
aggression, 182
akrasia, 136
altruism, 181, 186. *See also* benevolence
Ambrose, Saint, 65, 65n8
Ames, Roger T., 128–29, 130, 133n23
Amis, Kingsley, 91
analytic philosophy, 92, 94, 193
anger, 114–15n24
Annas, Julia, 3–4, 53n66, 87n13, 88n17, 209n23
Anscombe, Elizabeth, 1n1, 209n23
anthropomorphism, 12–13, 14, 23
Anti-Christ, The (Nietzsche), 96
Antigone (Sophocles), 91
Aquinas, Saint Thomas, 5; on cardinal virtues,

scope of, 71–74; on cardinal virtues as distinct, 68–71; on cardinal virtues as pervasive, 65–68, 69; influence of, 1; on morality and cardinal virtues, 64–65; negative virtues in, 127n3; theodicy of, 202–3n14; on virtues and prudence, 62–64; and virtues as system, 60–62, 74–77
—Works: *De Virtutibus Cardinalibus,* 64, 65, 66, 69, 70; *Scriptum de Sententiis,* 63, 64; *Summa contra Gentiles,* 76. See also *Summa Theologica*
aretaic judgments, 32n7, 182–83
Aristo (heretic): Inwood on, 39, 45; on precepts, 41n28; Seneca and, 31, 56; Stoic moral rules criticized by, 30–31; Stoics and, 42, 55n74
Aristophanes, 95–96, 98, 99
Aristotelianism: *eudaimonia* in, 32n9; human nature in, 17–18; naturalism in, 13, 14–15, 18n14; objections to, 4, 18n14; self-respect and, 5–6, 102–3; virtue as insufficient for happiness in, 19–20; virtue as necessary for happiness in, 4, 21–22, 26
Aristotle, 51n58; on anger, 114–15n24; on benevolence, 150; on cardinal virtues, 66–71; on children and virtue, 149, 150n22; on courage, 71–74, 106–10; on friendship, 119–20; on gender differentiations, 18–19; on happiness and virtue, 19–20, 93; influence of, 1; on magnanimity, 76; moral development neglected in, 143; on moral maturity, 118; on negative virtues, 130–31n16; negative virtues in, 127n3; on passions and virtue, 5, 81, 83, 86–87, 106; on praise/blame, 135–36; on pride, 110–13, 114n22; on prudence, 63; on

flourishing (*continued*)
necessary for, 147–48, 153–54, 155; virtue as
necessary for, 4, 26, 93; virtue as sufficient for,
4, 19–20, 26
Foot, Philippa, 4, 12, 13, 117, 179–80, 209n23
footbinding, 137–38
Frankena, William, 84, 85n9
Frankfurt, Harry, 94, 95
free will, 168
Freud, Sigmund, 91, 92
friendship: erotic love and, 82; as moral virtue, 5,
81, 83; partiality and, 176; as personal, 90; as
selfish, 93n29; self-respect and, 119–20
Fromm, Erich, 84, 88, 182, 186

Gardiner, Stephen, 20n15, 87, 111n18, 117n29
Garfield, Jay, 32n8
Gaut, Berys, 163
Gay Science, The (Nietzsche), 125n1
gender differentiations, 18–19, 23
generic goods, 196, 197, 209
generosity, 68, 90, 190
Godwin, William, 177n82
good(s)/goodness: excellence and, 179; external,
19–20, 21; generic, 196, 197, 209; meta-ethics
and, 12; perfectionist, 195, 197, 198–201, 202–
3n14, 206; tree roots example, 12–13; undistorted will to power and, 179; of virtue, 196
good life. *See* flourishing
good will, 118–19
Gorgias (Plato), 179
Graham, A. C., 129, 133n23
grandiosity, 186
gratitude, 6, 150–52, 154, 155
Gregory I, Saint, 65

habits, as virtues, 86
Hale, Stephen D., 181
Hall, David H., 128–29
Hampton, Jean, 102n4
happiness. *See* flourishing
Harris, George, 7
health, Nietzsche and, 7, 184–87, 191
hedonism, 179, 198
Herman, Barbara, 40
Hershock, Peter D., 134n31
Hesiod, *Theogony*, 91
Higgins, Kathleen, 6
Hill, Thomas, 102n4
Hippolytus (Euripides), 91
holism: moral rules and, 40, 41–42, 45–46n36;
self-respect and, 104–5, 116; virtue ethics and,
58
Horney, Karen, 185, 186
Huizi (logician), 134

human development: false belief and, 202; in
Nietzschean virtue ethics, 187–92; traditional
virtue ethics and, 6. *See also* character development
human nature: as constraint on ethical theory, 4;
rationality and, 4; rationality and, strong version, 22–28; rationality and, weak version, 17–
22; transcendence of, 11–12
Human Nature and Conduct or Ethics (Dewey), 146
Hume, David, 6; act-utilitarian interpretation of,
164, 166–67, 168n37; aesthetics of, 170n45;
common point of view in, 174–76, 178; descriptive ethics of, 160–61; impartiality in,
173–77, 178; influence of, 1; on justice, 165–
66; minor virtues and, 150; "monkish" virtues
attacked by, 75, 172; motivation in, 163, 165–
66, 168–69; motive-utilitarian interpretation
of, 169; on natural virtues, 166, 166n31; neglected in virtue ethics, 159; normative positions of, 161–64; objections to utilitarian
interpretations of, 170–73; on praise, 136; right
action in, 164–67; on self-interest, 165–66,
173–74; as skeptic, 163–64; virtue and utility
in, 170–73; as virtue-centered commonsense
moralist, 166–69, 173, 177–78. See also *Enquiry concerning Human Understanding, An*; *Treatise of Human Nature, A*
humility: magnanimity vs., 61, 76–77; as potential
part of temperance, 75–76
Hurka, Thomas, 7, 183; epistemic pessimism of,
205–6; on ignorance, 201–5, 208n22; knowledge as perfectionist good, 198–201; on pleasure, 202–3; value of knowledge, 200–203;
on vices, 204–5; virtue defense of theism re-
futed by, 196–97; virtue ethics opposed by,
195–98
Hursthouse, Rosalind, 4, 209n23; on cluelessness,
117; on end of virtuous activity, 87n13; on human nature and rationality, stronger relation,
22–28; on human nature and rationality,
weaker relation, 17–22; on impersonal benevolence, 16–17; on naturalistic ethical evaluation, 13–16; on virtue ethics/other traditions,
58n85; Zhuangzi contrasted with, 132
hypocrisy, 118

ignorance: boredom and, 207–8; as evil, 201–3,
208n22; vices of indifference toward, 204–5
immoralism, 179–80, 181
immorality, 114n23
impartiality, 173–77
importance, cardinal virtues and, 70–71
indifference, 204
inferiority complex, 185, 186
infused virtues, 60, 127n3